Eco-History

ECO-HISTORY: AN INTRODUCTION TO BIODIVERSITY & CONSERVATION

Ian D. Rotherham

British Library Cataloguing in Publication Data
A catalogue record for this book is available from the British Library

ISBN 978-1-874267-81-2

TABLE OF CONTENTS

BIOGRAPHICAL SKETCH

Ian Rotherham was born in Sheffield (UK) in 1956. He graduated with a First Class degree in Ecology from the University of Lancaster and then was awarded his Ph.D. in Botany from the University of Sheffield. He is Professor of Environmental Geography and Reader in Tourism and Environmental Change at Sheffield Hallam University, and is a Distinguished International Visiting Scholar at the National Sun-yat Sen University in Taiwan. He has written over 400 papers and articles and a number of books. His research includes landscape history, the economics of landscape change, issues of invasive alien species, urban ecology and aspects of tourism and economic development. Ian works extensively with the popular media and with grassroots conservation groups. He chairs a number of national and international committees and working groups and his work informs the development of relevant policies and strategies. He has acted as an advisor to a number of governments internationally.

ACKNOWLEDGEMENTS

Many friends and colleagues helped this project, a long-term journey over many years, with ideas, insights and encouragement. Christine Handley, Ted Green, Frans Vera, Jill Butler, Mauro Agnoletti, Chris Smout, Rob Lambert, Mel Jones, Paul Ardron, the late Oliver Gilbert, and many others, were supportive and inspirational. Professor Colin Beard provided some early ideas on the educational merits of the environmental time-line that he developed as a teaching aid. My wife Liz has shown endless patience during this endeavour. The editors at the White Horse Press, particularly Sarah Johnson, are thanked for their support, encouragement, critical insight and efficiency.

PREAMBLE

This short volume is not intended to be comprehensive; within a book of this size, it would be impossible to do more than touch the surface of key issues. However, despite the wealth of volumes on ecology, biodiversity and nature conservation, there is a gap in the current literature, which this book fills. The intention is to provide ready access to ideas on the nature of biodiversity and on the eco-cultural nature of landscapes and the history of their conservation. This approach considers key issues in short, focused chapters and then presents a timeline based on the British Isles, to describe the changes in ecology and landscape, and the emergence of nature conservation and environmental movements over the last millennium. Much of the current literature available to researchers, students or the interested public, overlooks or even misunderstands the interactions between people and Nature, the eco-cultural nature of landscapes. Attempts to conserve wildlife or ecology, and to heal the wounds of human impacts, are weakened if we do not understand our own history. It is essential that we comprehend how, over countless centuries, we have forged today's ecologies from our impacts on, and utilisation of, Nature.

Adder.

Photograph: Ian D. Rotherham.

Ian D. Rotherham

The book introduces the background to humanity's interactions with Nature and the forces at work in shaping today's world. In particular, it is essential reading for anyone wishing to understand the nature of today's global crisis and how we, the people, got here.

The text is not one of facts, figures, numbers and details, but of ideas, of history and of people. My intention is to stimulate thoughts and questions about reasons and processes. The 'spine' of the book is a thousand-year time-line history of biodiversity and nature conservation, which takes Britain as a case study example. A selection of references is included and guidance is given in terms of further reading. This is not definitive and cannot intend to be so, since the literature in this field is vast. The aim here is to direct readers to some standard sources but also to books and papers which they might otherwise be unaware of.

The book will be of interest, and hopefully of use, to anyone interested in the ecology and biodiversity of our planet, past, present and future. In particular, this will be a stimulating guide to students and teachers or lecturers from sixth form and college to university. It will also appeal to the ordinary wildlife enthusiast wishing understand the past, and to know what might be in store for the future.

SUMMARY AND OVERVIEW

Biodiversity both as a word and as a concept has exploded into the popular psyche and into academic literature in about twenty years. Yet, whilst its general reference to the diversity of life and species is clear, the meaning of the term and the significance of related issues are often misunderstood. Since its first usage, biodiversity has become inextricably intertwined with nature conservation and to a degree with ideas of sustainability. However, why and what we choose to conserve, and indeed how successful our attempts are, remain enigmatic. Furthermore, many of those working on biodiversity and ecology have only limited understanding of the historical context and the drivers of change that affect these. Since human impacts first began to alter and adapt landscapes and ecosystems, people and nature have adapted to each other and have ebbed and flowed like the tides. Human impacts have

Meadow Cranesbill.

Photograph: Ian D. Rotherham.

Ian D. Rotherham

fluxed with the evolution of social systems and of technological innovations and with political and economic forces and fashions.

Ideas of conservation and biodiversity become mixed with implied issues of *'wilderness'* and of *'nature'* and *'naturalness'*. Nevertheless, it is increasingly recognised that much of the biodiversity that we may hope to conserve is, in fact, the result of long-term interactions between people and nature. It is a 'cultural ecology', the product of the environment, history and tradition. The landscapes around us are *'eco-cultural'* not 'natural' and recognition of this fact presents the key to understanding contemporary biodiversity and major challenges for ideas of future conservation and sustainability. It is surprising how little of this concept or its implications is recognised by either researchers or site managers.

Today, with ever-increasing environmental stresses, with natural and anthropogenic climate change, with burgeoning human populations and ecosystems haemorrhaging their biodiversity, it is vital that we understand better where we have come from and perhaps where we might be going.

PART 1.

NATURE, ECOLOGY AND HISTORY

For I have learned
To look on nature, not as in the hour
Of thoughtless youth; but hearing oftentimes
The still, sad music of humanity,
Nor harsh nor grating, though of ample power
To chasten and subdue.

William Wordsworth. 'Lines, Composed a Few Miles above Tintern Abbey'.

1.

PEOPLE AND NATURE AND THE ECO-CULTURAL WORLD

Imagine a countryside where

Reedbeds are dry and clogged with brambles, heathlands have vanished as scrub begins to take over. Wetlands have dwindled and rivers and canals have become clogged by invasive plants which threaten native species. The loss of money for wildlife-friendly farming has seen farmland birds resume their slide into extinction. Bat populations are clinging on to survival in isolated pockets, facing starvation due to dwindling insect populations, while the country's flower meadows have all but vanished. England's uplands have become degraded; their wildlife is in decline and their ability to lock away carbon and to provide clean drinking water for millions sadly reduced.

This is the Wildlife and Countryside Link vision of a future 'austerity countryside' as expressed in August 2010 (*The Guardian*, 14 August 2010). The problem is that it is already happening.

Bluebell.

Photograph: Ian D. Rotherham.

Chapter 1

Introduction: cutting the umbilical cord of people and Nature

In May 2010, *The Guardian* newspaper carried a headline stating that the 'Case for saving species [is] "more powerful than climate change"' (Jowit, 2010). This was in response to the United Nations report on biodiversity. Nevertheless, the underlying reasons for biodiversity decline are still largely overlooked. In this short book, I highlight some key issues of the lessons of history and the challenges that result. Nature provides the umbilical cord linking humanity to Mother Earth but, in recent decades, not only has the physical cord been severed, but the emotional and psychological one too. In western countries such as Great Britain, a new generation has grown for the most part unable even to recognise and identify the most commonplace animals and plants. At this point, the umbilical cord of nature linking communities to their local environment is truly cut. There are major implications of separating people and nature and this process and its consequences have been growing in intensity for centuries. However, in the late twentieth century, severance and change accelerated around the globe at unprecedented rates. The consequences for ecology and biodiversity and for people are on a scale that approaches that of human-induced climate change. Surprisingly this is a topic overlooked by both popular and scientific media in recent years.

Today's landscapes and their associated biodiversity are changing on a scale almost beyond human comprehension (see Rotherham, 2010 for example). Currently most popular and scientific literature attributes the bulk of the change, and attaches the greatest elements of environmental risk, to climate change. Indeed much of this seems to isolate climate change as the sole driver and even suggests that human-induced climate change is acting almost alone – a naïve and dangerous assumption. Furthermore, the human-induced elements of climate change are reduced further, to causation by gases with the ability to generate and enhanced greenhouse effect in the earth's atmosphere. Finally, the gases responsible are attributed to modern urban and industrial activities and agri-industry in their various guises. Reading both popular and scientific media today it could easily seem that this encapsulates the entirety of the global environmental crisis. This assumption is dangerously wrong.

There is no disputing the intensity of the above, or the scale of the associated impacts. However, it is not the whole story in terms of environmental change and associated risks. It is certainly not the only, or even the major, threat to biodiversity and to the vast landscapes around the world that are not natural, but semi-natural and cultural in their origins, where the dramatic scale of abandonment of traditional and sustainable utilisation is the major threat. The process of abandonment of these eco-cultural landscapes is what I call *'cultural severance'* (Rotherham, 2007, 2009) and represents the widespread ending of traditional land management. This occurs at a number of levels but includes both the physical ending of subsistence usage and dependence, and the psychological distancing of individuals and communities from their environments.

Human resource use in the natural landscape is a fundamental driver (Agnoletti (ed.) 2006, 2007). Indeed, the interactions between people, civilisations and nature have been widely discussed (e.g. Fowler, 2002; Hayman, 2003; Perlin, 1989). People interact with the ecology and other environmental factors through complex social, legal, economic and political mechanisms, facilitating and constraining usage. Almost all the landscapes observed across Europe and many other parts of the world are 'Cultural Landscapes' (Agnoletti (ed.) 2006, 2007; Rotherham, 2009, 2010), or perhaps 'eco-cultural', often managed in traditional ways for millennia. In this context, observations have been made on such traditional uses and their effects. My research (e.g. Rotherham, 1999, 2005, 2007, 2009) to date has documented in detail the impacts of people over time for selected environments such as:

1. Wooded and forested landscapes
2. Marsh, meadow and fen
3. Heath, bog and common
4. Cultivated landscapes – field systems etc.

Yet far too often when conservationists and ecologists discuss landscapes and nature they seem to overlook this most basic and deeply embedded aspect of the 'natural' environment; that it is not 'natural' but 'semi-natural', an 'eco-cultural' resource. Within these landscapes, there are often strong links back to a more primeval ecology (see Rotherham (ed.) 2012), but also forwards through long time-periods of continuity and predictability. Importantly the human and natural processes centred on micro-disturbance rather than macro-disturbance, the effective recycling of nutrients within ecosystems and the extraction from systems of biomass. The ecological habitats produced tend to be predictable, have a strong degree of continuity through time and are meso-trophic or oligotrophic rather than eutrophic. Human cultural utilisation has often relied on careful management of recycled nutrients sustainably within the system. When this failed, as it sometimes did, the results were catastrophic

(Rotherham, 2005). Overall, human usage reduced biomass and macronutrients, especially nitrogen, were at a premium. Severance quickly reverses these trends to generate macro-disturbance, major disruption and unpredictability, lack of continuity and massive eutrophication, especially by nitrogen. These changes favour competitive and cosmopolitan species, including some ruderals, over stress tolerators and ruderals associated with traditional regular management.

A further and final impact of cultural severance on these traditionally managed or utilised landscapes is that they lose economic and hence local utilitarian value and are destroyed by conversion to other uses. These are often disputed territories with competing social and political actors. The ecological consequences of this severance and the ending of social and economic utility is often the complete collapse of the system and / or its transformation to other, often agri-industrial or urban-industrial uses. Oliver Rackham made the point very strongly in his seminal book *The History of the Countryside* (1986) when he argued that an ancient wood generally survived in England as long as it had local economic value. The same applies not merely to the physicality of the woodland, but also to its traditional management. Lose either or both and the site will be lost and its land-use converted to some other function. This same line of logic is pertinent to all other traditionally managed landscapes too, but I develop this argument further to include social and cultural values as well as economic value. So a woodland or heath may survive today and

Red Squirrel.
Photograph: Paul Hobson.

be valued highly, and so protected, but for its leisure and amenity or nature conservation functions. Whilst this modern cultural attachment to a site and its functions may protect it from destruction and even provide a modicum of management, it is still separated from its traditional origins and vulnerable to a slow decline through ecological succession. Importantly too, in these times of increasing austerity, rather than generating an economic or resource output, the sites then require input of public funding to maintain them.

Common lands and lands in common

Traditional, and especially subsistence, management of the landscape and its resources was often organised as 'common' either formally or informally. Common usage was then often embedded over time within a formal structure and administration of a 'common' such as a fen, heath, bog or wood. The story of the formalisation of commons and their ultimate widespread demise in Britain is well documented. Similar patterns occur around the world but with local and regional variants on the resource, the timescale and the speed of landscape transformation when common use declines or ends. Some of the issues of perceived mismanagement of commons were highlighted in the 1968 landmark paper by Garrett Hardin, 'The Tragedy of the Commons' (Hardin, 1968) and that seemed to help justify the ending of common rights and the imposition of other 'modern' systems of management and exploitation. He stated that human society had an inherently destructive relationship with nature and naturally over-exploited common resources. This is too complex an issue to discuss in detail here, but it seems to me that the essay overstates the negative effects of traditional common utilisation and to a large degree. His arguments also resonate back through history to so-called 'improvers' and others who sought justification for taking the common from the commoner.

Hardin's essay can be criticised on the grounds of historical inaccuracy and often failing to distinguish between 'common property' and 'open access resources'. Later ideas published by Elinor Ostrom (Ostrom, 1990) and others suggested that to use Hardin's work in arguing for the privatisation of resources was to overstate the case. His use of over-grazing for example has been strongly criticised. It has been noted that these were often carefully regulated commons that avoided misuse. Nevertheless, these later authors accept the existence of genuine problems in managing common resources and that the concept of the tragedy of the commons does apply to many real situations. However, it is an idea that should not be taken too literally. The concept relates to a complex structural relationship and the consequences of the interrelationships that ensue. The phrase itself summarises a concept but does not provide a precise description. Indeed the 'tragedy' as such should not be viewed necessarily as 'tragic' in a conventional sense. Furthermore, it should not be presumed that the argument is of necessity a condemnation of the processes ascribed to it. Today researchers in agrarian studies are turning to an understanding of traditional commons management to help provide insights into how common resources might be protected and conserved, but without alienation of the local people whose subsistence they provide.

It also seems that Hardin's use of the term 'commons' has been widely misunderstood or misquoted, which has led Hardin himself to state that he should have titled his work 'The Tragedy of the Unregulated Commons'. However, despite the limitations and issues which arise, the idea of the tragedy of the commons is very relevant in analysis of behaviour in economics and game theory, taxation and politics, and evolutionary psychology and sociology, and can relate to the outcomes of individual interactions within complex systems. The relationships between this concept and the assumed imperative to privatise commonly owned resources are especially contentious. In particular, this relates to resources traditionally managed communally by local communities and subsequently enclosed or privatised, a key thrust of this essay. The excuse presented politically and economically is usually that this act 'protects' the resources for the present and the future. However, the argument frequently and sometimes very carefully overlooks former management and resources are appropriated and indigenous (often poor) communities are alienated. The consequence is often that private or state-managed use results in a long-term deterioration of the resource and furthermore in what we now call 'ecosystem services'.

A key issue in Hardin's debate is the degree to which individuals always behave selfishly or self-interested individuals find ways to cooperate. The argument is that collective restraint may benefit collective and individual interests. Hardin's essay was criticised by Appell (1993) as follows: 'Hardin's claim has been embraced as a sacred text by scholars and professionals in the practice of designing futures for others and imposing their own economic and environmental rationality on other social systems of which they have incomplete understanding and knowledge.' This approach raises important issues for conservation and ecology. Indeed, his advocacy of clearly defined property rights has often been used to justify privatisation or private property per se. From these discussions and debates, the opposite state to the 'tragedy

People and Nature and the Eco-cultural World

of the commons' has been described, the 'tragedy of the anticommons'. This is where rational individuals acting alone collectively waste or destroy a particular resource by underutilisation, and again is an emerging theme of the current essay.

Hardin drew on examples of latter day 'commons', such as the oceans and rivers and their fish stocks, the atmosphere, national parks and others. The example of fish stocks led others to describe this as the 'tragedy of the fishers'. One of his key themes is the growth of human populations in relation to the resources of the planet Earth as a general global common. He advocated potential management solutions to commons problems and these included privatisation, polluter-pays regulations and management regulation. Relating to his pasture and grazing analogies Hardin described the 'enclosure' of commons and the historical progression from the use of all resources as commons with unregulated access to all, through to systems where commons are 'enclosed' and subject to various methods of 'regulated use'. Here the access to the resource is prohibited, restricted or controlled. He argued that reliance on individual conscience to police commons utilisation would not work because selfish individuals, termed 'free riders', are favoured over others who are altruistic. In relation to the need to avoid over-exploitation of common resources Hardin quoted Hegel's statement as used by Engels: 'freedom is the recognition of necessity'. Hardin indicated that 'freedom' completed the tragedy of the commons and so, in recognising resources as 'commons' and understanding that they therefore needed management, people could 'preserve and nurture other and more precious freedoms'.

Attempts to articulate solutions to the perceived or real tragedy of the commons are a key thrust of contemporary political philosophy. Without enlightened self-interest, there is a need for authority of some sort to deal with collective actions. Government regulation can restrict or allocate the amount of a common good made available for use by an individual. Permit systems are applied to extractive economic activities such as livestock raising, timber extraction, mining, fishing, hunting and the like. Another approach to protecting the commons is to place limits on pollution discharges, and today of carbon emissions, through government or international regulation. Common resources can also be the subject of cooperative regulation by the resource users themselves for mutual benefit. Finally, some resources can be converted from 'common goods' into 'private property' and it is then assumed that any new owner will have an incentive to manage it sustainably. (In fact, it is palpably clear that this is often not the case. A private owner is often inclined to capitalise the stock – in other words to cash in the value and then cut and run). In practice, this is often manifested in the imperative to increase productivity and profitability at the expense of long-term sustainability and the delivery of wider ecosystem services and benefits. The private owner has little incentive to maintain or increase any wider communal benefit and ironically, in cases such as Britain, whilst the early stages of 'improvement' were generally privately funded, the later stages during the twentieth century, were publicly subsidised by cash or by tax breaks. (see Rotherham, 2013a, 2013c)

Human utilisation and the cultural landscape

We now recognise that such traditional cultural utilisation, whilst not always sustainable, has generated and driven many of the landscapes we now value so highly. It is important at this stage to acknowledge and recognise that much communal use of ecological resources has not been benign. Indeed, many resources were over-used to the point of extinction and with others the uses over time transformed landscapes dramatically. However, such overuse was generally a result of sheer human population pressure and, in the case of transformation, the resulting cultural landscapes were often created over centuries; sophisticated systems for producing sustainable outputs with minimal external subsidies. Cultural uses created the conservation landscapes we value today and many are or were species-rich and diverse systems (Rotherham, 2009, 2010). Furthermore, and at present neglected in many debates on conservation and the environment, a massive proportion of our most highly valued ecology and biodiversity depends for existence on these traditional or customary uses. The reasons and mechanisms for this are too complex to examine here in detail, but they range from direct environmental impacts (like lowering of nutrient levels and micro-disturbance), to indirect effects through social and economic impacts (allowing people to remain and live on the land or in a particular region). A consequence of these long-term, intimate relationships between people and nature has been the creation of complex landscapes and often rich and distinctive ecologies. Many of these have evolved through generally stable and predictable patterns of human utilisation of the natural world, and the consequent response from biodiversity to adapt and evolve. A direct result of these processes is the heritage of biodiversity and landscapes that we inherit today. This includes within it the locally- and regionally-distinctive landscapes and their ecological character highly valued for nature conservation and increasingly now for tourism and leisure (Doncaster et al., 2006; Rotherham, 2008a, b).

People and Nature and the Eco-cultural World

Landscapes and ecology – character and distinction

It is very clear that the wealth of distinctive landscapes that exists around the world and the associated characteristic ecology are a consequence of the backdrop of natural conditions and the history of human traditional exploitation (Agnoletti (ed.) 2006, 2007). Very few locations and ecosystems can be accurately described as purely 'natural'. Yet, increasingly discussions on restoration focus on the 'natural' and not on the 'cultural' origins of desirable conservation areas. This is leading to serious problems in terms of the likely success or otherwise, and the sustainability, of even the highest profile and most well prepared and presented projects. Unfortunately, the perceived origins are generally misunderstood and therefore the hoped-for results of restoration are unlikely to be achieved (e.g. Rotherham, 2011). Importantly, most restoration or conservation projects are separated from economic or local community functions and in most cases there seems little chance of such fundamental long-term drivers being effectively established. Of great concern is that in most cases it seems these issues and the absence of the key mechanisms are unrecognised by project- or site-managers. If they are, then this omission is not publicly acknowledged.

Many so-called re-wilding or re-naturing programmes have great merits and should form an important part of any large landscape-scale restoration programme. However, they mostly lack any recognition of the cultural origins of most conservation landscapes or the dependence of many of the biodiversity targets on human utilisation (Rotherham, 2011). Even the selection of suitable target areas frequently lacks any real understanding of landscape history and human cultural origins. Many even lack realistic assessments of ecosystem carrying capacity and even suitability for the species targeted for reintroduction. This severely prejudices hopes for long-term success in achieving many of the environmental, ecological and even economic outcomes and targets. Misunderstanding and misinformation follow into the more popular media such as when Vidal (2005) in *The Guardian* newspaper ran a story on re-wilding entitled 'Wild herds may stampede across Britain under plan for huge reserves' which was potentially exciting but, in its content, sadly misleading. Suggesting that the high Pennine moors might support free-roaming herds of Heck cattle or reindeer is ludicrous. Furthermore, to say that this is a 'wild and natural' landscape, when it is a cultural landscape of 5,000 years standing, is entirely misleading. In regional economics terms, the idea that current upland farmers might be replaced in the economy by 'ecotourism' shows zero understanding of basic tourism economics (Rotherham, 2008; Anderson (ed.) 2004)).

Chapter 1

So what is 'cultural severance'?

I define '*cultural severance*' as the breakdown of the fundamental, often subsistence, relations between human communities and their local environment as manifested in the landscape and its ecology as an eco-cultural resource. This is essentially in terms of people and communities as active exploiters of the landscape and its ecology and so is different from passive 'users' of a landscape space (such as modern tourism, leisure or recreational actors). As noted above, this may be a social and community phenomenon as well as operating at the stratum of the individual and their perceptions. It has elements that are inherently practical in nature but is also strongly psychological at every level. This separation of people and nature has evolved at various times, in different places, and at rates that vary from dramatically quick and sudden to relatively slow and drawn out. A key process is the break in local community 'ownership' and use of the natural resource and the imposition of essentially individual, capital-based, value and exploitation. The separation may be inherently a locally-based social one, or can involve ownership and exploitation removed to a remote stakeholder without subsistence ties to the particular locale. Whilst reality may be far more complex, this is the essential process. In recent times, a major transformation has been from an essentially working countryside to one that is largely a leisure or tourism resource. The participants are still actors and competing for the space, but their interaction with the resource is largely passive. (see Rotherham (ed.) 2013c)

Over long periods, human cultural interaction with the landscape evolves and changes and various phases may be displaced as communities develop and as nature evolves. In recent times, perhaps over the last 200 years in the developed industrial countries, this relationship moves to and beyond the point of severance from nature (Figure 1). However, it is clear that in recent history there have been a limited number of key tipping points in this process, and these relate to four major trends which are themselves closely interrelated. These key processes are:

1. Agricultural improvement
2. Industrialisation
3. Urbanisation
4. Globalisation

Each of these represents a complex of human interactions with natural resources, of economic and cultural evolution and of social change with competition for the control of space and other resources.

Figure 1. British Eco-cultural landscapes now largely severed from their subsistence past include:

1. Fens and marshes
2. Bogs
3. Coppice woods
4. Ancient forest, parks and chases
5. Moors, heaths and commons
6. Ancient meadows and grazing lands such as sheep-walk downland
7. Ancient sand dune systems
8. Ancient arable lands

The net result, though, is a loss of traditional management, often of established patterns of ownership; frequently a dramatic decline in locally- or regionally-distinct landscapes; and, associated with these, a loss or transference of economic process, and a catastrophic reduction in ecological conservation value (Figure 2). Distinctive wildlife and plant species associated with particular niches maintained in these landscapes are quickly lost. Invasive and often aggressive species, sometimes including exotics, may then displace the native or at least long-established ecology.

The mechanism of impacts

One consequence of severance is a move to different land management, perhaps for features managed consistently for centuries as part of social and economic systems. This might be, for example, woodland or heath having lost social and economic functions being converted to farmland, the original habitat destroyed. All associated species are consequently lost. Alternatively, traditional management may cease or change radically, but the site remain physically intact. For example, mediaeval coppice wood being abandoned and then replanted with native or exotic hardwoods as high forest, or cleared and replanted with exotic conifers as a working plantation (Rotherham and Jones, 2000).

A heath, once central to the local economy, if its function and value to local people is lost, may be grubbed up and 'improved', and so destroyed (Webb, 1986, 1998; Rotherham, 2009b, c). Sometimes the site might be physically intact but abandoned in terms of management and use. This severance triggers a successional change to birch wood and a gradual loss of open heathland species (Rotherham, 2009b, c).

14

Chapter 1

Figure 2. The impacts of severance on selected British eco-cultural landscapes

---

1. **Fens:** spread mostly over period from 1600 AD until mid-1900s with almost total loss of function and ultimately of around 99 per cent of the resource; examples include the Yorkshire or Northern Fens, with 3–4,000 km² lost between 1650 and 1900, and the East Anglian or Southern Fens with 4,000 km²+ lost between 1650 and 1950.

2. **Bogs:** gradually abandoned, drained or worked-out as fuel turbaries over several centuries, followed by rapid drainage and removal in both upland and lowland environments from 1800 through to the late 1900s. Almost all lowland raised mires destroyed and those that remain are hugely modified.

3. **Coppice woods:** from enclosed mediaeval woods, to wooded commons and early industrial coppice woods, these were a resource of huge important to communities across the country. Many were converted to high forest in the 1800s as wood charcoal for industry became less important. From 1850 to 1950, almost all the others were abandoned, converted or grubbed out for agriculture. From 1950 to 1990, many more were lost and a sizeable proportion converted to conifer plantations. Traditional skills of woodmanship were almost entirely lost.

4. **Ancient forest, parks and chases:** these complex, economically functional landscapes provide insights into how large areas of primeval Europe may have looked and the ecologies it may have generated. The landscapes of these areas were essentially multifunctional to provide many resources alongside hunting and meat. A very few locations have remained largely intact, though most were lost from 1600 AD onwards. This was through conversion to farmland or to ornamental landscaped parks. Sites that remain physically intact have lost most of their complexity and are separated from their social and economic functions.

5. **Moors, heaths and commons:** until around 1700 AD, through to the late 1800s, these were the distinctive open landscapes of all parts of the country. Many sites probably included extensive wooded commons and were managed as such. At the end of the Parliamentary enclosures, they were reduced in area dramatically with a few lowland groupings of intractable heathland, such as the Lizard in Cornwall or the New Forest and Dorset heaths, and extensive upland moors but now separated spatially and economically from the landscapes down in the valleys and lowlands. However, even where sites remain, their traditional functions were abandoned or changed to specific economic uses. The latter, especially sheep grazing and intensive grouse farming, were often separated from the wider local community.

6. **Ancient meadows and grazing lands such as sheep-walk downland:** like moors, heaths and other commons, until around 1700 through to the late 1800s these were the distinctive open landscapes of all parts of the country. Through the impact of Parliamentary enclosures, they too were drastically reduced in area. Twentieth century wartime improvements removed most sheep-walk areas and a decline in mixed farming, often with local subsistence, and in the use of marginal lands too, meant most areas were destroyed or abandoned.

7. **Ancient sand dune systems:** although severely damaged by coastal urban development and conversion to recreational or tourism uses the remaining locations are of major conservation value. Many sites and dune systems were 'stabilised' by the planting of exotic conifers during the 1800s and 1900s. However, in the pre-improvement landscapes these ecosystems were exploited as a part of the complex of heaths, grasslands and other commons.

8. **Ancient arable lands:** with post-medieval improvements in farming, and especially because of parliamentary enclosures, almost all open field arable land was lost. With the advent of modern herbicides and cultivation systems, the distinctive ecology of these systems was quickly driven to extinction. With mechanisation and improvement, the economic and social functions of these landscapes were transformed and communities squeezed off the land and into the emerging cities. It is also likely that the original open field landscapes were in fact far more complex, diverse and ecologically rich than has previously been recognised.

People and Nature and the Eco-cultural World

Figure 3. Some examples of species declines in Britain through cultural severance

The White Admiral butterfly (*Ladoga camilla*): this strictly woodland butterfly does not cope well with the regular disturbance of coppicing but is a high forest species in woods with shady rides and some open areas for male territorial displays. Mid-twentieth century abandonment of coppicing in lowland English woods benefited this butterfly and it even colonised into young conifer plantations too. It declines in the latter as conditions become too shady. Conversion of woodland to farmland clearly removes the insect entirely.

The Nightjar (*Caprimulgus europaeus*): open heath and open areas in woodlands such as traditional coppice are favoured habitat but this bird also does well in young conifer plantations. However, this is a short-term benefit unless the habitat is opened up by clear felling and numbers swiftly decline after twenty years or so.

Hen Harrier (*Circus cyaneus*): one of our birds of prey most closely associated with moors and heaths, it also does well in young conifer plantations and so breeding numbers may increase in the first twenty years after conversion. However, from that time onwards, the effect of the plantation is to displace the traditional habitat and the bird's population then declines.

Black Grouse (*Tetrao tetrix*): this large game bird favours mixed heath, unimproved grassland and a mosaic of woodland. Again, it does well in the early years of conversion to conifer agri-forestry but declines as the trees mature.

A further option is that, like the coppice wood, it is planted with exotic conifers. Alternatively, heath or similar commonland maintained as open grazing loses other socio-economic functions; its ecology is changed and major successional shift occurs. The traditional and customary uses that maintained the ecosystem included harvesting gorse, bracken, ling and small wood for fuel; cutting wood for construction, bracken for bedding or turf for fuel or roofing; using holly, bramble and gorse as fodder; and cutting grass meadows. The site becomes nutrient-enriched and the low, open vegetation is replaced by taller, more rank, species. Rich mosaics of ecological habitats are converted to a few distinct areas but with limited diversity and stress-tolerant and habitat specialist species are generally lost (Figure 3).

In both these examples, the ecological consequences vary from total loss and replacement by a very limited ecology of intensive agriculture or agri-forestry, to a deflection at varying speeds into a new ecological successional process. This may reflect natural drivers of the ecological systems released by the ending of traditional management, but generally fuelled too by eutrophication (nutrient-enrichment) influences. The ecological changes are modified if new or different management is overlaid to displace that traditionally applied. In such cases, there is an interaction between the abandoned drivers and those of the newly imposed systems. A general observation is that the new approaches are usually 'owned' and managed at a distance from the resource and they replace labour-intensive systems sustained by the local community, with technologically applied management. The latter is often delivered by a few people, sometimes living locally but, increasingly over time, by small numbers of specialist contractors who have no long-term relationship to the resource.

A further consequence of these changes is that a landscape resource, which was utilised in many differing ways by specialist, locally-based, craftsmen, is reduced in complexity to become a much-simplified system. The inherent complexity of a subsistence ecology linked through traditional management to a locally functional subsistence economy is broken. Economic and social functions are operating at political levels and at key points in history for each landscape these are contested spaces operated upon by socially, politically and economically polarised actors. Throughout history and over long periods there are critical tensions between the competing interests, which may balance to produce stability and continuity for this shared resource. However, when, for varying reasons, the social, economic, political or ecological sustainability breaks down, periods of dramatic and sometimes catastrophic change ensue. Throughout history, such changes have generally led to moves towards less communal ownership, reliance, utilisation and determination of functions, to ones that are more individual and centralised and that often apply technology and chemistry to the landscape in place of skill and physical labour. Furthermore, demand for individual profit and financial return for the few resource owners, replaces the need for local sustainability. Acquisition of control of these resources is a political act as well an economic one and it further manifests itself it terms of enhanced political power and influence, as well as in sheer material wealth.

In England during the eighteenth century, enclosures of commonland were swiftly followed by the imposition of grand stately houses and halls with their gardens and parks. These were clear statements of power and unfettered political and economic influence and, surrounded by parklands, have sturdy walls to keep out the commoners. The peasant communities, displaced from their lands, became wage-slave labourers or tenant farmers, or drifted to the growing cities to power emerging industries. The consequence was the ending of traditional use but also a contestation of spaces and functions, which in

People and Nature and the Eco-cultural World

The Big Oak at Pontfadog in Wales, one of the oldest in Britain.

Author's collection.

this case ran for centuries. Separated from their legitimate means to subsist in their landscape, these peasants and commoners became poachers. Their overlord was both judge and jury in the local legal system and employed armed gamekeepers to ensure compliance in the new landscape. In uplands and lowlands, access to land was denied and it took 200 years before the access to countryside legislation re-established recreational access where subsistence access was once a right. In the absence of local communities with common rights undertaking traditional management and depending on customary, often subsistence, utilisation, landscapes and ecology change dramatically. Huge tracts of land were progressively 'improved' for capital-intensive farming and most wildlife species declined sharply or became extinct. At the same time, people moved to the towns and cities, which sprawled across the landscape, consuming all in their path and spewing out sewage, coal-fire smoke and mountains of refuse.

Summary

Interactions between people and nature have shaped modern-day ecology and biodiversity. Traditional, often customary, utilisation, frequently allowed species and communities present in Europe's primeval landscape to survive or thrive in the eco-cultural landscape. However, in the period since around the eighteenth century, local, often subsistence, uses have been replaced by increasingly intensive exploitations subsidised by energy from coal and then petrochemicals, and by industrial fertilisers. Local people have been replaced as actors in the landscape by capital-based systems and often by landowners removed from a region. Also, and increasingly, traditional land-uses have ceased and lands have been abandoned.

References

Agnoletti, M. (ed.) (2006) *The Conservation of Cultural Landscapes*. CABI: Wallingford.
Agnoletti, M. (ed.) (2007) *Guidelines for the Implementation of Social and Cultural Values in Sustainable Forest Management. A Scientific Contribution to the Implementation of MCPFE – Vienna Resolution 3*. IUFRO Occasional Paper No. 19 ISSN 1024–414X.
Anderson, P. (ed.) (2004) *Upland Ecology, Tourism and Access*. Proceedings of the 18th Con-

ference of the Institute of Ecology and Environmental Management, Buxton, 25–27 November 2003. IEEM: Winchester.

Appell, G.N. (1993) *Hardin's Myth of the Commons: The Tragedy of Conceptual Confusions.* Working Paper 8. M.E. Phillips (ed.) Social Transformation and Adaptation Research Institute, Indiana University, USA.

Doncaster, S., D. Egan, I.D. Rotherham and K. Harrison (2006) *The Tourism Economic Argument for Wetlands: a Case Study Approach.* Proceedings of the IALE Conference, Water and the Landscape: *The Landscape Ecology of Freshwater Ecosystems,* pp. 296–300.

Fowler, J. (2002) *Landscapes and Lives. The Scottish Forest through the Ages.* Canongate Books: Edinburgh.

Hardin, G. (1968) 'The Tragedy of the Commons'. *Science,* **162** (No. 3859, December 13): 1243–1248.

Hayman, R. (2003) *Trees. Woodlands and Western Civilization.* Hambledon, London.

Jowit, J. (2010) 'Case for saving species "more powerful than climate change"'. *The Guardian,* 22 May: 1.

Lowenthal, D. (1985) *The Past is a Foreign Country.* Cambridge University Press: Cambridge.

Ostrom, E. (1990) *Governing the Commons.* Cambridge University Press: Cambridge.

Perlin, J. (1989) *A Forest Journey.* Harvard University Press: Cambridge, Mass.

Peterken, G.F. (1981) *Woodland Conservation and Management.* Chapman and Hall: London.

Peterken, G.F. (1996) *Natural Woodland – Ecology and Conservation in Northern Temperate Regions.* Cambridge University Press: Cambridge.

Rackham, O. (1980) *Ancient Woodland: its History, Vegetation and Uses in England.* Edward Arnold: London.

Rackham, O. (1986) *The History of the Countryside.* Dent: London.

Rotherham, I.D. (1999a) 'Peat cutters and their Landscapes: fundamental change in a fragile environment', in Peatland Ecology and Archaeology: management of a cultural landscape. *Landscape Archaeology and Ecology* **4**: 28–51.

Rotherham, I.D. (ed.) (1999b) Peatland Ecology and Archaeology: management of a cultural landscape. *Landscape Archaeology and Ecology* **4.**

Rotherham, I.D. (2005) 'Fuel and Landscape – Exploitation, Environment, Crisis and Continuum'. *Landscape Archaeology and Ecology* **5**: 65–81

Rotherham, I.D. (2006) 'Historic Landscape Restoration: Case Studies of Site Recovery in Post-industrial South Yorkshire, England', in M. Agnoletti (ed.) *The Conservation of Cultural Landscapes.* CABI: Wallingford. pp. 211–224.

Rotherham, I.D. (2007a) 'The implications of perceptions and cultural knowledge loss for the management of wooded landscapes: a UK case-study'. *Forest Ecology and Management* **249**: 100–115.

Rotherham, I.D (2007b) 'Cultural Severance – Causes and Consequences', in *Cultural Landscapes – Changing Landscapes,* pp. 43–44. Delegate Handbook, The International Association for Vegetation Science: 50th Annual Symposium, University of Swansea, 22–27 July 2007, Swansea.

Rotherham, I.D (2007c) 'The Ecology and Economics of Medieval Deer Parks', in I.D. Rotherham (ed.) *The History, Ecology and Archaeology of Medieval Parks and Parklands.* Wildtrack Publishing: Sheffield. pp. 86–102.

Rotherham, I.D. (2007d) 'The Historical Ecology of Medieval Deer Parks and the Implications for Conservation', in R. Liddiard (ed.) *The Medieval Deer Park: New Perspectives.* Windgather Press: Macclesfield. pp. 79–96.

Rotherham, I.D. and K. Harrison (2009) 'South Yorkshire Fens Past, Present and Future: Ecology and Economics as Drivers for Re-wilding and Restoration?' in M. Hall (ed.) *Greening History: The Presence of the Past in Environmental Restoration*. Routledge: London. pp. 143–153.

Rotherham, I.D. (2008a) 'Tourism and recreation as economic drivers in future uplands'. *Aspects of Applied Biology* **85** Shaping a vision for the uplands: 93–98.

Rotherham, I.D. (2008b) 'Lessons from the past – a case study of how upland land-use has influenced the environmental resource'. *Aspects of Applied Biology* **85**, Shaping a vision for the uplands: 85–91.

Rotherham, I.D. (2009a) *The Importance of Cultural Severance in Landscape Ecology Research*, in A. Dupont and H. Jacobs (eds.) *Landscape Ecology Research Trends*. Nova Science Publishers: Hauppauge, NY. pp 1–18.

Rotherham, I.D. (2009b) 'Habitat Fragmentation and Isolation in Relict Urban Heaths – the ecological consequences and future potential', in I.D. Rotherham and J. Bradley (eds.) (2009) *Lowland Heaths: Ecology, History, Restoration and Management*. Wildtrack Publishing: Sheffield. pp. 106–115.

Rotherham, I.D. (2009c) 'Cultural Severance in Landscapes and the Causes and Consequences for Lowland Heaths', in I.D. Rotherham and J. Bradley (eds.) (2009) *Lowland Heaths: Ecology, History, Restoration and Management*. Wildtrack Publishing: Sheffield. pp. 130–143.

Rotherham, I.D. (2010) 'Cultural Severance and the End of Tradition'. *Landscape Archaeology and Ecology* **8**: 178–199.

Rotherham, I.D. (2011) 'The Implications of Landscape History and Cultural Severance in Environmental Restoration in England', in D. Egan, E. Hjerpe and J. Abrams (eds.) *Integrating Nature and Culture: The Human Dimensions of Ecological Restoration*. Island Press: Washington DC. pp. 277–287.

Rotherham, I.D. (ed.) (2013a) *Trees, Man, & Grazing Animals – A European Perspective on Trees and Grazed Treescapes*. EARTHSCAN: London.

Rotherham, I.D. (2013b) *Re-interpreting Wooded Landscapes, Shadow Woods and the Impacts of Grazing*. EARTHSCAN: London.

Rotherham, I.D. (ed.) (2013c). *Cultural Severance and the Environment. The Ending of Traditional and Customary Practice on Commons and Landscapes Managed in Common*. Springer: Dortrecht.

Rotherham, I.D. and M. Jones (2000) 'The Impact of Economic, Social and Political Factors on the Ecology of Small English Woodlands: a Case Study of the Ancient Woods in South Yorkshire, England', in M. Agnoletti and S. Anderson (eds), *Forest History: International Studies in Socio-economic and Forest Ecosystem Change*. CABI: Wallingford. pp. 397–410.

Vera, F.H.W. (2000) *Grazing Ecology and Forest History*. CABI : Wallingford

Vidal J. (2005) 'Wild herds may stampede across Britain under plan for huge reserves'. *The Guardian*, 27 October.

Webb, N.R. (1986) *Heathlands*. Collins: London.

Webb, N.R. (1998) 'The traditional management of European heathlands'. *Journal of Applied Ecology* **35**: 987–990.

2.

BIODIVERSITY AND ITS HISTORY

Introduction

Interactions between people and wildlife, both plants and animals, can be problematic. In many cases and across all continents, the human footprint is evidenced by catastrophic change and mass species extinctions. Today the process goes on and, with human-induced climate change for example, the consequences may be even worse than previous impacts. Yet despite the damaging impacts of people on the environment and its ecology, it is clear that in pre-industrial, often subsistence, societies there is an intimate long-term relationship between people and nature. Indeed, much of the ecology we now value is present because of the continuity of traditional management approaches over hundreds and sometimes thousands of years.

Ancient field maple coppice.

Photograph: Ian D. Rotherham.

Chapter 2

The lessons of history

Even a cursory look at history shows that in recent centuries humankind has been rushing headlong towards urbanisation and industrialisation with, by the early twenty-first century, over half the global population being city-dwellers. Agri-industry and agri-forestry have replaced traditional farming and woodland use, and the process of 'cultural severance', separating people from direct dependence on nature has swept in. This is what I call *'the end of tradition'* and relates to customary practices and long-term traditional interactions with nature. These changes are happening incredibly quickly and abruptly today in some places and in others, such as much of Britain, happened in large part two centuries or more ago. Over the intervening period, the remaining linkages to nature and natural resources have become stretched evermore thinly, to the point in some cases of a total rupture. This severance is likely to cause loss of biodiversity as significant as that from say climate change or other major environmental shifts. We have already

Grazed wood pasture.

Photograph: Ian D. Rotherham.

witnessed massive declines of ecology and biodiversity in Britain and are now experiencing the painful and often expensive consequences, such as flooding, drought, disrupted rural economics and communities, wildfires and associated damage, a haemorrhaging of native wildlife species and the increasing spread of aggressive alien colonisers. This is only the beginning of the process. Yet, so far, this threat to conservation, to humanity and to nature itself has crept in with barely a murmur and most environmentalists remain unaware of the defining shift in the ecological resource.

To understand the problems we need a good knowledge of the broad issues of biodiversity and its changes through time, both natural and human-induced. However, it is also necessary to learn from history and to be able to relate human activities – economies, politics and cultures – to the changing landscape and its ecologies. From this base, we can then consider the development of what we now term nature conservation and how this impacts on and even reflects the changes in the biodiversity resource. If we can gain effective insight into these processes, we can then question the degree to which we have real impacts and effects. In essence, are environmentalists merely spectators who catalogue the changing kaleidoscope of nature, or do we have a real and tangible impact on the outcome? History tells us that the changes we see over centuries are reflections of deep-seated politics and economics within society: issues of supply and demand, of competition, exploitation and abandonment. This suggests that in order to alter the processes and to influence the outcomes of change to achieve effective nature conservation, activities must be at political and economic levels within society. If this is the case, then in a democratic system it is likely that there will be serious challenges in terms of effective engagement and empowerment of people and communities in determining the nature that they desire. Indeed, these tensions are already emerging as nature conservation organisations themselves become large land-owning corporate bodies of professionals with views and agendas often imposed down on local communities rather than reflecting the aspirations of local people. Much modern conservation is of the highest quality, achieving restoration and remediation on a scale which, even twenty years ago, was inconceivable. Yet in terms of achieving genuine sustainability and a halt to human-induced biodiversity losses, much of the work is fundamentally flawed. Almost all the nature conservation work is dependent on short-term grant aid and subscription-based voluntary groups. Very little modern-day conservation work is embedded in long-term economic or political processes. Furthermore, there is little understanding by key stakeholders of the cultural nature of the resource or of the likely impli-

CALTHA PALUSTRIS. *MARSH—MARIGOLD, ¼.*

Marsh marigold.

Author's collection.

cations of cultural severance on biodiversity in our eco-cultural landscapes. In addition, there are significant issues about the lack of accountability or democracy in the determination of policies and agendas by many of the significant players. Nevertheless, without effective local '*ownership*' of environmental and conservation projects, any hopes of long-term sustainability must be questionable. The evidence of history and the lessons of the past inform our view of the present and the potential futures. With escalating urbanisation and still-growing human demands on the planetary resource, the challenges will continue to raise the stakes in the environmental lottery from which there may emerge no winners.

Ecological diversity changes with the environment and with time, varying spatially and temporally. Over the last few millennia, human impacts, either directly on wildlife and vegetation or indirectly on environmental resources, have had major influences on ecological diversity. Each phase of human development, from hunter-gatherer to settled agricultural communities to industrialisation and urbanisation, has wrought increased human impacts on ecology and environment. These effects have increased dramatically in recent centuries and in the last few decades, and the consequences of habitat destruction and species loss have led directly to concerns over loss of '*biodiversity*'. This was a term coined by the American ecologist E.O. Wilson in the 1980s (1998, 1992), and which has gained widespread recognition, albeit with much misunderstanding, across a broad arena of debate. Whilst the impacts of early human land-use, such as forest clearance and localised agricultural intensification were undoubtedly significant and dramatic, it is in the last 500 years that the colossal scale of change has become widespread and the effects so deeply engrained. The first big impacts of forest clearance and agricultural probably began around 5,000 years ago in areas of relatively dense population, such as around the Mediterranean and in China. There were devastating periods of drought, erosion of fertile soil and probably major floods associated with human impacts. The deterioration of the environmental resources clearly had dramatic consequences for communities dependent upon them but, generally, the overall effects were relatively localised. It is in more recent times that human impact has been on a scale that can only be described as immense; and indeed the current period in the Earth's history has recently been named the Anthropocene to reflect the determinant nature of human influence.

This remarkable transformation has been driven by twin processes of industrialisation and urbanisation, and related to these both the capability and the necessity for agricultural intensification and industrialisation. It is reasonable to say that today there is no place on the planet not in some way affected or modified by human-related change. Human activity has triggered mass extinction of fauna and flora on a scale previously unprecedented except in the most dramatic environmental catastrophes such as meteor impacts, mega-volcanic eruptions and ice ages. In recent years, it has also become clear that people are changing and have changed the planetary climatic condition. The debate still rages as to the precise cause, and even the nature, of the change but that change has occurred and a significant part is driven by human activity is clear and indisputable.

The realisation of these massive impacts and of the likely or at least potential effects on the environment, and on what we now call '*sustainability*', has become widespread. Because of the increasingly visible and tangible damage to the environment and to people, there has been a gradual emergence of concern and even fear about the consequences of unrestrained

Stag beetle.

Photograph: Ian D. Rotherham.

Biodiversity and its History

exploitation. Whilst this has developed gradually over the last two hundred years or so, particularly in Europe and in North America, it has emerged as a protest force and even as a political movement in the last few decades of the twentieth century and during the early years of the twenty-first. Yet concerns over ownership, use and custodianship of natural resources go back to the earliest organised communities. In animals, and especially in humans, territorial zones, often manifested as tribal areas, have been essential to survival. Much human behaviour and many aspects of social etiquette are based around the establishment and protection of a resource-base. This is sustainability and survival at its most basic, with communities closely and obviously dependent on their immediate natural resources. With time, the human population has increased dramatically and, in parallel, the natural resources on which it depends have been eroded and reduced. With this scenario, it has become increasingly important for individual communities to protect and ensure the survival of their resource capital, the basis of their existence. For the earliest settled communities it was increasingly vital to establish their particular niche and then avoid over-exploitation, and to protect their resources from the depredations of competitors. As well as protecting their vital resources, people learned how to manipulate them to become more productive; though this is increasingly high output for high input. Massive increases in productivity and output are achieved but only through hugely increased input, subsidised by petro-chemical energy and fertilisers.

Such attempts to manage and control vital environmental assets have had mixed success over the millennia. History tells a story of over-exploitation and collapses of societies and civilisations, and of catastrophically changed environments. However, there have been successes, although many systems of resource use were not long-term sustainable. In many cases careful management regimes, evolved, refined and rigorously enforced, resulted in increased production of needed material resources, from fuel-wood to timber to food. This was sometimes possible over long periods and coppice woods, for example, may have evidence of active management for more than a millennium. However, whilst some systems of exploitation allowed a resource to be produced over centuries or more, they were not necessarily benign in terms of the environment. Indeed, they often caused major and irreversible changes in the resource. The original ecology was often radically changed; landscapes were modified almost beyond recognition. These changes are so deeply ingrained and indeed fundamental to many ecosystems, that many of our now most precious wildlife species co-evolved with the human systems of exploitation. The flora and fauna of traditionally managed grasslands

Chapter 2

Veteran with dead wood.

Photograph: Ian D. Rotherham.

and commons, from hay meadows to pastures are examples of these rich cultural systems. However, when tradition ceases and economically driven management ends, the landscape and its associated biodiversity deteriorate. This theme will be revisited later.

Yet many exploitation systems proved fatally flawed and, as a result, societies and even major civilisations collapsed. Underneath many, if not all, of the world's most extensive deserts for example, lie the ruins of a failed civilisation; humans over-exploited their resources and consequently perished. Forest clearance around the Mediterranean led to serious shortage of essential fuel wood and timber and declines in early civilisations. The clearance of upland forest and the cultivation of lands in Britain can be evidenced by downwashed sediments in lowland floodplains and areas such as the East Anglian Wash and the Nottinghamshire Trent Valley. Over-exploited in Bronze Age and Iron Age times, the skeletal soils simply eroded and leached away to leave a nutrient-depleted ecology and a permanently changed landscape; in the uplands, we now have, for example, the Peak District moors. Over-use of Spanish forests in medieval times meant the loss of timber needed for shipbuilding and a long-term decline in both economic and political power. In many, if not most, cases the consequences of such catastrophes proved long-term and irrecoverable.

Summary

Humans exploiting, foraging in and managing environmental resources have influenced ecosystems and biodiversity for millennia. Competition for resources has also been pivotal in the balance between different communities and civilisations. Indeed, the impetus of gaining specific resources was often the key driver for conflicts and conquest. This was the case from the Roman Empire to European imperialism and expansion in the post-Renaissance period and beyond. The consequences for ecology and biodiversity of these long-term interactions between people and nature are significant but generally under-appreciated.

Chapter 2

References

Gaston, K.J. (ed.) (1996) *Biodiversity: A Biology of Numbers and Difference*. Blackwell Science: Oxford.

Jeffries, M.J. (1997) *Biodiversity and Conservation*. Routledge: London.

Rose, F. (1976) 'Lichenological Indicators of Age and Environmental Continuity in Woodlands', in D.H. Brown, D.L. Hawksworth and R.H. Bailey (eds) *Lichenology: Progress and Problems*. Academic Press: London.

Rotherham, I.D. (1999) 'Urban Environmental History: the importance of relict communities in urban biodiversity conservation'. *Practical Ecology and Conservation* **3** (1): 3–22.

Wilson, E.O. (ed.) (1988) *Biodiversity*. National Academy Press: Washington D.C.

Wilson, E.O. (ed.) (1992) *The Diversity of Life*. Harvard University Press: Cambridge, Mass.

3.

NATURAL CHANGE IN ECOLOGY AND BIODIVERSITY

Introduction

Not all fluctuations in ecological diversity are attributable to human activities. Observations of natural ecosystems show how ecology varies spatially with environmental variables like soil, geology, water, topography and aspect and climate. Variation also runs through time, as distribution and ecological successions generate change, and over longer time-periods, through processes of evolution and extinction.

This latter point leads to one of the key misunderstandings in terms of extinction and biodiversity. A common and popular fallacy is that since extinction is 'a natural process' and 'species have always come and gone', then human-induced destruction of wildlife is itself 'a natural process'. Whilst species loss can be a natural process, the key issues are the *rates* of extinction and the *scale* of human-induced losses and especially of recent impacts. The recent changes amount to a mega-extinction and, although it is true that mass extinctions have occurred previously, they have generally been associated with globally catastrophic events such as meteor impacts, mega-volcanic eruptions and long periods of ice age. The present rates of human-induced extinction are comparable with those of earlier mega-catastrophes. This should be a salutary fact and not a reason for complacency.

The imprints of environmental change on biodiversity

One of the most obvious influences on biodiversity, and of great concern today, is climate change. The effects of long-term climatic fluctuations are visible in ecosystems around the globe. Furthermore, the impacts of human-related changes in, for example, forest cover and the spread of deserts through over-grazing are frequently interlocked with natural fluctuations. It is increasingly recognised that human-induced changes to landscapes, such as deforestation and the extensive drainage of wetlands, change climates at local, regional and even global levels. These changes are then reflected in

EPIPACTIS PALUSTRIS, CRANTZ.
Epipactis des marais.   *Marsh Epipactis*
Sumpf Dingel.
Europe centrale, septentrionale et orientale, dans les marais.
Juin-Août.

Marsh helleborine.

Author's collection.

biodiversity at every level from local and regional to global. One of the most pertinent examples of climate change and changed biodiversity, especially for those in the Northern Hemisphere, is the so-called 'Little Ice Age' from the 1400s to the 1800s. It is worth considering this episode in a little more detail.

An example of a natural change: the 'Little Ice Age'

The causes of the major deterioration in the climate of the Northern Hemisphere are still disputed. However, whatever the reasons, the result was a period of several centuries of incredibly harsh cold weather. It is difficult to be precise about the scale and the nature of the impacts on biodiversity because there was almost no scientific recording and therefore very little evidence exists of the detailed ecology of the time. However, it is clear that wildlife was squeezed out of northern regions and into more southerly, warmer areas. There must have been significant losses of climate-sensitive species particularly in the northern areas. We get some idea of the likely changes through the retreat of the growing areas for particular crops and fruits such as the Grape Vine (*Vitis vinifera*) and the widespread failures of harvests across Europe during this period. Some indication of biogeographic trends can be seen in the southward spread of northern species such as for example the Hooded Crow (*Corvus corone cornix*) and its more recent retreat back north. Other sources of information are locked away in the palaeo-ecological archives of peat bog profiles, through which we can see the losses of plants which require warmer climates. Remarkably, too, the peat has the remains of ancient beetle faunas and through these we can reconstruct a warmer climate and its subsequent deterioration. The icy grip of the Little Ice Age squeezed them out. Similarly, there may be evidence from long-lived trees, such as Small-leaved Lime (*Tilia cordata*), of previous climatic conditions and of extreme events. The evidence is relatively sparse and it is hard to separate the climatic trends and induced changes from those caused by other aspects of landscape change including human agricultural practices. Indeed, human and direct climatic effects are closely intertwined, as extreme weather influenced people, crops and stock, diseases and fuel use.

The suggestion would be that northern and boreal species of plants and of wildlife would have spread south during this time and that southern 'thermophilic' species would have moved south too and many may have been lost. Certainly, if we consider a national biodiversity resource such as that of the British Isles, there would have been undoubted gains and losses on a large scale. The extent to which the European fauna and flora would have gained or lost is very difficult to predict.

The effects of major environmental events: examples of volcanoes, floods and coastal erosion

Global and regional biodiversities have been grossly affected by the impacts of major volcanic eruptions, by both direct regional or local effects of volcanic ash, gas clouds and lava and by the discharge of particulates to the high atmosphere, causing intense periods of cold and dark weather. Some of these events are now known to have caused huge suffering amongst human populations and the abandonment of, for example, more marginal settlements in upland areas. They must have had impacts on biodiversity but, aside from the obvious removal of fauna and flora in the immediate vicinity of a volcanic eruption, there is little known about the detailed effects. Edward Wilson (1992) discusses the likely implications of the known major volcanic events on biodiversity. He also considers the effects of major meteor impacts and, of course, these are now recognised as having been responsible for mega-extinctions of fauna in prehistoric times. One of the major events of this kind occurred around 66 million years ago and was responsible for the extinction of the dinosaurs. Whether this was a single event or perhaps a series of smaller meteor impacts and volcanic eruptions is still debated. Extinction did not happen all at once but was spread out over a few million years; a long time to us, but the mere bat of an eye in Earth history terms.

Fluctuations in sea level have also occurred since the first oceans were established on the Earth. It is considered likely that major and cataclysmic sea level changes and consequent flooding occurred in the early periods of the emergence of major civilisations and are 'recorded' in flood mythologies and folklore around the world. The most widely recognised are the accounts of the biblical flood, which may relate to the post-glacial filling of the Mediterranean and then the Black Sea as the Atlantic rose and water poured through to inundate the previously dry basins. Again, we can only speculate as to the impacts on ecology and biodiversity of events of such magnitude. However, flooding and sea level related changes have occurred throughout history and prehistory. The east coast of England for example, has suffered major periods of inundation, of coastal zone erosion and of massive deposition and accretion. All these have affected the ecology and biodiversity of the region. Even the process and pattern of change have influenced our contemporary

Natural Change in Ecology and Biodiversity

fauna and flora as, for example, Britain was cut off from continental Europe by rising water around 7,000 years ago. The precise timing of sea level rise was hugely influential set against the process of northward re-colonisation of animals and plants in the post-glacial period as climate generally warmed.

Yellow Archangel.

Photograph: Ian D. Rotherham.

The Pine Marten (*Martes martes*) was a mammal, a mustelid, that made the move in time to get across before the English Channel closed and is a part of the British fauna. The Beech Marten (*Martes foina*), its southern cousin, failed. The tiny Harvest Mouse (*Mycromys minutus*), our smallest mammal, is believed to have crossed what is now the North Sea in the reed-like vegetation that lined the path of a great river running across the shallow flatland between Europe and Britain. If you could walk underneath the North Sea from England to Holland, for instance, you would pass over the habitations and settlement sites of long vanished communities.

Areas of massive coastal flooding were totally changed, with some zones becoming wetter and other areas gaining new ground. Coastlines like East Yorkshire or Suffolk today were rapidly eroding regions of soft sands and clays; others like twenty-first century south Lincolnshire were rapidly accreting or depositing shores to which land was actively added. Such regions would have had extensive marshes and flats and vast areas of dynamic sand-dune systems with all their various successional stages. It is likely that many of the species adapted to such dynamic landscapes were the so-called ruderals, often the so-called 'weeds' of today. The present-day natural habitat of such species has often diminished, though, as noted by Oliver Gilbert (1989, 1992), they or their cultivated descendants are often important in urban commons and other disturbed environments. Indeed, Gilbert compared the successional changes and sequences of a regenerating urban or post-industrial disturbance site to those of the post-glacial re-colonisation of Northern Europe, albeit telescoped in time sequence from many centuries down to a few decades.

Summary

Landscapes and their ecologies have fluxed and changed throughout history. Sometimes this has merely been slight changes, occurring slowly; sometimes dramatic, even catastrophic, transformations. A lesson of history is that stability is a myth. To understand changes in ecology and biodiversity, we need to comprehend the twin drivers of continuum and catastrophe (Rotherham, 2005).

Natural Change in Ecology and Biodiversity

References

Gilbert, O.L. (1989) *The Ecology of Urban Habitats*. Chapman and Hall: London.

Gilbert, O.L. (1992) *The Flowering of the Cities ... The Natural Flora of 'Urban Commons'*. English Nature: Peterborough.

Ingrouille, M. (1995) *Historical Ecology of the British Flora*. Chapman and Hall: London.

Jeffries, M.J. (1997) *Biodiversity and Conservation*. Routledge: London.

Ponting, C. (1991) *A Green History of the World*. Sinclair-Stevenson Ltd.: London.

Rotherham, I.D. (ed.) (2005) 'Crisis and Continuum in the Shaping of Landscapes'. *Landscape Archaeology and Ecology* **5**.

Stott, P. (1981) *Historical Plant Geography. An Introduction*. Allen and Unwin: London.

Vincent, P. (1990) *The Biogeography of the British Isles – An Introduction*. Routledge: London.

Wilson, E.O. (ed.) (1988) *Biodiversity*. National Academy Press: Washington D.C.

Wilson, E.O. (ed.) (1992) *The Diversity of Life*. Harvard University Press: Cambridge, Mass.

PART 2.

HISTORY, ECOLOGY AND THE BODY ODOUR OF HUMANITY

4.

THE ECOLOGICAL FOOTPRINT OF THE HUMAN RACE

Introduction

It is generally accepted that the major process of re-colonisation of the Northern Hemisphere reached its zenith around 5,000–6,000 years ago, with many of today's main vegetation zones and ecosystems in place. However, since that time, with both successional change and in response to long-term and short-term climatic fluxes, the situation has remained dynamic. Species' distributions across the region, and hence the biodiversity of any one area, have changed dramatically over the centuries. In trying to assign species and biodiversity to specific areas or regions, it is sometimes hard to take the

Dense birch scrub on commonland.

Photograph: Ian D. Rotherham.

Chapter 4

inherent dynamic nature of the resource into account. Such changes occur today with, for example, the spread of Collared Dove across Europe from the East during the latter half of the twentieth century and the more recent colonisation, or re-colonisation, of Britain by Little Egret (*Egretta garzetta*) and Cattle Egret (*Bubulcus ibis*). Despite such changes, it is clear that the basic structures and diversity of ecology across Northern and Western Europe were in place by a period perhaps several thousand years ago. Since that time, when human activity was relatively limited and had its greatest effects through the use of fire and also indirect impacts via influences on large grazing herbivore behaviour, the human footprint has become massive. Early peoples certainly influenced the landscape and, as in North America, the selective hunting of large game would definitely influence savannah and forest growth, species and patterns. Yet potentially important though some of these influences might have been, the phases of human social development that followed make the earlier impacts seem minuscule. There is still a debate about the nature of this primeval landscape across North Western Europe, and the discussions centred on the seminal work of Frans Vera (2000) have helped to clarify

Grazing commonland.

Photograph: Ian D. Rotherham.

how the early landscape might have looked and perhaps aid understanding of how their biodiversity relates to that which we see today. Our vision now is not one of wall-to-wall forest, but of more open plains or savannah, with a rich diversity of other landscape and ecological components too. Much of this variation would be related to basic environmental factors like climate and waterlogging, but Vera's key factor is the importance too of large grazing herbivores. Not everyone agrees with Vera's hypothesis, but the argument is compelling and a refined version of his original vision has a considerable body of supporting evidence. The landscape had vast expanses of wetland, marsh, fen and peat bog with extensive coastal wetlands too. Dense woodland and thickets would grow up in the protection of rings of prickly blackthorn and bramble and here would be the plants and animals that characterise our so-called 'ancient woodlands' today: the Bluebell (*Hyacinthoides non-scripta*), Dog's Mercury (*Mercurialis perennis*), Wood Anemone (*Anemone nemorosa*) and Yellow Archangel (*Galeobdolon luteum*), for example. Outside the prickly halos of the thorns was a wide-open savannah with heath, grassland and giant old trees such as Pedunculate Oak (*Quercus robur*), which could attain ages of a thousand years or more before collapsing into oblivion. A further powerful driver of succession and change in this landscape would be pre-human fire caused by lightning strikes, which would take out the great trees in the open plain. Further north and into the upland zones there would be a change to landscape dominated by great and similarly ancient Scots Pines (*Pinus sylvestris*) and again a strong influence from natural, lightning-related fires. Mountain zones would have large areas of disturbance through natural landslip and erosion areas and all the great rivers would include sometimes-vast floodlands and meandering patterns of erosion and deposition in an ever-changing yet stable landscape. Much of this environment would have limited quantities of available nutrients, especially nitrogen and phosphorous, and this too had a great influence on associated biodiversity. Localised areas such as mountain downwash zones and alluvial fans would have higher nutrient levels and the whole landscape would have abundant micro-disturbance through natural process, but only limited macro-disturbance. Erosion and deposition areas, animal-related disturbance, fire and successional and life-cycle related changes, such as the collapse of ancient trees, provided a template for a richly diverse fauna and flora with regionally distinct ecologies related to broad climatic influences and localised geological and topographic factors.

This was the landscape, the ecology and the biodiversity upon which the footprint of human activity would be stamped with increasing effect over the following five to six thousand years.

The hunter-gatherers

Early human impacts were relatively limited, as small bands of hunter gatherers roamed the landscape. Their main influences were probably through selective hunting of big game so that, as in North America, certain species flourished whilst others were lost. The knock-on effects of the animals that did well under this regime would bring about major changes in the native vegetation. Areas of forest and older trees were probably reduced and fire would be used specifically to clear and to maintain the cleared areas of open grassland. To some extent, this might be a shift in balance but in some cases it was almost certainly a tipping point for the survival and loss of some of the fauna. As shown quite recently in North America, there would be effects too through human influence on animal behaviour. This might be through the removal of carnivores and through people directly influencing the grazing herbivores. With these effects there would be major, if subtle, changes in this, as with patterns of tree regeneration and other landscape-scale variations in vegetation patterns. Tree removal in upland zones led to major erosion, downwash and acidification of soils. In regions such as the English Pennines, the result was skeletal soils that were now acidic and low in nutrients. Downstream in the lowland areas such as the Cambridgeshire and Lincolnshire Fens and the Wash, and in the rivers flowing into the Humber Estuary in Yorkshire and north Lincolnshire, the result was massive deposition of silts and other sediments as the watercourses spewed their load across the vast open floodplains. The major impacts of people on the landscape and on the biodiversity of the regions were beginning.

Human settlement and agriculture

One of the first major effects of people on the wider environment was through the conversion of land to agricultural use. This involved clearance of trees, scrub and boulders, sometimes drainage and at other times irrigation, and generally the tilling of soil. With the emergence of settled and more sophisticated agriculture around the fertile crescent of the eastern Mediterranean, the impacts increased, with the beginnings of a three thousand year process of soil erosion and nutrient enrichment that has since spread around the globe. Settled farming and increased production, together with the better predictability of food supplies, enabled permanent settlement and a process of population growth at both local and global levels. Improved food supply

The Ecological Footprint of the Human Race

and the ability to produce and store surplus to either trade or to use in leaner times both required and facilitated stable and larger communities. The other twin impact of early human development on the environment, urbanisation, was beginning. For the first time in human history there were great urban areas emerging as cities in and around Egypt, across India and in China. This began the great transformation of the planet, although it has taken until the twenty-first century for the majority of the human population to become urbanised i.e. to live physically within a conurbation. However, the reality is that for centuries many, if not most, people in many countries have been dependent upon or greatly affected by towns and cities, their people, their demands and their markets.

Cities have ecological and environmental footprints that extend way beyond their physical boundaries. Their economic and social footprints similarly extend across a wide hinterland of exploitation and rationalisation to supply the resources needed by the populace and to absorb the wastes which the cities generate in abundance. Over the centuries, the footprint

Overgrown commonland SSSI and abandoned wood.

Photograph: Ian D. Rotherham.

of urban humans, the body odour of urbanisation, has inexorably infiltrated almost every aspect of the planetary system.

Densely populated cities demanded more organised and intensive agriculture and, to meet this need, forests were felled and grasslands ploughed. Where possible, wetlands were drained and, in dry-lands waters were then 'harvested' for irrigation. The process of 'improvement' took charge as technologies were refined and ways to add and to recycle important nutrients were developed. Energy to power this transformation of landscape and of productivity was limited to people power and then animal power. There was some use of wind and, where feasible, of waterpower but, until the unleashing of the energy potential of petrochemicals, there were limits to the conversion that could be undertaken or sustained. Once coal power through steam engines and then petrol-power were discovered and the technologies were evolved to apply the power to land improvement and to agricultural processes, the achievements of this transformation appeared unlimited. Furthermore, the petrochemical revolution also solved the other key problems of 'improvement' and productivity – the limited supplies of essential nutrients. With petrochemicals came inorganic fertilisers and the human ability to transform what seemed to be barren wastelands to fertile farmlands was complete. This final phase of the process took place centred firstly on Europe and then North America, from the 1600s to the 1900s.

The long-term consequences of agri-industrial production have included widespread contamination of ecosystems by persistent pesticides and the nutrient-enrichment or eutrophication of land and water across many parts of the world. The impacts have been severe for many species of animals and plants, which cannot persist in such high-nutrient environments. Biological production has often increased, but biodiversity has generally plummeted. In many situations, this all-pervasive contamination has penetrated into water-bearing bedrocks and other substrates and so water supplies may be affected for many decades to come.

The general effects of most agricultural systems in the late twentieth century included the drastic simplification of the ecological system. Whilst this often supported at least short-term increased productivity, it also caused obvious and often dramatic loss of biodiversity.

Summary

Human influence on the environment has increased dramatically over the centuries. The ecological footprint of humanity is now visible in almost every landscape across Europe. Urbanisation and the consequences of large collections of people in towns and cities have transformed many areas. Some of this is the direct impact of the urban settlements and some of it derives from the changes in agriculture and forestry needed to supply the urban centres.

References

Agnoletti, M. (ed.) (2006) *The Conservation of Cultural Landscapes*. CABI : Wallingford.

Perlin, J. (1989) *A Forest Journey*. Harvard University Press: Massachusetts.

Ponting, C. (1991) *A Green History of the World*. Sinclair-Stevenson Ltd.: London.

Rackham, O. (1986) *The History of the Countryside*. Dent: London.

Rotherham, I.D. (1999) 'Peat cutters and their landscapes: fundamental change in a fragile environment'. *Landscape Archaeology and Ecology* **4**: 28–51.

Rotherham, I.D. (2010) *Yorkshire's Forgotten Fenlands*. Pen and Sword Books Ltd.: Barnsley.

Rotherham, I.D. (2011) 'A Landscape History Approach to the Assessment of Ancient Woodlands', in E.B. Wallace (ed.) *Woodlands: Ecology, Management and Conservation*. Nova Science Publishers: Hauppauge, NY. pp. 161–184.

Rotherham, I.D. (2013) *The Lost Fens: England's Greatest Ecological Disaster*. The History Press: Stroud.

Rotherham, I.D. and P.A. Ardron (2006) 'The Archaeology of Woodland Landscapes: Issues for Managers based on the Case-study of Sheffield, England and four thousand years of human impact'. *Arboricultural Journal* **29** (4): 229–243.

Rotherham, I.D. and J. Bradley (eds) (2011) *Lowland Heaths: Ecology, History, Restoration and Management*. Wildtrack Publishing: Sheffield.

Rotherham, I.D., D. Egan and P.A. Ardron (2004) 'Fuel economy and the uplands: the effects of peat and turf utilisation on upland landscapes'. *Society for Landscape Studies Supplementary Series* **2**: 99–109.

Rotherham, I.D. and D. Egan (2005) 'The Economics of Fuel Wood, Charcoal and Coal: An Interpretation of Coppice Management of British Woodlands', in M. Agnoletti, M. Armiero, S. Barca and G. Corona. (eds) *History and Sustainability*. European Society for Environmental History: Florence. pp. 100–104.

Rotherham, I.D. and C. Handley (eds) (2011) *Animals, Man and Treescapes*. Wildtrack Publishing: Sheffield.

Rotherham, I.D. and M. Jones (2000) 'The Impact of Economic, Social and Political Factors on the Ecology of Small English Woodlands: a Case Study of the Ancient Woods in South Yorkshire, England', in M. Agnoletti and S. Anderson (eds) *Forest History:*

International Studies in Socio-economic and Forest ecosystem change. CABI: Wallingford. pp. 397–410.

Rotherham, I.D. and D. McCallam (2008) 'Peat Bogs, Marshes and Fen as disputed Landscapes in Late Eighteenth-century France and England', in L. Lyle and D. McCallam (eds) *Histoires de la Terre: Earth Sciences and French Culture 1740–1940.* Rodopi B.V.: Amsterdam and New York. pp. 75–90.

Smout, T.C. (2000) *Nature Contested – Environmental History in Scotland and Northern England Since 1600.* Edinburgh University Press: Edinburgh.

5.

THE IMPACTS OF INDUSTRIALISATION

Introduction

The details of the processes of agricultural intensification and of industrialisation are debated in terms of precise timing and which depended on the other. In practice they are closely intertwined as they are with the third process, that of urbanisation. Farming improvement such as happened in the period from around 1500s AD to around 1900 AD would not have been possible without industrialisation. However, for effective industrialisation there needs to be urbanisation to provide the labour supply and the technological 'growth-poles' and synergies, and the economic markets for products. As noted already, urban centres demand regular and substantial supplies of food and they need effective disposal of wastes and other by-products of industry and urban life. The growth of town and cities, the industrialisation

Making armour plate at Cammell Laird in Sheffield, WW1 with a 12,000 ton press.
Author's collection.

of manufacturing and the footprints of these two phenomena, demand intensive and highly productive agriculture. The latter needs the technologies and products of industry in order to convert the landscape to meet these demands. In many ways success breeds success and the circle of production and demand is closed. Once again, when industry depended on the power of humans or of animals, supported sometimes by wind-power or by waterpower, then the degree to which this path could be followed was limited.

Energy and subsidy

With the advent of first coal-powered steam engines, and then petrochemically-driven machines, the immediate limits were removed. The three driving forces of agriculture, of industry and of urbanisation formed a closed circle of landscape and environmental change, each feeding and feeding off the others. The pinnacles of such applications were seen during the twentieth century in both western capitalist systems and the old Soviet bloc state

Stocksbridge Steel Works, around 1900.

Author's collection.

capitalist systems. In both these contrasting systems the less intensive and more traditional systems of land management with often labour-intensive and locally sustainable but less productive harvests were swept away. The key to this was often a rationalised social system and the application of colossal amounts of very cheap or at least subsidised petrochemical energy. Agriculture and industry in many ways became one, so the food production and processing systems of the later twentieth century are largely agri-industrial, are heavily dependent on cheap oil, employ few people full-time and have small numbers of low-paid transient workers to undertake menial tasks which cannot be mechanised. Another trend of agri-industry has been a separation of arable farming and animal husbandry both in process and geographically. This is the application of the logic of economies of scale and the rationalisation of specialisation. However, there are also serious resulting issues of waste disposal, of recycling and of disintegration of the social systems in rural farming areas. In the short-term market place, intensive agri-industrial farming is competitive. Whether it supports systems that are either environmentally or socially sustainable is open to question.

Thorncliffe Works, Sheffield, 1909.

Author's collection.

Chapter 5

Pollution

The other obvious impact of the move to industrialisation, and again one which cannot be separated fully from agriculture or urbanisation, is that of gross environmental pollution. Whilst localised pollution through manufacturing or through urban living and for example the burning of coal is known from very early days, it was with the Industrial Revolution in tandem with Victorian urbanisation that pollution came into its own. From the early 1800s to the late 1900s, wastes and other materials from industry and from urban living grossly affected air, land and waters around the planet. In the wider countryside too, the runoff of nutrients from inorganic fertilisers and the ecosystem-wide effects of herbicides and pesticides rapidly took their tolls and the impacts became obvious and alarming. By the 1960s, the effects of organo-chlorine pesticides like DDT were becoming obvious, as an entire tier of the food-chain, comprising the top carnivores and similar species, was killed off. At the same time, many rivers in Europe and in North America became biologically dead through a heady mix of chemical pollution and overloading with raw sewage. When Rachel Carson published her *Silent Spring* in 1967, it was a bombshell to the corporate psyche of public trust in post-war techno-solutions. Kenneth Mellanby followed this with his landmark book, *Pesticides and Pollution*. A hint of what was to come had already been experienced on the River Thames in London when the nauseating stench of the Victorian river caused Members of Parliament to choke and faint. Legislation was passed to try to resolve the problems, or at least their most obvious manifestations, but it would take more than a century for the wider problems of water quality to be resolved. Today many of these problems have been exported around the world and the rivers of many emerging countries and economies such as mainland China are derelict and despoiled.

Summary

The modern economic and social successes of humanity depend on revolutions in both agriculture and industry. Inextricably tied to urbanisation, these shifts allowed people to exploit and dominate nature in ways previously beyond comprehension. The toll in terms of ecological decline and especially of pollution, parallel the benefits for economy and society.

References

Carson, R. (1965) *Silent Spring*. Penguin: Harmondsworth.

Mellanby, K. (1967) *Pesticides and Pollution*. Collins: London.

Perlin, J. (1989) *A Forest Journey*. Harvard University Press: Cambridge, Mass.

Ponting, C. (1991) *A Green History of the World*. Sinclair-Stevenson Ltd.: London.

Rackham, O. (1986) *The History of the Countryside*. Dent: London.

Rotherham, I.D. (2005) 'Fuel and Landscape – Exploitation, Environment, Crisis and Continuum'. *Landscape Archaeology and Ecology* **5**: 65–81.

Rotherham, I.D. (ed.) (2005) Crisis and Continuum in the Shaping of Landscapes. *Landscape Archaeology and Ecology* **5**.

Rotherham, I.D. (2009) 'The Importance of Cultural Severance in Landscape Ecology Research', in A. Dupont and H. Jacobs (eds) *Landscape Ecology Research Trends*. Nova Science Publishers Hauppauge, NY.

6.

THE IMPACTS OF URBANISATION

Introduction

Linked to both agricultural development and to industrialisation, has been the growth of towns and cities. In terms of impacts on biodiversity and ecology, it must be understood that urbanisation has not been a simple or linear process. There were great cities in Egyptian and Roman times for example, which exceeded greatly in size the biggest settlements of medieval England. Therefore, through history there have been phases on urban development and the growth of an ecological footprint in the wider landscape, through resource use and particularly agriculture. However, these have come and gone in pulses of activity as particular civilisations and cultures have waxed and waned. The Romans of around 100 BC to 500 AD transformed large areas of landscape to produce food and wine for their urban populations.

Badger.

Photograph: Ian D. Rotherham.

Chapter 6

Through both forest clearance and land tillage, the ecology was radically altered. They also began the long history of hunting for sport and pleasure and not just food, again something which, over subsequent centuries, would have massive effects on biodiversity. Hunting would alter the social and economic balances between competing land uses and between key social groups. Through the related processes of resource management and legal enforcement, this deep-rooted interest in the chase rather than just in food production would influence ecology and biodiversity across Western Europe through the medieval period and even to the twenty-first century. Some of our richest sites for wildlife are the few surviving descendants of the great medieval parks and chases; and, according to Vera, some at least may be the closest we have to the primeval European savannah and forest. Even here though, we see the influence of the urban centres because, to a large degree, these were reservations for the pleasure of urbanised elites.

Overgrown commonland SSSI with Rosebay.

Photograph: Ian D. Rotherham.

The Impacts of Urbanisation

Urban impacts

When urbanisation came, sophistication and complexity of organisation followed and, through these, there were increasing demands on the surrounding landscapes and their ecology. Cities needed food and drink, water and fire, building materials and transportation. The ecological footprint of a major urban settlement extended well beyond its physical boundaries. Forests were cleared, wetlands were drained, lands were ploughed and wastes were excreted into the ecosystems. Generally, all these processes have grown as the cities have expanded. Limitations to this growth were the capacity of the landscape to support it, or the wider area to provide imported materials to subsidise the system. As noted earlier, the forms of available energy also limited urban extent and, with the advent of readily available petro-chemicals, the impacts on biodiversity have increased dramatically. In earlier civilisations, as noted particularly around the Mediterranean, when a city exceeded its capacity often its supply chains for essential commodities such as timber became stretched and vulnerable and ultimately collapsed, with retrenchment following. As cities shrank or were abandoned, nature to some extent returned, but always in a form much changed from the original landscape. Recognising the changes and differences

Sheffield from above the Midland Station in 1909, A. Holland.

Author's collection from an original by A. Holland, with thanks to Sheffield Museums.

Chapter 6

has proved problematic for today's researchers and often landscapes regarded as somehow pristine and primeval are in fact anything but. Understanding the often subtle influences of former land use and long-gone societies is hugely important in assessing human impacts on biodiversity.

Following the decline of the great Mediterranean civilisations, and particularly the Roman Empire, there was a move away from great cities and not until the Middle Ages did a new urban society begin to emerge. Even so, the cities of the Normans in France and in England for example, were a fraction of the size of some of the centres that preceded them by perhaps a thousand years. Gradually through the period from 1100 AD to the early 1600s, there was a move to new towns and cities and a rationalisation of land use to supply resources to these centres of population and of trade. Then, following the Renaissance and the emergence of new political, economic and social forces driving innovation and industrialisation, came the rapid development of great industrial urban cities and towns. These reached a peak in Western Europe from the mid-1800s into the 1900s with the dramatic expansion of industrial cities like Birmingham, Manchester and Sheffield in England. The impacts of these centres on biodiversity have already been

Urban Pipistrelle Bat.

Photograph: Paul Ardron.

described in terms of their use of resources and their output of gross pollution. However, there were many other influences that changed regional ecosystems and which still influence patterns of biodiversity. One of the key factors has been the way in which urban centres have expanded and subsumed rural and 'natural' landscapes throughout their hinterland. The city and the town modify societies and communities and change land-use, making huge demands on their hinterland or catchment. They suck in resources of materials, products and people, and spew out wastes, the so-called '*body odour*' of urban development, as the green becomes grey.

The processes and impacts witnessed in Western Europe and North America during the Industrial Revolution and the early twentieth century have been emulated around the world but, like 'Topsy', they have grown. Across China, India, South America and elsewhere the urban process is swift and catastrophic. By the early twenty-first century, one of the biggest changes in human interaction with the environment has been the move globally from a predominantly rural society to an urban one and, with this, from a traditional community to a technological one.

Cultural severance from nature

The consequence for biodiversity and nature conservation is the process the present author calls '*cultural severance*' that, in simple terms, is the end of traditional or customary uses and practices. All across the planet, the traditional and ancient ways of managing the natural resource, which in many cases are now essential for species survival, are being lost. Even more worrying is that in many cases scientists and others do not even realise the cause behind the losses. They see 'abandonment' of landscapes as a process of so-called '*re-wilding*' and are surprised when the species do not return. Wilder landscapes may bring some benefits to wildlife, but abandonment is not re-wilding and is often catastrophically damaging. However, it should not be assumed that 'traditional' management of natural resources was always benign – it was not, and many ancient societies consequently suffered environmental, economic and political traumas. Nevertheless, when local people and local communities have control of their natural resources, it is in their interests to manage them sustainably; their very survival may depend upon this. Certainly too, in a pre-petro-chemically subsidised economy, careful recycling of energy and resources is essential. Mostly, over long periods, communities develop sophisticated ways of living within the constraints of

Chapter 6

their immediate environment. These uses of the landscapes change them but mostly in gradual ways, which allow nature to adapt and evolve through time. The 'severance' or breakdown of the systems by over-use is often disastrous and the impacts of capital-based exploitation, of corporate control distanced from local communities and of consequent depopulation and abandonment of rural areas are catastrophic.

Associated with the emergence of industrial societies driven largely by petro-chemicals has been the use of pesticides. Some of these synthetic chemicals are relatively benign and have brought undoubted benefits to humanity but others, such as DDT from the 1940s to the 1970s, proved hugely damaging to ecology. The rapid decline in both wildlife species and their habitats across whole areas of landscape presents serious problems for claims of sustainability. Some species losses are clearly attributable to particular causes, for example the DDT pollution that wiped out birds of prey for many decades over vast areas. It is only now in the new millennium that, across Britain, birds such as Peregrine Falcons, Kingfishers and Grey Herons and mammals like Otters have recovered. Other animals have gone because of very specific persecution and plants because of collecting. Intensive farming and forestry have simply squeezed out many species and their habitats. Many

Woodland destruction.

Photograph: Ian D. Rotherham.

species are lost due to release or addition of gross levels of nutrients to the environment associated with such use. However, many species in many areas today are affected by combined pressures of habitat loss and fragmentation and degradation of what is left; and by abandonment of traditional management as people leave the countryside for an urban existence.

Abandonment allows ecological successions to progress unfettered, often resulting in accumulations of nutrients and of organic matter that change fundamentally the ecological resource. The changes which then occur range from micro-climatic alteration in critical habitats – for example for many insect species – to landscape-scale transformation from open grassland, savannah and scrub with some high forest, to rank scrub and secondary woodland. Some species will be able to utilise these new areas but many will be lost. Others will do well in particular successional stages, but will decline once their time has passed.

Summary

Urban living has transformed societies and caused fundamental shifts in the ways that communities exploit nature.

As noted earlier, traditional management did not create some sort of utopian landscape; in many cases and in many ways, it could cause serious change and damage. However, it happened over very many centuries and the landscape, human cultures and wildlife species co-evolved. This means that, on abandonment, these are cultural landscapes, not natural ones, and the changes that subsequently occur are not necessarily those that conservationists either expect or desire. There are three key aspects of traditional, and especially subsistence, management of a landscape in terms of the maintenance of associated biodiversity:

Micro-level disturbance;
Removal of biomass for fuel, building and grazing;
Continuity and predictability.

With abandonment or a move to intensive landscape utilisation, these key factors are lost or at least compromised. The consequences are now witnessed around the globe.

Chapter 6

References

Ponting, C. (1991) *A Green History of the World*. Sinclair-Stevenson Ltd.: London.

Rackham, O. (1986) *The History of the Countryside*. Dent: London.

Richardson (1992) *Pollution Monitoring with Lichens*. Naturalists' Handbooks No. 19. Richmond Publishing Co. Ltd.: Slough.

Rotherham, I.D. (1999) 'Urban Environmental History: the importance of relict communities in urban biodiversity conservation'. *Practical Ecology and Conservation* **3** (1): 3–22.

Rotherham, I.D. (2005) 'Fuel and Landscape – Exploitation, Environment, Crisis and Continuum'. *Landscape Archaeology and Ecology* **5**: 65–81.

Rotherham, I.D. (2009) *'The Importance of Cultural Severance in Landscape Ecology Research'*, in A. Dupont and H. Jacobs (eds) *Landscape Ecology Research Trends*. Nova Science Publishers Hauppauge, NY.

Rotherham, I.D. (2013) *'Searching for Shadows and Ghosts'*, in I.D. Rotherham, C. Handley, M. Agnoletti and T. Samoljik (eds) (2013) *Trees Beyond the Wood – an Exploration of Concepts of Woods, Forests and Trees*. Wildtrack Publishing: Sheffield. pp. 1–16.

Rotherham, I.D. (2013) *The Lost Fens: England's Greatest Ecological Disaster*. The History Press: Stroud.

7.

POLLUTION OF LAND, AIR AND WATER

Introduction

The consequences of human activity for planetary ecosystems have been the degradation, despoliation, and pollution of land, air and water. These impacts have been manifested in obvious problems such as the death of wildlife or the declines of birds for example due to failure to breed. However, there are many longer-term and less immediately obvious effects of environmental pollution, and most are still prevalent today.

Polluting the land

Ever since humanity increased in numbers, settled in towns and cities and then developed the technologies of exploitation and development, we have polluted and changed the land and the soil. The scale of impacts and the consequences have increased through time and step-changes have occurred with key transformations such as the Industrial Revolution and the Agricultural Revolution and with increased urbanisation. Today, globalisation has accelerated and compounded the impacts. In urban and industrial areas, lands have been polluted with a vast array of chemicals and waste products from manufacturing and processing. In the wider rural landscapes, chemically subsidised intensive farming has combined with atmospheric fallout from power stations and from motor vehicles to pollute and contaminate soils and groundwater. In developed countries such as Britain, nitrogen is endemic and causes massive changes in ecology. Fertilisers, pesticides and other contaminants such as radionucleotides from accidents like Chernobyl, occur from the highest mountains to the coastal seas.

Interestingly though, in some cases and especially old, contaminated, industrial or ex-industrial sites, biodiversity, and especially rare species, can be abundant. Extreme conditions of soil pH from highly acidic to highly basic, very dry or waterlogged conditions and low levels of nutrients encourage stress tolerant plants and animals. These are often the species squeezed out from the wider landscape by nutrient-loving competitors. Furthermore, very old, large industrial complexes often took lands from the landscape at a time before agriculture became increasingly intensive. Therefore, these sites frequently include relicts from the medieval environment. Now, visually and chemically degraded, these areas are generally regarded as 'brownfield' lands of little worth and yet hold some of our richest hotspots for biodiversity.

Polluting the air

Air pollution was another obvious consequence of industry and urban life. In the twenty-first century, the possibility of gross air pollution in cities like Athens or Beijing causes jitters for the organisers of events like the Olympic Games. Yet air pollution is an everyday occurrence in most cities around the world. Although some recovery is now taking place, the impact of two centuries of air pollution annihilated populations of pollution-sensitive species both in the cities and in a wide footprint around them. In Great Britain for example, lichens and plants such as ferns were removed from whole areas of the landscape. The ecology and associated biodiversity of many areas was irreparably changed. Acid rain and other acidic fallout from industry and from domestic coal fires removed arboreal lichens and also sensitive trees and other species. However – more long-term perhaps – they also transformed soils, with decreased pH and associated loss of nutrients. In cities like Sheffield, this has undoubtedly transformed entire ecosystems and caused the massive loss of sensitive plants and animals. Other effects seen widely across cities like Sheffield are the deposition in watercourses and on land of large amounts of air-borne, long-residence pollutants such as lead. The implications of such widespread and long-lived pollution are unknown, though most are believed to be benign. Some of the other post-industrial legacies of more active and biologically available toxins, especially heavy metals, in river sediments such as along the River Rother in both Yorkshire and Derbyshire, remain elusive.

The effects of pollution on biodiversity are not simply to reduce or even remove particular species, but also sometimes to set in train a longer-term displacement of some species by others. Therefore, the contamination of soil and water by nitrogen rich inorganic fertilisers, for example, produces conditions which suit the more aggressive and faster-growing competitor species and these displace the stress-tolerators, which require lower levels of available nutrients. One of the most elegant examples of this process is the impact of air pollution on lichens in urban areas (Richardson, 1992). Drastic air pollution in English industrial cities progressively removed the pollution sensitive species such as *Usnea* and *Ramalina* and facilitated the appearance and ultimately the dominance of species such as the 'pollution lichen', *Lecanora conizaeoides*. Indeed, through assessments of the selective impacts of air pollution they can be used as environmental indicators or '*bio-indicators*'. If air is badly polluted, particularly with sulphur dioxide given off as gas by burning of mineral coal, then there may be zones with no lichens at all. At the other extreme, if the air is clean, then a range of shrubby, hairy and leafy lichens may be abundant and the diversity of lichens increases dramatically. Some lichens are able to tolerate relatively high pollution levels. These species are commonly found in urban areas on pavements, walls and the bark of trees. However, any evaluation of air pollution levels also has to be set in the context of the trees and bark available since the acid barks of trees such as Pedunculate Oak (*Quercus robur*) are rather poor for most lichens whereas those with more alkaline bark such as Ash (*Fraxinus excelsior*) or Willow (*Salix* sp.) are far more suitable.

The lichens which are most sensitive to air pollution are shrubby and leafy, since their 'branches' protrude out into the pollution-laden atmosphere. Those that are most tolerant tend to be the somewhat structurally reduced forms or crustose lichens. Following the emergence of heavy industry in the

A Sheffield forge on the River Don, 1907.

Author's collection.

late 1700s and 1800s the more sensitive shrubby and leafy lichens (such as *Ramalina, Usnea* and *Lobaria*) species had very limited geographical ranges and were largely removed from anywhere near to or down-wind of an air pollution source. They were then, by the 1970s, confined to regions of Britain with unpolluted air and today are especially abundant in northern and western Scotland, west Wales, Devon and Cornwall. Since the decrease in atmospheric sulphur during the 1980s and 1990s, many of these species have expanded back into their original ranges.

In terms of biodiversity, human impact has had clear effects on lichen communities around cities. The results of air pollution and modifications to substrate availability have generated lichen zone patterns, which can be seen around most big towns or cities and around individual industrial complexes. The driving force here is the mean level of sulphur dioxide in the atmosphere and in rain. There are zonal indices such as that produced by Hawksworth and Rose (1970). This has a scale of 1 (poorest air quality) to 10 (purest air) and is a good general 'index' of ambient air quality. An interesting observation regarding human impact on biodiversity is that whilst the Hawksworth and Rose zonation applies well in situations with rising sulphurous air pollution, the reverse does not apply as levels fall. As sulphur dioxide decreases with air pollution controls, with a shift from coal burning in domestic fires or with

Eels.

Author's collection.

the closure of heavy industrial factories, the lichens do not re-colonise in the same sequence in which they were lost. More random effects of propagule dispersal and substrate suitability probably have greater influence on the subsequent distribution patterns.

In the early to mid-twentieth century in most British towns and cities, air pollution was greater than it is today. Sulphur dioxide pollution was worst in the inner city and declined out to the suburbs. In this situation, a lichen pollution zone scale would highlight Zone 1 as the inner city with progressive improvement to the cleaner air at the transition to the countryside beyond the town. However, since the 1970s, sulphur dioxide concentrations have been falling in both the inner and outer city zones with far less difference between them. This reduction in sulphur dioxide from the 1970s to the present day has triggered re-colonisation by a number of lichen species. Interestingly too, it has meant a drastic reduction in the pollution indicator *Lecanora conizaeoides* which is now once again becoming quite rare and is generally confined to very acidic tree barks such as those of Scots Pine.

Polluting the waters

The precise impacts of river pollution depend on many factors, from the type of pollutant to the nature of the river and hence its capacity to absorb or to recover from a pollution incident. Furthermore, the impacts of pollution on biodiversity vary with the season and hence the vulnerability of particular organisms and between regular repeated pollution releases and one-off incidents. The range of pollutants and their effects is infinitely wide and varies from relatively benign materials such as sewage, which simply use up available oxygen in their degradation, to highly toxic chemicals such as mercury, arsenic and dioxin. This means that the effects on aquatic ecosystems are similarly varied. However, just as with the air pollution zonation found with lichens and sulphur dioxide, there are specific and predictable patterns of biodiversity, which occur in polluted waters. Through detailed understanding of these patterns, quite sophisticated assessments can be made of the levels of water pollution occurring at a site over time. These effects are seen in micro-organisms such as bacteria, algae, blue-green algae and fungi. However, they are especially obvious in aquatic arthropods, such as crustaceans and insects with larval stages in water, and in fish. Just as with air pollution in cities, the pollution can squeeze species out and then if conditions recover, a process of re-colonisation may occur.

Chapter 7

'Work-a-day Sheffield' by Hayward Young; painting of the River Don and Blonk Bridge in the early 1900s.

Author's collection.

Pollution of Land, Air and Water

Human impact on rivers and streams is not simple and physical disruption through canalisation, culverting, diversions and increases in sediment loads can all affect the ecology. In some cases, these impacts may be at least as significant as the levels of pollutants. However, the effects can be dramatic as well as unexpected. In industrial cities in northern England, such as Bradford, Sheffield, Leeds and Manchester, the combination of chemical, physical and biological pollution plus the structural manipulation and modification of many urbanised watercourses led to the almost entire removal of all biodiversity from entire stretches of river and stream. These systems and the banks immediately adjacent were generally degraded and despoiled and in some cases biologically dead.

However, as the pollution levels dropped, and plants and animals re-colonised there was a further human twist to the biodiversity mix. Exotic species of plants, sometimes escaping from the former Victorian 'wild' gardens to which they had been introduced by plant collectors, slipped out almost unnoticed into the new wilds. In some cases, they were assisted through deliberate introductions by exotic plant enthusiasts. Therefore, these urban watercourses once almost devoid of life in the same way that urban areas had become lichen deserts, received a new recombinant flora. This is dominated by alien trees such as Sycamore (*Acer pseudoplatanus*) with aggressive peren-nial herbs like Japanese Knotweed (*Reynoutria japonica*), robust biennials such as Giant Hogweed (*Heracleum mantegazzianum*) and vigorous annuals, particularly Himalayan Balsam (*Impatiens glandulifera*). As Oliver Gilbert demonstrated in the 1980s, these dense stands of exotic trees and herbs were forming a new and distinctive urban plant community, though perhaps with more human influence than Gilbert imagined. However, what he did show was the re-colonisation of native plants typical of ancient woodland environments, washing downstream from wooded sites in the headwaters and establishing an 'ancient woodland' flora beneath the pseudo-canopy of the dense knotweed and balsam (Gilbert, 1989).

There is a further demonstration here too of the intimate relation-ships between human influences and contemporary biodiversity. These urban rivers not only suffered chemical pollution and massive inputs of human sewage effluents, but became artificially heated too. Rivers such as the Don in Sheffield were used to cool the great industrial processes such as steel manufacture and as such had their ambient temperatures raised to a more-or-less constant 20–23°C, winter and summer. This situation continued until the 1970s when many of the factories closed and the remaining sites became more self-contained and more rigorously controlled. However, the combination of thermal pollution and the widespread sewage pollution, which occurred again until the late 1970s, brought together the seeds of the Mediterranean Wild Fig (*Ficus carica*) with the conditions they require for germination. They require a consistent high temperature and, imported from the Mediterranean, and having passed through the human gut and so into the abundant raw sewage, they were able to germinate and grow along the urban rivers. These figs now sucker and grow and in some areas have formed unique 'urban fig forests' along our most urban watercourses. In Sheffield, these trees are protected as an especially iconic symbol of the Industrial Revolution and its very special impact on regional biodiversity (Bownes et al., 1991).

For an island complex like the British Isles, much of the pollution from the land ends up in watercourses and much of that subsequently ends up in the seas.

Summary

Human impact on ecosystems and wildlife has occurred through many different mechanisms. However, the most insidious and widespread effects of people on the planetary systems are probably through pollution and despoliation through the release of chemical wastes of various sorts and through myriad processes, into land, air, freshwater and seas.

References

Carson, R. (1965) *Silent Spring*. Penguin: Harmondsworth.

Freedman, B. (1995) *Environmental Ecology – The Effects of Pollution, Disturbance and Other Stresses*. Second Edition. Academic Press: San Diego.

Gilbert, O.L. (1989) *The Ecology of Urban Habitats*. Chapman and Hall: London.

Gilbert, O.L. (1992) *The Flowering of the Cities ... The Natural Flora of 'Urban Commons'*. English Nature: Peterborough.

Goldsmith, E. and R. Allen (with help from M. Allaby, J. Davoll and S. Lawrence) (1972) *A Blueprint for Survival*. *Ecologist* **2**(1). Also published by Penguin: Harmondsworth.

Meadows, D.H., D.L. Meadows, J. Randers and W.W. Behrens (1972) *The Limits to Growth*. Pan Books: London.

Mellanby, K. (1967) *Pesticides and Pollution*. Collins New Naturalist: London.

Richardson (1992) *Pollution Monitoring with Lichens*. Naturalists' Handbooks No. 19. Richmond Publishing Co. Ltd.: Slough.

Rose, F. (1976) 'Lichenological indicators of age and environmental continuity in woodlands' in D.H. Brown, D.I. Hawksworth and R.H. Bailey (eds) *Lichenology: Progress and Problems*. Academic Press: London.

Rotherham, I.D. (1999) 'Urban Environmental History: the importance of relict communities in urban biodiversity conservation'. *Practical Ecology and Conservation* 3 (1): 3–22.

Rotherham, I.D. (2008) 'Landscape, Water and History'. *Practical Ecology and Conservation* 7: 138–152.

Rotherham, I.D. (2008) 'Floods and Water: A Landscape-scale Response'. *Practical Ecology and Conservation* 7: 128–137.

Rotherham, I.D. (2012) 'Post Coal-mining Landscapes: water, heaths, and commons as a resource for wildlife, people and heritage', in I.D. Rotherham and C. Handley (eds) (2012) *Between a Rock and A Hard Place*. Landscape Archaeology and Ecology Special Series. Papers from the Landscape Conservation Forum (2). Wildtrack Publishing: Sheffield. pp. 49–58.

Rotherham, I.D. and P.A. Ardron (2006) 'The Archaeology of Woodland Landscapes: Issues for Managers based on the Case-study of Sheffield, England and four thousand years of human impact'. *Arboricultural Journal* 29 (4): 229–243.

Rotherham, I.D., J. Lunn and F. Spode (2012) 'Wildlife and Coal – the nature conservation value of post-mining sites in South Yorkshire', in I.D. Rotherham and C. Handley (eds) *Dynamic Landscape Restoration*. Landscape Archaeology and Ecology Special Series. Papers from the Landscape Conservation Forum (1). Wildtrack Publishing: Sheffield. pp. 30–64.

Rotherham, I.D., F. Spode and D. Fraser (2003) 'Post–coalmining landscapes: an under-appreciated resource for wildlife, people and heritage', in H.M. Moore, H.R. Fox and S. Elliot (eds) *Land Reclamation: Extending the Boundaries*. A.A. Balkema Publishers: Lisse. pp. 93–99.

Stamp, D. (1969) *Nature Conservation in Britain*. Collins New Naturalist: London.

Taylor, G.R. (1972) *The Doomsday Book*. Panther Books Ltd.: London.

8.

POPULATION AND RESOURCES

Introduction

In terms of human impacts on the environment and on biodiversity, it is obvious that the sheer numbers of the human population are a major issue. Any attempt to address this is fraught with issues of massive political, social and even economic significance. However, to be in denial about the scale of the problem and the need to apply resources more equitably and to utilise them more sustainably, is naive.

Furthermore, a specific issue with regard to human populations is the demographic shift to older communities and, especially in recent years, from largely rural to mostly urban dwelling. These trends have massive implications for human demands for natural resources and for the sustainability of the wider landscapes. For the first time in human history, in the early twenty-first century, we became a predominantly urban species. Rural areas become depopulated, with large swathes of countryside either abandoned or taken over by agri-industrial farming and forestry.

Additionally, as the global population expands and becomes urban and the aspirations for consumption continue to grow across the planet, ecosystems are increasingly stressed and unable to absorb and balance human demands. The changes wrought by human existence are so great that we have now entered a new phase in planetary history, the so-called Anthropocene, which is the era in which people, not Nature, determine the future patterns of global ecology.

The scale of loss, of species reductions in distribution, in extinctions and in, for example, the spread of alien invasive species around the planet, has become unprecedented.

Following from all these pressures and changes has been the broad-scale destruction of 'natural' and 'eco-cultural' landscapes and associated wildlife habitats. Furthermore, areas that remain reasonably intact are increasingly fragmented, with consequent impacts on species mobility and the ability of ecosystems to recover from the traumas of human impacts or of natural catastrophes.

Chapter 8

Examples

1. The Northern Heaths

Across much of northern England, changes in land-use caused massive loss of heath and low-lying moor, with huge inroads into upland moorland. This was particularly from around 1600 AD until the early 1900s. The remaining, generally unenclosed, landscape of the high moorland and blanket bog has also changed dramatically. For example, there was more medieval removal of peat from the South Pennines than from the entire Norfolk Broads (Ardron et al., 1999). Most peat was removed in the early medieval period, whilst the greatest, catastrophic losses of lower-lying sites probably occurred during the sixteenth, seventeenth and eighteenth centuries. These were associated with Parliamentary and private 'enclosures' of heath, moor, common, bog and 'waste'. The resulting landscape has heather moorland restricted largely to the upland north-west of the region and the remaining lowland sites in the east are generally small and fragmentary.

The scale of cultural utilisation

Much of this landscape was subjected to cultural utilisation including peat cutting, 'turf-getting', 'moss-gathering', bracken and rush harvesting and a multitude of other uses. On upland landscapes especially, this was far greater than previously suspected. For example the extent of well-defined peat cuttings located around remaining areas of blanket mire in the Peak District (and other similar areas such as the North York Moors) is considerable. Furthermore, thin peats and turf on low-level moors were also stripped away, with in many areas extensive 'turf-cutting' and 'paring and burning', in upland landscapes but also on valley-sides and down to the lowlands. Therefore, the Derbyshire, Nottinghamshire, Lincolnshire, and South Yorkshire heaths were extensively utilised for fuel, grazing and building materials. This affected valley mires, raised bogs and fens and, importantly, many areas of lowland heath and common mostly now obliterated. Where suitable landscape remains intact, be it upland or lowland, the widespread occurrence of drainage features and other cutting infrastructure indicates that little if any 'peatland' was unaffected. Often associated with land improvement for agriculture and the creation of in-bye land, this extends downhill into the extensive lowlands. In most situations, the evidence on the ground has been swept away by enclosures and agricultural intensification.

Population and Resources

A major conclusion is that the nature and scale of associated change in these landscapes are fundamental to their present-day condition. Firstly, this relates to long-term use for subsistence farming, over many, many centuries. The scale of this impact has been grossly under-estimated. Secondly, the separation of these landscapes into lowlands and uplands often masks the human element. These are very much enclosed and improved, and unenclosed and unimproved landscapes; with the impact far greater in the lowlands. Enclosure, cutting and drainage and, finally, often catastrophic agricultural intensification or creeping urbanisation, have radically altered the lower ground, almost beyond recognition.

Red Grouse - a bird of heath and moor.

Author's collection.

Chapter 8

2. The Yorkshire Fens

The Northern Fens of Yorkshire and north Lincolnshire extended across around 3,000 square kilometres or 1,900 square miles of largely flat lowland landscape (about 400,000 large football pitches). Much of this survived intact until perhaps 400 years ago and a significant proportion well into the 1800s. The county of Yorkshire has many wetlands and water-bodies. Many of these are 'natural' but today most are probably to an extent more or less artificial creations of people. From water supply reservoirs to fish ponds, from medieval millponds to mineral extraction sites, the region is pockmarked with water features large and small. Yet if you examine an old map closely, even one from, say, the early twentieth century, you find evidence of a former wetter landscape. In today's technologically driven and manicured landscape of the twenty-first century, much of the water has been inexorably squeezed from the environment. Across the lowlands, ponds and meres have been drained,

Grey Heron.
Photograph: Ian D. Rotherham.

Population and Resources

fens and marshes have been 'improved'. In the uplands of the eastern Peak and the flanks of the great Pennine chain the moors and bogs were drained and stripped for medieval peat fuel and then intensively '*gripped*' for sheep and grouse farming. The resulting 'wild' uplands are modified hugely from their more natural origins. The evidence of former wetlands is seen in the landscape through the networks of drains and dykes, through the ranks of rectilinear walls and hedges of the eighteenth and nineteenth-century improvers and often through place-names associated with the past. 'Marsh Lane' was generally the old road down to the common marsh, 'Turbary Lane' or 'Peat Pits Lane' would have led to the common turbary for peat fuel, 'Land's End' was where land and water met, 'Willow Garth' was the place where willow was grown for basket-making; there are many others. Many areas have names with 'Moor' and very often, this was the old-fashioned, lowland wet moor, such as the Somerset 'Moors and Levels', not an upland heath.

Stand on relatively high ground looking across a lower-lying valley and you will see the evidence of the former wetlands and of their progressive loss and ultimate demise. They are all around us, but we have to look in order to see. In order to understand the wetland past, it is necessary to remove yourself from today and the modern living with which you feel comfortable and to immerse yourself in the waters of medieval Yorkshire, be it peat bog, marsh or fen. Only then can you gain some insight into this once vast resource. Even now, it is possible to get a glimpse of how this landscape might have looked, perhaps how it functioned and even of its importance to local communities. Stand in the heart of Thorne Moors, for example, grossly modified though they are by centuries of peat stripping and drainage, and you feel something of the magnificence of a landscape (or waterscape) of unfettered nature. Horizon to horizon, no sign of human artefact or construction: today this is an unusual or maybe even unique experience in lowland England. Seek out the great floodlands of Wheldrake Ings near York during a winter flood and you have a tantalising view of the medieval or even primeval wetlands of ancient Yorkshire. Sadly, though, most have gone and those that remain are tattered remnants of a once vibrant ecology. The greatest challenge today is to restore and repair what is left and even to help reinvent and reconstruct new additions to Yorkshire's Fens.

The waters did not exist in isolation but were joined by meandering, often sluggish, rivers – the living arteries of the vast landscapes of ancient times. These channels gave winter deposits of silts from high grounds to low, to provide fertility for summer grazing meadows and for harvests of hay. They provided transportation routes for mobility and trade, they drained the drier lands, which surrounded them and gave back to local people immense supplies of fish, fuel, withies and much more. Wetlands and rivers also brought fear of flooding and the ever-present spectre of disease especially of malarial 'ague'. Around the rivers and water-bodies was higher land that was used for farming and for settlement. Even here the landscape past was much wetter than today. Every farming field that you see will have been intensively 'under-drained' for maybe two centuries, the result being a desiccated and increasingly dry landscape and increased flood-risk downstream.

The fate of the rivers sits alongside that of the bogs, marshes and fens: manipulated, constrained and controlled to do human will. Only at times of catastrophic flooding such as in York in 1998 and 2000, do the rivers break out of their artificial channels to once again, albeit temporarily, become the masters of their own horizons. Rivers are straightened and embanked, dredged and drained, culverted, concreted and canalised. Whereas bog, marsh and fen were squeezed dry, the rivers were progressively strangled by generations of engineers charged with bringing order to chaos and productivity and capitalist profit to what was once a common resource.

It is clear that much contemporary intensive farming in this lowland region is environmentally unsustainable. To resolve deep-seated issues of centuries of land drainage and 'improvements', requires farmers to 'buy into' a new approach. Without their co-operation, further progress will be slow. The future vision needs to incorporate bold and large-scale reversion to wetlands and conversion of a wider landscape to wetter farmland. Farming diversification and tourism combined can provide economic drivers, but there needs to be a strategic vision with effective funding. Human exploitation of this once extensive waterscape has transformed it beyond recognition. Increasingly prone to both drought and flood, and often now below sea level, the situation is not sustainable.

3. Changing influences in Sheffield's Ecclesall Woods

Ecclesall Woods in Sheffield is the region's premier conservation woodland today, but detailed studies of deadwood indicators of ancient woodlands, undertaken in the 1980s, identified it as an anomaly. Ecclesall Woods lacks key species of invertebrates that its assumed antiquity would suggest that it should have. Following in-depth studies of field archaeology and archival research however, the circumstances make eminent sense. Ecclesall Woods was open farmland with small areas of very wet carr woodland and riverside woodland. This was the case throughout a long period from the Late Neo-lithic and through the Bronze Age, Iron Age and Romano-British periods,

Population and Resources

even until the late Saxon era. Following the Norman Conquest, the lands changed hands and the site has its origins as a medieval hunting park. In 1317, Robert de Ecclesall was granted a licence to impark and this is reflected in modern place names such as Parkhead, Warren Wood, Park Field and Old Park. Rotherham and Ardron (2006) present an overview of the issues of interpretation of the landscape here. There is further evidence of the use of the Woods for hunting from a set of depositions taken on 2 October 1587. These were from George, Sixth Earl of Shrewsbury. He stated that he, his father and his grandfather: 'used sett and placed Crosbowes for to Kyll the Deare in Ecclesall Afforesaied and to hunte at all tymes when it so pleased them there.' Thomas Creswick noted that 'ye said Erle George grandfather to ye said now Erle of Shrewsbury hath sett Netts & long bowes to kill deare in Ecclesall and hunted dyvers tymes there and he thinketh that ye said Erle ffrancis father to ye Erle that now is did the lyke.' Richard Roberts confirmed that 'he hath sene the lord ffrancis hunting in Ecclesall byerlow and that said lords officers sett decoers there at such places as they thought convenyent.'

In the early 1700s, there were also livestock pastured in the woods, with horses, mares, foals, cows, heifers, calves and sterks recorded. Gelly's map of 1725 shows a 'laund' in the centre of the Woods and this was planted up in

Woodland and pollards.

Author's collection.

Chapter 8

1752. In the 1587 deposition, it is also clear that wood and underwood are also being taken and it was this use that was to dominate the former deer park for the next few centuries. It seems perhaps that the hunting use was falling from fashion by the late 1500s, with references to deer hunts certainly from the late 1400s and early 1500s. Was this the reason for the deposition? Excitingly, in the late 1990s, Paul Ardron, working with the present author, located the western boundary bank of the medieval park (Rotherham and Ardron, 2001). Here we have some insight into the evolution of a specific wooded landscape, for which the medieval imparkation was probably the critical moment in it becoming woodland today. However, this 'ancient' woodland is not all it seems and its ecology and pedology reflect its unique history. From the 1500s onwards, the Woods were individually named and being exploited for intensive manufacture of charcoal and whitecoal. By the mid-1800s, the coppice exploitation ended. Gradually the woodland was converted to high forest with exotic tree species. It was then largely abandoned as 'amenity woodland'. This site is now locked within a sea of urbanisation and separated from its past by the process of 'cultural severance'. However, the key issue is that for long periods of time this site was mostly unwooded and included large areas of arable land. For

Ancient Oak tree – wonderful and irreplaceable heritage.

Photograph: Ian D. Rotherham.

much of the rest of its history it was grazed parkland. Today, culturally severed from its working past and managed as an urban amenity space, it is rapidly becoming 'parkified' but, aside from occasional deer and rabbits, there is no grazing. Importantly, the absence of the ancient dead wood invertebrates now makes eminent sense; the site lacks essential continuity.

The Woods today reflect the long time-line of human influences and interactions, from prehistoric hunter-gatherers, to Dark Ages farmers, to medieval deer hunters and later industrial exploitation. As the urban population of Sheffield grew, suburban housing and major transport routes transformed the rural setting of the Woods. Furthermore, the site was polluted from both air and water. In the last century, now an urbanised amenity woodland, the ecology of the Woods was driven by the forces of cultural severance, as the tree canopy closed with the abandonment of coppice management, and by the accidental and deliberate releases of exotic, alien plants into the site.

A wider context

Many fundamental drivers in the wooded landscape have gone or changed. Woods and forests are now more highly valued for recreation and for tourism, not for subsistence and survival. Rackham (1986) noted the fact that woods were under threat when their economic importance waned. Today's forests and wooded landscapes risk severance from their direct, local economic functions. In place of this, they provide a backdrop to tourism and leisure, to the visitor's gaze and the community's recreation. This has real value and, along with the value of ecosystem functions such as carbon sequestration, provides a real economic reason for forest maintenance. The problem seems to be that in the past the economic value, management cost and control of the resource and its management were placed or held at least by the same community, if not by the same person. This is no longer the case and today's 'value' and 'cost' are generally separated. Furthermore, it was the day-to-day community impacts of management over centuries, that made the forest and woods what they are; they are not merely 'natural'. They are complex palimpsests of culture and nature. It is clear that, with the loss of cultural memory and knowledge, these landscapes are misunderstood. The woods are seen as ancient, natural and primeval, on the one hand, and young and secondary, on the other. To let nature take its course as is so often advocated will lead inevitably to major changes and these may not represent sustainability.

In the 'cultural forest', we can see the woodman through the trees, such as relict coppices, ancient pollards, pits and platforms; and in soil, vegetation and lack of water. The woodman has left an indelible imprint on the woods, along with loss of soil and loss of water. These are cultural landscapes and the future vision of Europe's forests and wooded landscapes must recognise this. Across much of Europe there is far more local fuel-wood use, often for local, domestic supply, than is the case in Britain. Perhaps such local, cultural attachment might be encouraged, to give local people a real functional link to the forest landscape. This would be community-led fuel lots rather than economically-led industrial exploitation.

Our wooded landscapes have been affected dramatically by a number of specific human impacts, for example air pollution, as described earlier. However, two major impacts were the enclosure and naming of woods under the Act of Commons (1235) and then the widespread enclosure of common-lands and open spaces through Parliamentary enclosures during the 1700s and 1800s. The impacts of these two seismic events were, in the first place, to fix spatially and name the 'woods' and their boundaries and, secondly, to separate the woods from the commons. The first enclosure also affected the balance of pasture woods and coppices, with the removal of most grazing and browsing animals from the woodland environment. The second period of wider enclosures took the commons from the commoners and the local people from their woods. I suggest that this has broken the ancient connection of community and wood. Commoners became poachers and trespassers and cultural severance began in earnest. Only recently have community groups begun once more to be actively involved in their woods, but the nature of the relationship is changed. Even groups that began in the 1980s as nature conservation campaigners, are now mostly delivering access and footpath works. Biomass removal and ongoing, small-scale micro-disturbance through subsistence and early industrial uses maintained open areas and often-distinctive vegetation. Increased biomass, closed canopies and pulses of macro-disturbance by machines now replace these former impacts. The predominant uses for the woods today are as recreational pleasure grounds where the users do not interact as managers but demand well-surfaced, metalled, drained footpaths and ever-wider access routes to all areas.

Summary

These three examples provide insight into the issues now arising through long-term impacts of human exploitation and especially of the current pressures of cultural severance, intensive agriculture and conversion to leisurely landscapes. As human populations have increased and become urbanised, the impacts have become greater and, where sites remain intact, they are still altered fundamentally in their ecological character and processes.

References

Agnoletti, M. (ed.) (2006) *The Conservation of Cultural Landscapes*. CABI: Wallingford.

Ardron, P.A. (1999) Peat Cutting in Upland Britain, with Special Reference to the Peak District. Unpublished Ph.D. Thesis, University of Sheffield, Sheffield.

Ardron, P.A., I.D. Rotherham and O. Gilbert (1999) 'An evaluation of the South Pennines peatlands with reference to the impact of peat cutting'. *Peak District Journal of Natural History and Archaeology* 1: 67–75.

Bownes, J.S., T.H. Riley, I.D. Rotherham and S.M. Vincent (1991) *Sheffield Nature Conservation Strategy*. Sheffield City Council: Sheffield.

Buckingham, H., J. Chapman and R. Newman (1999) *Hidden Heaths – A Portrait of Limestone Heaths in the Peak District National Park*. Peak District National Park Authority: Bakewell.

Çolak, A.H., S. Kirca, I.D. Rotherham and A. Ince (2010) *Restoration and Rehabilitation of Deforested and Degraded Forest Landscapes in Turkey*. Ministry of Environment and Forestry, General Directorate of Afforestation and Erosion Control: Istanbul.

Cutter, S.L. and W.H. Renwick (1999) *Exploitation, Conservation, Preservation – A Geographic Perspective on Natural Resource Use*. Third edition. John Wiley and Sons Ltd.: New York.

Freedman, B. (1995) *Environmental Ecology – The Effects of Pollution, Disturbance and Other Stresses*. Second Edition. Academic Press: San Diego.

Meadows, D.H., D.L. Meadows, J. Randers and W.W. Behrens (1972) *The Limits to Growth*. Pan Books: London.

Rotherham, I.D. (ed.) (2005) Crisis and Continuum in the Shaping of Landscapes. *Landscape Archaeology and Ecology* 5.

Rotherham, I.D. (2005) 'Alien Plants and the Human Touch'. *Journal of Practical Ecology and Conservation Special Series*, No. 4: 63–76.

Rotherham, I.D. (2008) 'Landscape, Water and History'. *Practical Ecology and Conservation* 7: 138–152.

Rotherham, I.D. (2008) 'Floods and Water: A Landscape-scale Response'. *Practical Ecology and Conservation* 7: 128–137.

Rotherham, I.D. (2009) 'The Importance of Cultural Severance in Landscape Ecology Research', in A. Dupont and H. Jacobs (eds) *Landscape Ecology Research Trends*. Nova Science Publishers: Hauppauge, NY.

Rotherham, I.D. (2009) *Peat and Peat Cutting*. Shire Publications: Oxford.

Rotherham, I.D. (2010) *Yorkshire's Forgotten Fenlands*. Pen and Sword Books Limited: Barnsley.

Rotherham, I.D. (2012) 'Traditional Woodland Management: the Implications of Cultural Severance and Knowledge Loss', in I.D. Rotherham, M. Jones and C. Handley (eds)

Chapter 8

(2012) *Working and Walking in the Footsteps of Ghosts. Volume 1: the Wooded Landscape.* Wildtrack Publishing: Sheffield. pp. 223–264.

PART 3.

REPAIRING THE DAMAGE AND ADAPTING TO CHANGE

9.

INTRODUCING CONSERVATION AND ITS HISTORY

Introduction

Since the Earth is around 4.6 billion years old and life began here about 3.8 billion years ago, we have a long time-line to consider. Some environmental and landscape features are themselves ancient. The Amazon rainforests are perhaps over 100 million years old, at least in terms of some linkage back to their primeval origins. Northern and southern hemisphere temperate zones have less obvious continuity since they have been periodically affected by long, deep, gripping Ice Ages. These brought about major changes and many extinctions, but many species simply moved south in the northern hemisphere as the ice moved southwards, and the reverse of this in the southern

Autumn at Froggatt in the Peak District National Park.

Photograph: Ian D. Rotherham.

hemisphere. As described earlier, it was against this backdrop of landscape and environment that humans gradually brought about change. There are debates about where and when humans first arrived on the scene, and the earliest hominids undoubtedly did influence landscape and wildlife. Even though 'people' were present at low population densities, they affected animals though selective hunting and through removal of carnivores and these, together with subtle changes in grazing animal behaviours, altered vegetation. Another impact of people from an early date was the use of fire both to burn vegetation and to hunt; and, through this, soils and landscapes were modified. However, the major impacts began to show as human numbers increased and the sophistication of societies grew, and as *Homo sapiens* displaced others. As described earlier, we then see a progression of more and more intensive use of the landscape and a transformation and often loss of species.

It was in response to these changes and to the increased awareness of human impacts that the conservation movement evolved. The precise stages and the processes and responses have varied from place to place, though, as a global community, we see increasingly frequent worldwide responses by the late twentieth century. The massive impacts of modern urbanisation, industrialisation and intensive farming became most quickly and dramatically apparent in North America and in Western Europe and triggered significant responses. Therefore, these two regions have influenced the emergence of the nature conservation movement to the greatest extent. This is not a simple evolution, though, since conservation has emerged in tandem with outdoor education, with outdoor sports and activities such as walking and rambling. In particular, nature conservation has grown in parallel with pollution control and environmental awareness generally. It has also had close links to game management, hunting, shooting and fishing, and these are now sometimes very tense relationships. It is worth considering some key points in the development of nature conservation and taking first the example of Britain. The timeline that appears at the end of this volume was prepared using an approach developed with Colin Beard (Beard, 1997) and also applied at a local and regional scale for wooded landscapes by Rotherham and Jones (2000) and Rotherham (2007).

Some examples of ecological consequences of human impacts

The overall trend in ecology wrought by these changes at every level from local to international is a catastrophic decline in diversity and local distinc-

Introducing Conservation And its History

tion (Figures 4 and 5 Chapter 10) (Rotherham, 2009, 2010). There is a loss of stress-tolerant species as they are replaced by homogenous and simplified landscapes and by ecological competitors. With globalisation, this has ultimately generated a 'Disneyfication' of ecology and landscape. However, whilst this general and widespread trend is obvious and is undeniable, the specific impacts vary and the short-term effects of some modifications and functional changes can be beneficial to certain species. Clearly, when habitats such as bog, woodland, fen and heath are simply lost by conversion to other uses, then wholesale extinction of associated species results. In this case, the calculation of loss is simply an assessment of the plants and animals associated with the particular landscape and its habitats factored against the areas of land converted. I give a few examples later, but essentially this is total loss. Where some element of the original landscape remains, then there is the potential for a degree of recovery or for some species to adapt and to thrive. Unfortunately, this may sometimes be a transient gain and the species decline as ecological successions change the conditions to disfavour them.

Wildflower meadow.

Photograph: Ian D. Rotherham.

Chapter 9

Embedding culture in nature

The last ten years have witnessed a remarkable debate on the origins of ancient landscapes, and centred on Europe, a revisiting of ecological and evolutionary origins (see Rotherham (ed.) 2012). This has developed to a significant degree through the seminal writings of three individuals namely Frans Vera (2000), Oliver Rackham (1980, 1986) and George Peterken (1981, 1996). Essentially the discussion has been around a vision of how Western Europe looked in prehistoric times and, associated with this, how its ecology functioned and developed. Much has been said about the evidence-base for such a vision and the interpretation of that same information. In summary, it is likely that this vast primeval landscape had the following attributes (Rotherham, 2009, 2010, 2013):

> **Wooded landscapes:** woodland and forest of various types, in varying proportions depending on terrain, topography, geology and climate; from high mountain forest, to lowland floodplain forest and more isolated woodland patches within a mosaic of other habitats.
> **Open grassland, heath, sand dunes and savanna:** in varying amounts as above and again juxtaposed with other habitat types; and in upland and northern zones both Alpine and Tundra forms of these.
> **Wetlands:** from vast valley-bottom floodlands and their great meandering rivers to expansive peat bogs and fens and with large areas of wet woodland; scattered throughout these landscapes would be a complex and intimate matrix of pools, ponds, marshes, bogs, fens and drier ground with considerable temporal and seasonal fluctuation.
> **Disturbance features:** scattered across all the other communities, from mountain rock-fall zones and erosion areas to riverine erosion and deposition habitats and wildfire areas caused by lightning strikes.
> **Coastal zone landscapes:** flats, cliffs, dunes and extensive marshes, fens, grasslands and heaths.

These habitats would be in some long-term balance and in proportions that can be debated and argued about. The landscapes and their habitats occurred in a context of a vast continuum of a mosaic of interacting ecologies, which fluxed seamlessly across the entirety of the continent. These were not static but changed through their internal and interactive dynamics and in response to climate change and sea level rise and fall. It is onto the basic template that the human footprint was imposed indelibly and increasingly – from the first hunter-gatherer communities to the techno-fix cultures of today. However, for several thousand years the basic process was one of gradual imposition of human influence and the assimilation of nature into locally and regionally distinct landscapes. Over time, whole areas and regions were transformed beyond recognition but much of the basic ecosystem function remained, though altered, within the now not natural but eco-cultural landscapes. Even today, we can see a degree of resonance with aspects of the primeval ecology in the contemporary landscapes of the very few remaining medieval deer parks. We can also see evidence of human modification and utilisation in, for example, the great worked trees, be they pollards or coppices, which remain scattered throughout today's countryside.

For individual regions, countries and cultures we can recognise pulses of increased human impact and often periods of retraction and release. Nevertheless, gradually throughout history the impact of human usage and landscape transformation has increased. However, until the advent of petrochemically subsidised economies, most landscape use had to be inherently self-sustaining and often at a local subsistence level. When the utilisation became unsustainable, as happened not infrequently, the society and its systems changed, declined or died out entirely. A society that lived beyond the means of its regional environment to support it, or above the level that modest trading could subsidise, could not survive (Rotherham, 2005).

Summary

The consequence of these limitations was the evolution of often regionally distinctive and often complex systems of landscape resource utilisation to regulate exploitation and to ensure sustainability. A result of this long-term predictable land management was the development of distinctive cultural landscapes from the original primeval environment, and the selection and development of ecologies best able to adapt to these new scenarios. In Western Europe, these systems and their distinctive landscapes and ecologies were generally well established by the medieval period and many of the particular landscapes and the most highly valued habitats and ecologies we have today descended to us from this time. It is the traditional utilisation and management of these unique and often semi-natural and eco-cultural landscapes that is rapidly ending across Britain and now all over Europe. For heritage and nature conservation, the implications are potentially catastrophic and yet largely either unrecognised or ignored.

When human communities have depended on local environments for their subsistence, they have altered the ecologies in many ways, sometimes dramatically. However, whilst nature becomes eco-cultural, there is a vested interest in local communities maintaining and conserving the resources on which they depend. The consequences of this imperative are witnessed in the plethora of social protocols and traditions in, for example, managing the commons and, in some places, concepts such as 'sacred groves' or protection for particular species. In England, by medieval times, the landscape and its resources were managed according to strict laws, established rights and traditional protocols. The implications of these ranged from the protection and conservation of game for royal prerogative to the controlled allocation of essential resources for local subsistence.

By the seventeenth century, the fundamental drivers of social, political and economic forces in England were changing. Local community controls were weakened and, with increasing enclosures, people were squeezed from their traditional countryside and into the expanding towns and cities. The twin horns of agricultural and industrial revolutions combined to transform society and ecology. The term conservation was now more likely to mean the protection of game for landed gentry and of 'forests' or woods for timber, not for locally-consumed produce. Over the next two centuries, the traditional and customary uses of woods, commons, fens and other areas declined almost to extinction, and with this decline was set in train an inexorable decline in nature.

By the late nineteenth century, the idea of 'conservation' as we know it today was emerging as a response to the now obvious demise of ecology.

References

Beard, C. (1997) *Wildlife Conservation and the Roots of Environmentalism. The Facts and Figures*. Privately Published.

Peterken, G.F. (1981) *Woodland Conservation and Management*. Chapman and Hall: London.

Peterken, G.F. (1996) *Natural Woodland – Ecology and Conservation in Northern Temperate Regions*. Cambridge University Press: Cambridge.

Rackham, O. (1980) *Ancient Woodland: Its History, Vegetation and Uses in England*. Edward Arnold: London.

Rackham, O. (1986) *The History of the Countryside*. Dent: London.

Rotherham, I.D. (2005) 'Fuel and Landscape – Exploitation, Environment, Crisis and Continuum'. *Landscape Archaeology and Ecology* **5**: 65–81.

Rotherham, I.D. (2007) 'The implications of perceptions and cultural knowledge loss for the management of wooded landscapes: a UK case-study'. *Forest Ecology and Management* **249**: 100–115.

Rotherham, I.D. (2009) 'The Importance of Cultural Severance in Landscape Ecology Research', in A. Dupont and H. Jacobs (eds) *Landscape Ecology Research Trends*. Nova Science Publishers: Hauppauge, NY.

Rotherham, I.D. (2010) *Yorkshire's Forgotten Fenlands*. Pen & Sword Books Limited: Barnsley.

Rotherham, I.D. (2013) *The Lost Fens: England's Greatest Ecological Disaster*. The History Press: Stroud.

Rotherham, I.D. and M. Jones (2000) 'The Impact of Economic, Social and Political Factors on the Ecology of Small English Woodlands: a Case Study of the Ancient Woods in South Yorkshire, England', in M. Agnoletti and S. Anderson (eds) *Forest History: International Studies in Socio-economic and Forest Ecosystem Change*. CABI: Wallingford. pp. 397–410.

Vera, F. (2000) *Grazing Ecology and Forest History*. CABI: Wallingford

10.

A BRITISH CASE STUDY

Introduction

The timeline case study that appears at the end of this volume describes around 1,000 years of fluxes, changes and influences in terms of biodiversity and nature conservation in Britain. This approach is one I have used previously to describe the key changes in woodlands and the factors (political, economic, and social) that have affected them. Instead of merely taking ecological facts and figures, the intention is to raise awareness of causes and influences through history.

The case study

The case study presents a simplified and subjective description and evaluation of the development of nature conservation in Britain over 1,000 years.

Bustard.

Author's collection.

Many of the trends and the notable events parallel those in other countries or regions around the world, though obviously many are displaced or disjunct in time. Furthermore, it is important to consider that nature conservation has evolved in parallel with but again often disjunctive from the development of environmentalism, the two often but not always being closely allied. A simple inspection of the timeline presented highlights gradual change from protection, control and exploitation of natural resources including wildlife and the productive landscape (e.g. forest, marshes fens, and farmland), to preservation and conservation for ethical and leisure reasons (such as wildlife tourism *etc*). There is also a clear shift from very minimal but often rigorously enforced protection (such as by the Forest Laws), which controlled the rights to utilise the resource, to increasingly complex legal protection for conservation purposes. These changes further basic shifts in the social and economic systems within the landscape, from subsistence – largely rural economies and communities strongly dependent on their immediate environment for survival – to urban industrial societies and intensive agri-farming. These changes and trends influence the ecology of the resource itself with massive changes as described earlier. They are discussed in more detail in the publications provided in the references (e.g. Rotherham, 2011a and b, 2012, 2013; Rotherham and Ardron, 2006; Rotherham and Bradley, 2011).

Within a landscape setting, a variety of different stakeholders strongly contests many of the natural resources. I argue that the outcome of such competition, between say aristocratic landowners, the Crown and the peasantry, has been defining in terms of the biodiversity that has survived and the form in which this manifests itself. A key landmark event in this development, and a reflection of the competition for resources running deeply throughout society and within the landscape, was the Statute of Merton, the 'Magna Carta of the landscape' (Dick Greenaway pers. comm.; see Rotherham, 2013). This began the long process of fixing and determining the once fluid landscape of heath, bog, fen, marsh, common, wood and field in an increasingly set landscape of discretely managed elements. The next seminal moment was the passing of legislation to facilitate the enclosure of common or 'waste' lands by Act of Parliament. In easy steps, these processes transformed the landscape and its associated biodiversity on a scale that has yet to be fully appreciated. However, this was not just a case of an environmental change; it wrought social and economic transformations on a dramatic scale too. Commoners displaced from their lands migrated to the emerging cities or remained to become tied workers or seasonal labour, and in many cases to reassert their rights through poaching and trespass.

Box 10.1. The Common Crane in England

The name Common Crane reflects the wide breeding range of the species in Europe and across Asia and its former relative abundance in our wetlands. It nests on the ground in marshy vegetation. With a seven-foot wingspan and a loud bugling call, the Common Crane is a genuine wildlife spectacle. However, persecution and the large-scale drainage of the Fens for agriculture led to its loss as a British breeding bird by about 1600. A small number returned to the Norfolk Broads as early as 1979 but, perhaps because of the still precarious state of wetlands during the late twentieth century, although they have bred there successfully, the population has remained isolated and vulnerable. Their return to the newly-created Lakenheath Fen in the early twenty-first century suggested they were beginning to spread into the East Anglian Fens. Within a few years, they had re-colonised Yorkshire too.

Common Crane.

Author's collection.

Common Cranes were once a familiar sight across Britain's wetlands, giving rise to place-names and family names such as Cranfield, Cranmer, Cranwell, Crane, Cranbourne and Cranbrook. Obvious and distinctive birds, Common Cranes have a long cultural history in Britain: they feature on illuminated manuscripts and cranes appeared on the menus for major feasts. An example is King Henry III's feast at York in 1251.

Common Cranes occur widely in Europe, where, again, populations have suffered historically from major wetland loss. By the mid-twentieth century just small numbers visited eastern and southern England each year on migration. Large, stork-like birds, they are grey all over rather like a Grey Heron, but with black, white and red markings on the head and neck. They feed on roots, shoots and leaves of meadow and marshland plants as well as on small animals such as voles and frogs. The resurgence of the Common Crane in England has shown how large-scale habitat creation can combine with species protection to trigger recovery. ♣

Chapter 10

Box 10.2. Fen Ragwort

It might seem surprising to be concerned about a Ragwort, but Fen Ragwort (*Senecio paludosus*) is the rarest and most impressive native British Ragwort. It can grow to two metres high and has a bright yellow flower head. However, unlike the familiar weeds with which farmers are most familiar, and the Oxford Ragwort which has famously spread along railway lines and into urban heartlands, this magnificent plant is not invasive or an aggressive coloniser. Until the rediscovery of a solitary population near Ely in Cambridgeshire, it was actually believed extinct in Britain. The site of this relict population was subsequently designated an SSSI (Site of Special Scientific Interest). In the old days, this plant was found throughout the Fenland areas of eastern England; its habitat was fens, marshes and other suitable wet environments. However, as with so many fen species, its sites were drained for agriculture.

E.B. 650.

Senecio paludosus.   Great Fen Ragwort.

Great Fen Ragwort.

Author's collection.

As described by Rotherham (2013), a few wetlands like Wicken Fen survived the worst of these impacts, albeit reduced and desiccated. Now, through careful management, such areas are being restored and they represent the very best of their kind that we still have. Bearing this in mind there is now a programme to re-establish the Fen Ragwort at suitable sites across the area that was once its natural range. It has so far been re-introduced to two sites including Wicken Fen. By the mid 1990s, up to 22 plants were thriving at Wicken and flowering profusely. Detailed ecological research has also begun to unravel the specific requirements of this beautiful plant and hopefully it now has a much brighter future. ❧

A British Case Study

Figure 4. Examples of species increases with cultural severance in Britain

---

There has been a huge increase in range and abundance of common, catholic, competitive species and especially of invasives. The later include large numbers of aggressive alien invasives. Some of the major increases are noted below

---

1. **Bracken** (*Pteridium aquilinum*): across moors, heaths and grasslands as a cultural artefact of changes in management

2. **Birch** (*Betula pendula & B. pubescens*): massive spread over heaths and moorland fringe as a result of abandonment of traditional management

3. **Sycamore** (*Acer pseudoplatanus*): huge spread and colonisation throughout many woods and grasslands too as a result of cultural changes and especially of disturbance and eutrophication of soils; the debate on whether this species is native or alien in Britain still continues

4. **Grey Squirrel** (*Sciurus carolinensis*): another aggressive invader but the success is largely due to cultural severance as coppice woods were re-planted or abandoned to high forest.

5. **Tall False Oat Grass** (*Arrhenatherum elatius*): this is one of a number of competitive species that have spread across abandoned and eutrophicated grassland.

Landscapes of subsistence became ones of intensive production (of food and other goods) and of leisure or pleasure. The gentleman's hunt replaced the subsistence common. It can be argued that the competition for these resources had always been present, with the preservation of extensive lands for royal deer hunts being an obvious example from the early medieval period. However, even in this case, the peasants and the paupers were still able to utilise parts of the landscape and generally to subsist through such allowance. Enclosure, mostly by royal warrant, of common land for deer parks was perhaps the first serious move, which significantly displaced the rights of the poorer members of society. Nevertheless, by the eighteenth and nineteenth centuries, the process was largely complete and the common was literally wrested from the commoner. It was only by the late nineteenth century, and mostly reflecting demands for access to open space for the urban populations, that the processes of enclosure were finally and successfully opposed. However, during this period, open lands were enclosed and 'improvement' for intensive agriculture followed. This process was driven by the fear of crop failure and widespread starvation that had haunted Europe

---

Figure 5. Examples of species declines with cultural severance in Britain

1. Wetland birds: massive declines of species such as Bittern (*Botaurus stellaris*), Spoonbill (*Platalea leucorodia*), Marsh Harrier (*Circus aeruginosus*), Night Heron (*Nycticorax nycticorax*), Crane (*Melornis grus*), Black Tern (*Childonias niger*), Black-tailed Godwit (*Limosa limosa*) in traditionally-managed lowland fens and washlands, but with some very localised recovery with habitat creation.

2. Wetland flora: huge losses of typical species such as Fen Ragwort (*Senecio paludosus*), Fen Violet (*Viola stagnina*), Heath Dog Violet (*Viola canina ssp montana*), Milk Parsley (*Peucedanum palustre*), Snakeshead Fritillary (*Fritillaria melagris*) and Fen Woodrush (*Luzula pallidula*), in traditionally-managed lowland fens and washlands.

3. Wetland invertebrates: Large Wolf Spider (*Lycosa paludicola*), Raft Spider (*Dolomedes fimbriatus*) and Fen Raft Spider (*Dolomedes plantarius*), Large Heath (*Coenonympha tullia*), Large Copper (*Lycaena dispar*), Marsh Fritillary (*Eurodryas aurina*) and Swallowtail (*Papilio machaon*) butterflies, in traditionally-managed lowland fens and washlands.

4. Heathland and grassland birds: Skylark (*Alauda arvensis*), Woodlark (*Lulluala arborea*), Nightjar (*Caprimulgus europaeus*), Cuckoo (*Cuculus canorus*), Red-backed Shrike (*Lanius collurio*), Black Grouse (*Tetrao tetrix*), Stone-curlew (*Burhinus oedicnemus*) and Great Bustard (*Otis tarda*).

5. Heathland and grassland invertebrates: losses of many species such as Dark Green Fritillary (*Argynnis aglaja*), High Brown Fritillary (*Argynnis adippe*), Large Blue (*Maculinea arion*), Adonis Blue (*Lysandra bellargus*), Chalkhill Blue (*Lysandra coridon*), Glow-worm (*Lampyris noctiluca*), Orb-web Spider (*Araneus quadratus*) and Silver-spotted Skipper (*Hesperia comma*), through direct habitat loss and through successional change following abandonment.

6. Heathland and grassland flora: specific losses such as Pasque Flower (*Pulsatilla vulgaris*) and Dodder (*Cuscuta epithymum*) but removal of entire flora from most of the lowland landscape, and desiccation and degradation of upland areas too.

7. Heathland and grassland reptiles: Adder (*Vipera berus*), Smooth Snake (*Coronella austriaca*), Common Lizard (*Lacerta vivipera*), Sand Lizard (*Lacerta agilis*); massive declines of amphibians too.

8. Woodland birds: many species have declined but particular examples include Nightingale (*Luscinia megarhynchos*) and Woodlark (*Lulluala arborea*) in the lowlands and Capercaillie (*Tetrao urogallus*) in the north.

9. Woodland flora: loss of rare woodland species such as Herb Paris (*Paris quadrifolia*), and contraction in range of many other woodland 'indicator' flowers with destruction of sites e.g. Bluebell (*Endymion non-scriptus*), Wood Anemone (*Anemone nemorosa*); veteran trees largely removed.

10. Woodland invertebrates: Declines in particular species such as Stag Beetle (*Lucanus cervus*), Lesser Stag Beetle (*Dorcus parallipedus*), Purple Emperor Butterfly (Apatura iris), Duke of Burgundy Fritillary (*Hamearis lucina*), Purple Hairstreak Butterfly (*Quercusia quercus*), Wood White Butterfly (*Leptidea sinapis*), Chequered Skipper (*Carterocephalus palaemon*), and loss of many dead wood invertebrates from most areas.

for centuries, and facilitated by urbanisation and population increase and the expansion and development of technologies, fuels and processes for cultivating land and enhancing fertility by the addition of synthetic chemicals. The science of the Enlightenment enabled the technology to develop which transformed the landscape.

Alongside production sat pleasure for the now wealthy gentleman farmers and their more wealthy aristocratic neighbours. The woods, moors and heaths were enclosed and 'preserved' for fox hunting and the shooting of game. The local peasants, unless employed as keepers, were rigorously excluded from these areas. Mantraps were not only lethal but also legal. It took until the year 2000 for the ordinary people to regain their rights of access to even the remaining open, unenclosed lands. A social divide had been imposed with landscapes of 'leisure and pleasure' overlaid on those of increasingly industrial productive agriculture. The preserve and the domain of the landowner were now disputed by the displaced commoner and paupers.

A similar pattern can be seen in the wooded landscapes, with many mediaeval coppice woods established and enclosed to keep out livestock and people in the decades following the Statute of Merton. These provided vital supplies of wood, timber, acorns, beech mast, herbage and more. Sometimes these were within enclosed parks and at other times enclosed within the wider rural landscape. The parks too provided essential crops and products. However, by the seventeenth century, rigorously managed intensive industrial coppices were displacing traditional rural coppice. These provided wood to make charcoal for iron smelting. Then, once the process of smelting using coked mineral coal was perfected, many traditional 'woods' were transformed into plantations of high forest. Much of the replanting was with imported stock or with exotic species such as conifers.

Within these woodlands and wooded landscapes, these changes were paralleled and in part facilitated, by improved land drainage, a process happening across the wider landscape too. Over two to three centuries from the 1700s onwards, almost every significant wetland was affected and most were destroyed. In the Cambridgeshire and Lincolnshire Fens, more than 3,000 square miles of wetland were totally removed. By the twentieth century, almost every woodland and moor was 'gripped' and all farming fields were significantly under-drained. Insidiously, progressively, the landscape was desiccated. Ultimately, this had impacts in terms of both flood and drought, and devastating impacts on wildlife.

The twentieth century witnessed a continuation and intensification of all these processes, ultimately facilitated by technology driven by oil and

Chapter 10

Box 10.3. The Large Copper Butterfly

By 1864, because of wide-spread drainage, the Large Copper Butterfly (*Lycaena dispar*) became extinct in the Southern Fens and in England. Its food plant is the Great Water Dock (*Rumex hydrolapathum*) which occurs along ditches at Wicken Fen.

The extinction of the Large Copper Butterfly was due to loss of habitat across its core range of the Fens and East Anglia. The endemic English sub-species *Lycaena dispar dispar* was lost in 1848 due to the drainage of the only remaining sites, mostly around Whittlesey Mere. However, in 1927, there was a reintroduction, albeit with the Dutch sub-species, *Lycaena dispar batavus*, to both Wicken Fen and Woodwalton Fen. The former was at first the most successful, but the wartime

Large Copper Butterfly.

Author's collection.

drainage of Adventurers' Fen put paid to that. The population at Woodwalton has been maintained, in part through artificial support, ever since. Marsh Fritillary (*Eurodryas aurinia*) was also finally lost in the early 1940s.

This habitat loss and fragmentation is a problem for mobile species as suitable habitat becomes smaller in extent and separated by greater areas of inhospitable countryside. Climate change is predicted to make this worse for many species. ☙

electricity. With fertilisers, pesticides, and huge government subsidies to provide market stability for the production of food and other materials, the lifestyles of urban consumers were increasingly de-coupled from the environment on which they depended. It was only at the very end of the twentieth century that politicians and the wider public began a dialogue on issues such as sustainability and quality of life.

Following these trends through the timeline, we see key moments in the evolution of modern conservation. Sometimes these critical events were not recognised as such for many years after their occurrence. The protestors over bird plumage in ladies' hats in the late 1800s could hardly have foreseen the emergence of the RSPB as a conservation body owning hundreds of sites and with over a million members. Others such as, for example, the publication of Rachel Carson's *Silent Spring* (1965) had almost immediate impact and recognition.

The British timeline provides examples of these events and processes and these can be mirrored in other countries. However, with a relatively small land mass and a high population, the pressures on Britain's environment have been especially acute. The consequent scale and intensity of environmental damage then reflect Britain's role in the forefront of both industrial and agricultural revolutions. Finally, though, despite, and indeed perhaps because of, the obvious environmental damage, Britain has led the way in terms of responses to degradation and the emergence of active nature conservation. Particularly with respect to the role of community and voluntary organisations and conservation Britain has often been a world leader, even when government and agencies have lagged behind.

Examination of the timeline reveals numerous examples of species extinction and of catastrophic habitat loss or decline. The ones presented are just a selection and often of the most obvious plants and animals. So behind these headline species there are huge numbers of others which, in terms of ecosystem functioning, may be equally or even more important. It is also worth remembering that, until the nineteenth century, records of the species present in most areas were generally unreliable and always significantly incomplete. By the end of our period of study, the year 2000, there were numerous attempts, with marked differences in success rates, to reintroduce key species formerly lost. However, despite successes – such as the Red Kite and the Osprey, for example – there remain deep-seated problems in terms of the necessary habitat quality and the required landscape integrity and management. In most areas the wildlife habitat is highly fragmented and in very poor condition.

A final issue to consider in the timeline is the dramatic proliferation of wildlife- and conservation–related groups and organisations from the nineteenth century into the late twentieth century. This is matched by increasingly broad and complex legislation covering all aspects of envi-

Chapter 10

Box 10.4. The Raft Spider or Swamp Spider and the Fen Raft Spider

The Raft Spider or Swamp Spider (*Dolomedes fimbriatus*) is much more common than its relative from the Pisauridae family, the Fen Raft Spider (*Dolomedes plantarius*), which is endangered and found only in East Anglia.

These are two of Europe's largest, most beautiful but least common species of spider. They are the largest native British spiders. Both species require swampy conditions and are large and robust, capable of catching sizeable prey including damselflies and small fish.

Dolomedes - the Swamp Spider or Raft Spider.

Author's collection.

The latter are attracted to the surface by the spider vibrating the water with the front legs. Females of these species can lay up to 1,000 eggs in sacs which are ferried about underneath the abdomen and the young spiders are found in shrubs or trees rather than in the water.

The Fen Raft Spider is a wetland species dependent on permanent, standing or slow-moving water. It is generally associated with nutrient-poor water of near neutral or alkaline pH. Living on the water surface of pools and ditches, and around the emergent vegetation, it typically hunts from 'perches' on stems rising out of the water. Its wide range of prey items are taken on or below the surface. It also needs emergent, stiff-leaved vegetation with open, sunny conditions for breeding with nursery webs constructed for the young. There were no reliable British records of this species before its discovery in 1956, at Redgrave and Lopham Fen, on the border of Norfolk and Suffolk. However, in 1988, it was discovered at a second site, the Pevensey Levels c.160 km away in Sussex. Over the same period the population at Redgrave and Lopham Fen has declined and is now restricted to two, small, isolated centres. Systematic monitoring begun in 1991 showed numbers fluctuating at very low levels. The total population seems to be little over 100 adult females in most years and is considered highly vulnerable to extinction. The Pevensey population was estimated at 3,000 adult females in 1992. In Great Britain this species is classified as Endangered. It is given full protection under Schedule 5 of the Wildlife and Countryside Act 1981.

The common name of Raft Spider comes from the mistaken belief that the beast forms a raft of detritus and threads and so is able to drift across the fen waterscape in search of prey. It does not do this but it will readily go under water after prey or down a plant stem and underwater out of harm's way if disturbed.

Most historical records of the very rare *D. plantarius* are difficult or impossible to verify because of the frequent taxonomic confusion with the congeneric species *Dolomedes fimbriatu*. In addition, the cryptic or camouflaged nature of *D. plantarius* and the difficulty of locating it amongst tangles of emergent aquatic vegetation, make recording and assessment of very difficult.

SPECIES THAT MAY CAUSE CONFUSION

The case study of these two invertebrate species highlights the problems of identification and the reliability of records. The main source of confusion in the UK is with the semi-aquatic *Pirata* and *Pisaura* species of Wolf Spiders. Several have more or less distinct white lateral lines on the carapace, are very active and quite large, though not in the *Dolomedes* range. Mature *Pirata* can be a similar size to young perhaps 2/3 grown *Dolomedes*. They often inhabit rough and marshy grassland and will retreat down plant stems and under water. ⚡

ronmental impacts and actions. However, as the legislation has often been piecemeal and patchy, it is frequently difficult to enforce – a situation made more problematic by the ever-changing tapestry of responsible government agencies and departments. The Countryside Agency and Natural England, lasted barely eight and fifteen years respectively. The patterns within the timeline suggest that the rate of change and the degree of bureaucratic inertia both increase with time. Over the period at the end of the timeline, there is also an increasing separation apparent between scientists and conservation bureaucrats, and probably a decreased degree of democratic accountability within much of the process. The NGOs have also grown from small, amateur and sometimes part-time groups to big organisations sometimes with millions of members and hundreds of staff. On the one hand, this is an incredibly positive reflection of public concern about and engagement in natural history, nature conservation and the environment.

Box 10.5. The Native Pool Frog

Most people assume, wrongly, that in terms of threatened wildlife species, our biodiversity, we do know what we have and where it is. This example demonstrates some of the issues that arise. One of the most bizarre stories of extinction in the Fens is that of the Pool Frog (*Rana lessonae*), the last English native populations of which went extinct in the late twentieth century. This was probably for a combination of reasons, but primarily habitat loss (e.g. pond infilling) and habitat modification and destruction (notably large-scale fenland drainage in past centuries. Water abstraction and lack of site management were problems in the mid to late twentieth century. Thus far, the story is not unique – but there is an ironic twist. Following its discovery little attention was paid to the Pool Frog because it was assumed to be a non-native species, i.e. an introduction. With the name *Rana lessonae*, the species' scientific name, it lived anonymously in the fenlands and sadly, in recent centuries, faded from them in equal obscurity. Indeed, its true identity was only established internationally a few decades before its UK extinction in the wild. There were big questions to be answered. Firstly, was it a native species? Secondly, was the British population, like the Edible Frog, in fact a hybrid of Marsh Frog (*Rana ridibunda*) and Pool Frog (both from Europe), actually introduced from the continent in the nineteenth century? By the time these questions were answered, the animal was extinct.

The last remaining site was near Thetford in Norfolk with a population there until between 1993 and 1995. The last survivor from that population died in captivity in 1999. There followed a belated campaign to 'reintroduce' the now lost frog. Work was undertaken to assess its former status and according to Jim Foster, then a vertebrate ecologist with Natural England, it proved to be a 'huge needle-in-a-haystack exercise'. A specially commissioned palaeo-zoologist painstakingly sifted through hundreds of ancient frog bones unearthed by archaeological digs. Eventually the archaeological remains found at Saxon settlement sites in Ely in Cambridgeshire and Gosberton in Lincolnshire, were found to be of native Pool Frogs. So Pool Frogs existed in England more than 1,000 years ago and other evidence supporting this emerged after almost ten years' research across Europe to unravel the mystery.

There has since been a co-ordinated programme of reintroduction with animals taken from the wild in Sweden, under special permission from the Swedish authorities, and overseen by UK agencies. So, according to the project website and Brian Unwin, the scheme is underway and now nearing completion 'to restore to the English countryside a creature that most people didn't know ever existed'. ♣

A British Case Study

Box 10.6. The Fate of the Swallowtail Butterfly

One of the most exciting and characteristic insects of the old fenland was the Swallowtail Butterfly (*Papilio machaon britannicus*), one of the main entomological attractions of sites such as Wicken Fen. Though it was once a classic butterfly of the geographical Fenland and persisted at Wicken Fen until the 1950s, the Swallowtail is now confined in Britain to the Norfolk Broads. However, its distribution appears to be closely linked to that of its food plant, the milk parsley (*Peucedanum palustre*), itself a nationally scarce species. The

Swallowtail Butterfly.

Photograph: Ian D. Rotherham.

plant is almost confined to the old Fenland and the Norfolk Broads and has become extinct in most of the northern part of its range. By the 1950s, probably in 1952, the Swallowtail became locally extinct at Wicken, most likely because of a decline in habitat extent and quality for its food plant, the Milk Parsley. At this site, the carr woodland had spread to reduce Milk Parsley habitat from 120 hectares to only about eight hectares, a consequence of falling water-tables and abandonment of traditional management. At the time of extinction the nearest other colony of Swallowtails was 160 kilometres away on the Norfolk Broads.

Because of the unlikely event of natural recolonisation there were numerous attempts to reintroduce the Swallowtails artificially from Norfolk. However, these all failed because of the poor condition of the food plant. This seemed to have problems re-establishing in the newly managed and now suitable areas of Wicken Fen. To get round this problem, teams of conservation volunteers came in during 1974 to transplant Milk Parsley to new areas and over 2,000 Milk Parsley plants were planted around the Mere on Adventurers' Fen. In 1975, a further 228 Swallowtails (adults bred in captivity at Monks Wood Experimental Station from Hickling Broad stock, 124 females and 104 males), were released on the Fen. Despite 20,000 eggs being laid and 2,000 caterpillars pupating, numbers again fell steadily and, by the 1980s, the species was again locally extinct. By the 1990s, further work was being done to transplant eggs from Norfolk to raise larvae in glasshouses. The larvae are then placed on the food plants in the Fen and adults can be seen flying across the site in the summer months.

Following all this, the Reserve has been carefully managed to encourage the Milk Parsley. However, it is not enough that the plant is present – it must also be the 'right sort of plant'. The Milk Parsley needs to protrude above the surrounding sedge for the female butterfly to lay her eggs on it. In order to encourage this, the Milk Parsley fields are cut once every four years, allowing this biennial plant to gain a foothold before it is cut back. If the fields were not cut back, the sedge community would be invaded by Willow and Alder Buckthorn.

One final attempt to re-introduce Swallowtails was made, when captive-bred, Norfolk-sourced larvae were released onto the Fen. In 1993, Jack Dempster and Marnie Hall started a reintroduction project, jointly funded by the Butterfly Conservation Society and the English Nature Species Recovery Programme and supported by the landowner, the National Trust. Butterflies were released onto the Fen and good numbers of flying adults were seen in 1995. However, once again, the attempts failed and several years of summer droughts produced poor Milk Parsley growth; the Swallowtail was extinct again by 1996. No further attempts have been carried out and none are proposed as, at the present time, significant areas of suitable habitat are still not available and it has still not been possible to re-establish pre-drainage water levels on the Fen.

The Swallowtail story illustrates a hugely important point about these now isolated, scattered and (relatively) small relict sites. Many of the animals and plants have limited powers of dispersal and so cannot cover huge distances to get to new areas. Therefore, if they become locally extinct, recolonisation is very unlikely. ❧

However, there are other issues, which seem to be emerging as many of these organisations become more corporate and often seek to disengage their employed professionals from their amateur and volunteer roots and membership. Only time will tell how these organisations will resolve the challenges of their professional status, but it is significant that by 2008 major Wildlife Trusts were closing their amateur–led membership magazines. Their former nature reserve conservation committees (with real power, expertise and responsibility) are now becoming 'friends groups' whose sole purposes are to raise funds and to undertake physical conservation tasks as dictated by the employed professionals.

Box 10.7. The Swallowtail Story – A Twist in the Tale

The Fenland and Broadland Swallowtails seem very closely tied to their food plant, the Milk Parsley, a species of rich fen which grows in sedge and litter fields and is strongly affected by site management. It depends on suitable cutting regimes of sedge and litter.

However, whilst a key problem is the drying of the site and the ecological succession to scrub and carr, there are other problems linked to the history of drainage and then isolation. The Norfolk population and probably the relict Fen population prior to extinction have become genetically different from their predecessors, and this changed genetics is at the core of their current failures. Furthermore, studies on museum specimens of Swallowtail Butterflies in comparison with those of the Norfolk Broads, suggests that the two populations were different. So the Wicken butterflies were genetically different from those of Hickling Broad in Norfolk, probably a result of the fragmentation of the once extensive old Fenland habitat. However, there is still more to this story. Early records of the Swallowtail in Britain indicate a formerly much wider distribution in southern England. This is possibly associated with the use of a more extensive range of food plants and probably with more extensive fen and common. It is suggested that the food plants included the relatively common wild carrot (*Daucus carota*). If this were the case, then the establishment and maintenance of colonies would be so much easier. Obviously the landscape was also dramatically different, with extensive commons, 'wastes' and small wetlands, and this too would have favoured the Swallowtail.

The now endemic British subspecies, *Papilio machaon britannicus*, is strictly a fenland butterfly and it feeds only on milk parsley; yet the more widespread continental sub-species, *Papilio machaon bigeneratus*, has a less restricted diet. The early records could be just occasional vagrants from continental Europe. However, I suspect that this is not the case, since the Swallowtail was collected in some numbers in Dorset and perhaps elsewhere too.

The Swallowtail Butterfly had been locally abundant in the Fenlands of Huntingdonshire and Cambridgeshire but, by the late 1800s, with drainage and agricultural improvement, there were already concerns for its survival. As the fens became the last refuge of this butterfly in Britain, perhaps isolation then further defined our endemic subspecies?

One of the big issues for an isolated population of butterflies is the risk to survival and breeding of individual adults dispersing from their home site. In the undrained fens, this would be good: the insects moved out to breed and find new areas and the genetic mixing required for success took place. However, in an isolated pocket of habitat, literally an island in an unfavourable sea of farmland, the results are disastrous. Here we see evolution in action. The conditions most favour individuals that do not disperse widely, but remain in their original breeding site. This may help them survive but it also encourages inbreeding and dis- courages any wider dispersal to new areas. This appears to be what has happened to the Swallowtail in the Fens. Jack Dempster found that, by studying museum collections of Swallowtail Butterflies, he could track the physical changes, as manifestations of underlying genetic trans- formations. Following the drainage of the wider fen landscape in the 1800s, the Swallowtail population at Wicken began to develop smaller wings and a narrower thorax, both features associated with weaker flight and shorter flying distances. Interestingly, after the 1920s, the Norfolk Broads population began to show the same changes and so, in both populations, the adults that fly within the site survive and breed. Those that are stronger and fly outside the core site perish. Within only a few decades, the populations were showing remarkable evolutionary adaptation to their changed environment. In this remarkable case study, there is a serious message for conservation. The challenges of reintro- ductions, even if conditions are right, can be problematic. ❧

Summary

The timeline provides a unique insight into this particular case study, with relevance much wider than Britain. The presentation of an historic overview with key landmarks and turning points is intended to place the changes of ecology and hence 'biodiversity', in a framework of human society, politics and economics. Beyond being just informative, and hopefully stimulating, this is a unique teaching and learning resource, for students, teachers, lec- turers and parents. It is hoped that the account places a context on the present state of the planet and the immense challenges that future genera- tions face. I argue that, unless we know where we have come from, what we have done, when and how we did it, it is impossible for the decision- makers of tomorrow to make informed or correct choices. Today's students are tomorrow's politicians and decision-makers, and they need to do better.

Key issues from the time-line are the critical points in history, the tipping points, at which ecological systems and human relationships with them are transformed. The consequences of the Battle of Hastings for ex- ample, included the imposition of a feudal system of land rights and man- agement, and ultimately the development of hundreds of enclosed deer parks and the fixing of landscape components through the Act of Commons. Later watershed moments included the development of a system of parliamentary enclosures and the removal of commons for commoners, and commoners from the commons. Industrial Revolution and Agricultural Revolution transformed society and were compounded by urbanisation. Imperialism and globalisation shifted people and nature around the planet in processes that are ongoing today. Further consequences of these events and processes have been witnessed in climate change and associated stresses for ecology. Of critical significance, though, has been the separation of people from nature and the consequences of 'cultural severance'.

References

Carson, R. (1965) *Silent Spring*. Penguin Books Ltd.: Harmondsworth.

Rotherham, I.D. (2011a) 'Hanging by a Thread – a brief overview of the heaths and commons of the north-east midlands of England', in I.D. Rotherham and J. Bradley (eds) *Lowland Heaths: Ecology, History, Restoration and Management*. Wildtrack Publishing: Sheffield. pp. 30–47.

Rotherham, I.D. (2011b) 'Habitat Fragmentation and Isolation in Relict Urban Heaths – the ecological consequences and future potential', in I.D. Rotherham and J. Bradley (eds) *Lowland Heaths: Ecology, History, Restoration and Management*. Wildtrack Publishing: Sheffield. pp. 106–115.

Rotherham, I.D. (2012) 'Traditional Woodland Management: the Implications of Cultural Severance and Knowledge Loss', in I.D. Rotherham, M. Jones and C. Handley (eds) *Working & Walking in the Footsteps of Ghosts. Volume 1: the Wooded Landscape*. Wildtrack Publishing: Sheffield. pp. 223–264.

Rotherham, I.D. (2013) 'Searching for Shadows and Ghosts', in I.D. Rotherham, C. Handley, M. Agnoletti and T. Samoljik (eds) *Trees Beyond the Wood – An Exploration of Concepts of Woods, Forests and Trees*. Wildtrack Publishing: Sheffield. pp. 1–16.

Rotherham, I.D. (2013) *The Lost Fens: England's Greatest Ecological Disaster*. The History Press: Stroud.

Rotherham, I.D. and P.A. Ardron (2006) 'The Archaeology of Woodland Landscapes: Issues for Managers based on the Case-study of Sheffield, England and four thousand years of human impact'. *Arboricultural Journal* **29**(4): 229–243.

Rotherham, I.D. and J. Bradley (eds) (2011) *Lowland Heaths: Ecology, History, Restoration and Management*. Wildtrack Publishing: Sheffield.

11.

DISCUSSION OF THE KEY ISSUES

Introduction

This chapter seeks to introduce ideas of the development of biodiversity and its relationship with human impacts and particular changes in landscape and resource management. In doing this, the author has established some basic processes of landscape evolution and the concomitant changes in associated plants and animals. These are considered and illustrated by a subjectively determined timeline for nature conservation and ecological changes in Britain. The intention is to demonstrate some significant, perhaps landmark, events and to tease out important changes. The examples and processes are then embedded in the social, economic and political drivers over the 1,000 years that are considered. Many of the general trends and ideas are transferable to other places and times, and follow human social development from subsistence and traditional rural economies to modern, urban and industrial ones.

The nature and intensity of exploitation have affected many landscapes such as those highlighted across Great Britain (e.g. Rotherham, 2005, 2007f, 2008, 2009). This may be through the actual direct impact of extraction and processing, or of harvesting and processing, and of use. It may be that the processes have indirect impacts through landscape change, through pollution and through the disposal of associated wastes. Use had major effects through the social need to protect, or even to establish, the resource, such as coppice wood, peat bog, fen or common heath; important when otherwise these would have been removed from the landscape. Literature and records give insight into resource uses and availability, providing data for detailed interrogation on comparative values, costs and trends. These aid interpretation of the impacts, nature and intensity of landscape exploitation – directly through extraction or harvesting, processing and use, or indirect landscape change perhaps caused by pollution or waste disposal.

In determining these changes, both crisis and continuum have played a part (Rotherham, 2005). The transformation from traditional subsistence use to petro-chemically driven industrial exploitation has been defining in many environments. Environmental conditions and resources, economic and political or social forces, and the interactions or competitions involved in these,

Chapter 11

have been crucial in determining the impacts on land-use and landscape. In many ways, the landscape provides a continuum punctuated by crises for the community and for the environment. The interaction of community, resource utilisation and environment has been a driving force in the evolution of the eco-cultural landscape that we inherit. However, scholars, politicians and practitioners rarely appreciate the fundamental nature of this relationship and the sophistication and totality in which subsistence and other traditional communities interacted with their environment. The medieval landscape was rather like the traditional family pig, with everything used except the squeak. It is perhaps this totality of use that most eludes us today.

There are opportunities to rebuild connectivity with nature, but with society increasingly remote from the natural world as a resource, this is very difficult. We now seek ways to link people to nature through education and conservation but this must extend to a genuine long-term social and economic value system too. There are attempts such as those in Britain, particularly by the RSPB and the National Trust, to join landscape to communities and to the economy but much more will be needed in the future. Initiatives now seek to link the following in coherent local and regional projects in order to achieve this more joined-up vision:

Burnham Beeches fuelwood pollards.

Author's collection.

Discussion of the Key Issues

1. Nature conservation
2. Tourism, leisure and amenity
3. Local provenance food and drink and farming extensification
4. Economic function
5. Ecosystem function and value

Cultural severance

In being subject to cultural severance, local communities have been cut off from nature and from dependence on local resources. This process brings many financial and other benefits, but ultimately it frequently means that awareness of nature and of our ultimate relationship with and dependence upon it is reduced. Many children growing up today have no idea where food, energy or raw materials come from. Few people in developed countries have any direct connection with nature in terms of harvesting foods, energy or raw materials, and the situation is spreading round the globe as economies and societies are transformed. For wildlife or ecology, the

Grass Snake.

Photograph: Thomas Wood.

consequences can be especially severe, as landscapes and wildlife habitats, managed for hundreds and perhaps thousands of years, are abandoned. Some become agri-industrial or agri-forestry systems; others are simply released to predictable ecological successional changes. Without people utilising these landscapes in traditional ways, and often against a backdrop of pollution by nitrogen and other chemicals, open lands change rapidly to scrub and then to secondary woodland. Biomass increases quickly and this leads to further nutrient increase or eutrophication. In fire-sensitive landscapes, wildfires soon cut through the accumulated plant materials and, unlike the light fires used for traditional management, they burn hot and deep into soils and other substrates.

Following predictable successional pathways, the ecosystems change and their ecological diversity declines. In technical, ecological parlance, specialist, stress tolerant species and stress tolerant ruderals are some of the most obvious losses. Their demise follows the predictable pathways suggested by authors such as Philip Grime (Grime, 2003; Grime et al., 2007). The results for wildlife conservation are catastrophic and disastrous for species of plants and animals that are often the ones we wish to conserve.

Summary

The truth is that we cannot turn back the socio-economic clock and there are often good, sound reasons why traditional management is no longer undertaken. However, the impacts and implications of cultural severance from past tradition and the abandonment of eco-cultural landscapes are massive. We need now to recognise what is happening and to attempt as far as possible to reconstruct a viable and sustainable future. It will not be easy but the penalty of failure will be even harder to bear.

A key challenge is to re-establish local economic function in ways that do not compromise or destroy either ecology or heritage interest. Too frequently, in initiatives such as biofuel extraction from semi-natural ancient woodlands in England, or the imposition of industrial wind-farm landscapes across heritage-rich countryside, this is not the case. There are effective models for the use of areas as fuel lots in both Europe and in North America, and perhaps that could be a way to conserve lowland heaths and commons and to relink their connections to local economies and to local people. However, to be effective, such initiatives need to be sustainable and non-damaging utilisation, not industrial exploitation. Moreover, these ideas need to resonate with local communities and, where possible, to be immersed within them. Common and commoner need reuniting.

The alternative, and what is happening across Britain, and indeed the wider world today, is the inexorable, long-term loss of important wildlife habitats and intractable declines in those that remain.

In the longer-term, the only solutions that will be sustainable are those which place natural resources and ecology back at the heart of local communities. Nature conservation as a leisurely activity can help, and indeed provides a much-needed sticking plaster approach to a deleted nature but, in the long term, something more radical will be required.

References

Grime, J.P. (2003) 'Plants hold the key. Ecosystems in a changing world'. *Biologist* **50**(2): 87–91.

Grime, J.P., J.G. Hodgson and R. Hunt (2007) *Comparative Plant Ecology. A Functional Approach to Common British Species*. Second Edition. Castlepoint Press: Dalbeattie.

Rotherham, I.D. (ed.) (2005) Crisis and Continuum in the Shaping of Landscapes. *Landscape Archaeology and Ecology* **5**.

Rotherham, I.D. (2007) 'The implications of perceptions and cultural knowledge loss for the management of wooded landscapes: a UK case-study'. *Forest Ecology and Management* **249**: 100–115.

Rotherham, I.D. (2008) 'Landscape, Water and History'. *Practical Ecology and Conservation* 7: 138–152.

Rotherham, I.D. (2008) 'Floods and Water: A Landscape-scale Response'. *Practical Ecology and Conservation* 7: 128–137.

Rotherham, I.D. (2009) 'The Importance of Cultural Severance in Landscape Ecology Research', in A. Dupont and H. Jacobs (eds) *Landscape Ecology Research Trends*. Nova Science Publishers: Hauppauge, NY.

12.

ALIEN AND INVASIVE SPECIES – A BRITISH VIEW OF A GLOBAL ISSUE

Introduction

One of the major changes over the time-line's thousand years has been the introduction and often naturalisation of plants and animals not native to Britain. Many of these have become welcome additions to parklands and gardens and from there have 'escaped' into the wild. The process is not new and can be documented from early medieval and even Roman times. Now iconic and even specially protected species like the Brown Hare (*Lepus europaeus*) are not native but were probably Roman (or even Celtic) introductions,

Canada Goose.

Photograph: Ian D. Rotherham.

and then Norman reintroductions. Numerous plants were also introduced from the Mediterranean for herbal and culinary use and became naturalised around monasteries and similar locations, from there moving out into the wider landscape. Many of these species are welcomed and valued by both botanists and local people. Longevity perhaps leads to acceptability.

However, during the period from around 1700 onwards, as European seafarers travelled the world, they brought back more and more exotic species. These were welcomed as exotic additions to native fauna and flora and were often highly valued. The gardens and landscape parks of the eighteenth and nineteenth centuries were adorned with such species, both animals and plants. Indeed, by the 1800s there was a 'wild garden movement' to promote the naturalisation of spectacular exotic plants into wild areas and an 'acclimatisation society' to do the same for birds and mammals. Some of the exotic trees for example (such as Sitka Spruce (*Picea sitchensis*) and European Larch (*Larix decidua*)) became hugely important to the British economy as the mainstay of the forestry industry.

Nevertheless, there has been a penalty incurred by this giant experiment in ecology in that many of the species introduced have done exceptionally well. In fact, they have done so well that they are now considered one of the most serious long-term threats to native biodiversity. How to deal with this problem and to address it effectively, on the scale that is necessary, is now taxing conservationists and policy-makers. However, there is a problem in dealing with it, in that not all problem species are alien and many exotic plants and animals are not a problem. Furthermore, the public often like exotic plants and animals and are still actively involved in causing them to spread into the wild. Even worse, the basic concepts of what is '*native*' or '*natural*' in Britain are frequently seriously flawed. It seems that many people dealing with these issues have little understanding of landscape history or of associated social, economic and political processes.

Hybrid ecologies

There is little doubt that introduced species in some cases have changed the landscape and the indigenous ecology. Furthermore, these changes are often dramatic and even fundamental to the ecology seen today. Nevertheless, the trends and changes must also be considered in the context of wider fluxes in climate, in land-use and in the way in which landscape and ecology interact with people. This is often not the case, and judgments are made based on subjective assessments of '*worth*' and '*value*' and even an almost xenophobic fear of native wildlife under threat from alien invaders. Yet even the most cursory view of a British landscape will demonstrate there is often little that is truly '*natural*' or '*native*'; most is a '*cultural*' or eco-cultural landscape. Our ecology has been acquired through centuries of interactions between people and nature. At best, it has elements that can be considered 'semi-natural' and traditional and large areas of farmland, for example, which themselves are exotic in character and of modern origins. Therefore, it is against this backdrop that the problems of invasive species must be considered if we are to have any hope of prioritising effective and valid actions. We need to understand that our ecology has been hybridising for a very long time and the process of 'ecological fusion' runs deep.

The roles of both people and nature have been identified as interactions at the core of biological invasions. This chapter focuses on two specific aspects of the invasion paradigm, firstly that of the deliberate introduction of plants and animals around the world by the Victorian Acclimatisation Societies and secondly the Wild Garden Movement. These two nineteenth century phenomena led directly to many of the issues and challenges which

Fallow bucks.

Photograph: Ian D. Rotherham.

Chapter 12

face conservation today. Important within this consideration are the changing perceptions and attitudes of people towards nature, and especially to the exotic, over the period from the early nineteenth century to the end of the twentieth century. Whilst Davis et al. (2001) addressed the changing attitudes towards exotic plants and animals in Britain consequent on the writings and broadcasts of Charles Elton, this wider influence of fashion and taste in shaping responses to aliens has generally been overlooked. Furthermore, the critical role of the practical manifestations of fashion, such as the accidental or even deliberate introduction of now invasive species to the countryside, has not been recognised. This chapter provides insight into the importance of human cultural facilitation of invasions, and into how perceptions and attitudes have affected this. Crossing boundaries of ecological science and history it considers two specific British examples, which together created many of the invasions of the twentieth, and twenty-first, centuries.

Grey squirrel.

Photograph: Ian D. Rotherham.

Alien and Invasive Species – a British View of a Global Issue

The problem of aggressive and invasive plants and animals is not new but the scale of impact combined with rapid climate change and other environmental fluxes is dramatic. A starting point for discussion must be in deciding what is alien and what is a problem. An alien species is a plant, animal, or microorganism not 'native' to an area, but introduced by humans, accidentally or deliberately. It may or may not be invasive, and in fact only about 0.1 per cent of aliens are damaging. Furthermore, the spread of species across the planet is not new, but recent horror stories have stirred up a debate amongst ecologists, politicians, industry and the public. Indeed there are good reasons why this is so. Some fifteen per cent of Europe's 11,000 aliens have environmental or economic impacts and damage to the UK economy is estimated at £2bn *per annum*. Nevertheless, underlying the headlines are deep-seated questions of what is native and where, what is alien and when. From Spanish Bluebell to Eagle Owls and Canada Geese and from Big Cats, Beavers and Signal Crayfish to Wild Boar, which ones should get a free pass?

The historic perspective

These are issues that are frequently overlooked or ignored, but history is informative in such debates. In particular, it is worth considering how human actions have triggered invasions and, indeed, how many of these were deliberate acts. It then quickly becomes apparent that initially many invasive alien species were welcomed. Furthermore, human attitudes to these plants and animals are not fixed in time. Our responses to what we now see as problem alien species are often subjective and not objective and those regarded as problems are chosen very selectively. The past roles of two particular English or British groups are especially informative when we try to understand both the problems of today (some of which cannot be doubted) and the causes of many invasive colonisations. These two examples are the Victorian 'Wild Garden Movement' and the 'Acclimatisation Societies'.

The problems and challenges of the exotic

There are few doubts that the adverse impacts of invasive alien plants and animals pose some of the most serious threats to nature conservation. There is a large and expanding literature based on research into the issues, impacts and effects of exotic species. Overall, the adverse effects on wild animals and plants across the world have been compared to the likely impacts of human-induced climate change in terms of their severity and significance in the twenty-first century. In particular, the once-isolated faunas and floras of islands have suffered most and, in today's globalising world ecology, they are threatened and in many cases have been destroyed. Often these ecosystems have simply been erased by European colonisation over the last few hundred years. With the chronic environmental disruption of industrialisation, intensive farming, urbanisation and now climate change those species unable to adapt are declining dramatically, and those able to exploit changed conditions are spreading around the globe. For nature conservationists this is potentially the stuff of nightmares. Indeed a superficial consideration can result in a view of the processes that blurs and blends some essential aspects of both the science and the cultural aspects of this hugely important interaction of people and nature. The immediate unthinking response to exotic species which dare to naturalise, is firstly that we know which they are and secondly that they should be eradicated. However, in recent years there have been some significant publications that broaden the issues and debates and raise serious questions about how and why we label certain species as 'good' or 'bad', as 'alien' or 'native'. There is an extensive literature on this and related issues (see for example Rotherham and Lambert (eds.), 2011).

Therefore, whilst the seemingly reasonable response to aliens seems to be backed by rigorous scientific evidence, and the issues seem to all intents and purposes clear-cut, the reality is more complex. Engaging the media and others involved in a wider public debate and dialogue is challenging. The media loves 'sound-bites' and 'sexy issues', so an alien invasion with its clear and simple message is easy to cover whereas the more subtle and complex debate is less newsworthy. In essence, it seems that alien species which establish and then naturalise can have the potential to wreak havoc amongst native ecosystems. Simple observation also suggests that, with a very few exceptions, humans have been unwilling or unable to do much about this and that most bad invasions with harmful effects have gone unchecked and their impacts have run their natural course.

Many of the world's ecologies have already become 'Disneyfied', local or regional character and distinction being lost or diluted. Nevertheless, this process goes on against the uncomfortable backdrop of an evolving and changing landscape and environment, some of the flux being natural and some anthropogenic. As with climate change, not all the effects we see today are human-induced, but they represent a subtle mix of natural and inevitable change now dramatically catalysed by human intervention. In this context, it is worth recognising that species and ecologies are not static but dynamic. They ebb and flow, flux and change, over periods from decades to centuries or millennia. Changes during the period from around 1400 AD to the 1800s provide a good example of this, as Northern Europe, gripped by the harsh chill of the so-called 'Little Ice Age', experienced major transformations of its ecology.

The mixing pot of empires, acclimatisation and wild gardening

The consequences of all this are especially pertinent to Britain and to our attitudes. Indeed, observations in Europe and discussions with ecologists and landscape historians from Continental Europe are informative. In many cases, it seems that the Europeans worry more about '*problem species*' rather than necessarily '*alien*' ones. In Britain we are an island race, (or at least a collection of races now on a collection of islands); but the boundaries of the

Himalayan Balsam.

Photograph: Ian D. Rotherham.

Chapter 12

land and sea give clear definition as to what should be 'in', and what should be 'out'. Yet our perceptions of this and the attitudes and responses stemming from these are surprisingly recent in origin. Until the 1940s, we generally went out from our islands and travelled the globe collecting and selecting plants and animals to bring back to Britain. Not merely content with collecting this mixed bag of species, we then deliberately set about their release into the landscape to 'improve it' for people and for economic benefit too.

This movement spread around the world, with European Acclimatisation Societies established first, seeking to introduce and test new crops for economic purposes and especially their potential for food. However, these organisations developed in other ways and in Britain and the colonies, they looked to the introduction of animals and birds to new places in order to improve economies, gastronomies and landscapes. The impacts of Acclimatisation Societies had huge effects on New Zealand and Australian ecologies for example. Today their legacy has a huge impact on conservation, particularly in New Zealand.

The Acclimatisation Societies and the Victorian Wild Gardeners (Rotherham, 2005) were manifestations of processes that had occurred to greater or lesser degrees for centuries. We know that, through history, the waves

Signal Crayfish.

Photograph: Ian D. Rotherham.

Alien and Invasive Species – a British View of a Global Issue

of settlers or conquerors of Britain had done just the same. The Romans and then the Normans imported huge numbers of animals and probably plants too, many of which are keystone species in the modern ecology. The most obvious example is the humble Rabbit, but we can add the Fallow Deer and the Brown Hare to the list to consider later when we examine issues of perception and attitude. We also accidentally, unwittingly and uncaringly released many other animals and plants to make their own ways in the world. Many of these species went on to become an intimate part of what we now see as 'British' ecology. The Romans and Normans imported herbs and food-plants from southern Europe and the Mediterranean, as did the returning Crusaders and the various monastic dynasties that controlled much of the productive landscape for several centuries. Many of these species have been absorbed into the mix of native ecology. Most of these species are now tolerated and many (such as the Brown Hare for example) are celebrated and conserved.

By the 1500s, seafarers from Britain and Holland, for example, were beginning to chart their ways around the globe. From all the corners of the world they brought back exotic plants and sometimes animals; many of these introductions perished but others did not. Accidental imports had already included Black Rat and Brown Rat, plus a dash of Bubonic Plague, and, in return, the later explorers spread these around the planet along with dogs, cats and much more. The cultural homogenisation of ecology was speeding up. The collection and dissemination of alien species quickened as travellers went in search of exotic plants and animals for gardens and for menageries. As landscaping, forestry and gardening emerged in Britain through the 1700s and 1800s, the impacts on the environment increased. This process continues today with catastrophic consequences.

However, it should not be imagined that these changes to '*native*' ecology were isolated from other impacts. At about the same time, in the eighteenth and nineteenth centuries, the wider landscape was traumatised by the Parliamentary enclosures, with common land wrested from the commoners, the peasants and the poor and converted into intensive food production units. Much of the more natural landscape and its ecology were swept away by this sea of change. Traditional coppice woods were converted to high forest plantations and industrialising cities began to sprawl across the countryside. Lands that remained relatively untouched by this were often blended into leisurely landscapes for the pleasure of the landowners and industrialists and were often populated by the exotic plants and animals being brought in from around the world. Associated with these changes, there was also a seminal undercurrent of transformation from ecology dominated by native 'stress tolerators' to often exotic species of 'ruderals' and 'competitive' plants. This trend was noted for the twentieth century by Davis et al. (2001), but in reality began much earlier; the landscape flexed and changed and disturbance plus nutrient enrichment came to the fore.

Ecology transformed

The uncomfortable truth that emerges from these observations and the compounding effects of the abandonment of traditional countryside practices throughout the 1800s into the late 1900s, was a radically transformed ecology. *'Cultural severance'* (Rotherham, 2009b), which is the ending of traditional uses, values and management of the landscape and its ecological resources, has been a final compounding factor. Many areas, released from the subsistence exploitation of centuries have rapidly gained biomass and nutrients and the stress tolerant species that are often of high conservation value slip quietly away. Either abandonment or pulses of macro-disturbance replace micro-disturbance associated with traditional management. These stresses in the ecosystem are most obvious in urbanised zones where, combined with the exotic species described earlier, they are forming new ecological associations – the so-called *'recombinant ecology'* (Barker, 2000) – different and distinctive from what went before.

There are glimmers of the former landscapes in what we generally call *'semi-natural'* habitats, but even here the cultural drivers for these areas over centuries of human exploitation have changed and often ceased. Some of the results are subtle and long-term blurring of the ecology and in other cases the consequences are rapid and dramatic. One remarkable fact is that so much of the former landscape and its ecology remains visible through the modern veneer. Some aspects of the ancient ecosystems are surprisingly resilient unless totally swept aside by modern mechanisation. Nevertheless, there are major issues for conservation, such as the latter-day recognition, for example, of the importance of remnants of medieval parks and their links to the 'Frans Vera primeval landscape' (Vera, 2000); for decades these areas received little recognition or protection.

We are now searching for the so-called 'shadow woods' etched in the landscape from perhaps pre-Domesday but still surviving, though often unrecognised (Rotherham, 2013). Similarly, many relict heaths and commons hark back to this antique ecology and yet are sadly abandoned and neglected. A point to emerge from these observations is that what we value is not necessarily an ecology that is truly native, but one that is perceived to be so. Some of our most ancient landscapes still have little protection and often very unsympathetic management. On the other hand, some of the landscape features and their ecology now passionately protected, such as eighteenth and nineteenth century enclosure hedgerows, are actually imposed exotic features. Many of the 'native' oakwoods from which school children carefully

Wild fig.

Photograph: Ian D. Rotherham.

collect 'local' acorns to grow and then plant into 'local provenance' woods were actually not native at all. These are frequently, as the estate accounts confirm, imports from Dutch nurseries in the eighteenth century. Indeed, a forester today can often spot the distinctive manifestations of genetic traits that distinguish native trees from Dutch. There are wonderful ancient hedges from pre-Domesday and these cross ancient landscapes to link patches of wood, common and heath, but they are different and distinct from the imposed barriers that separated commoner from common.

Science, politics and environmental democracy

It is important to set the problems of alien invasive and exotic species into the broader contexts of environmental change, conservation and politics. Understanding the interrelationships between ecology and politics in terms of reactions to biological invasions is important. In bringing together science and politics it is necessary to acknowledge that many conservation decisions are not based on 'truths', often not even on science, and are not objective. But they are subjective decisions based on the best scientific understanding we have, blended with an emotional response to a situation based on and twisted by many social, cultural and historical influences.

Unfortunately, this applies to the professional conservation manager and to the wider public alike. Even the language used to define and to describe the issues is loaded with bias and the decisions are political and social. Why for example do we seek to eradicate Himalayan Balsam as a riverside and roadside invader but not Sweet Cicely, an alien from the mountains of central Europe first recorded wild in Britain in 1777? In the Peak District and South Pennines, it is spreading rapidly and its impact is dramatic. So if control is based on science and objectivity then why one and not the other? *Buddleia davidii* causes millions of pounds of damage to services and buildings, and is now expanding into woods, hedgerows and other habitats such as clifftops, but we welcome it as 'The Butterfly Bush'. In contrast, conservationists dislike Rhododendron, which they seek to bash and eradicate.

Summary thoughts and conclusions

Devolution in the (dis)United Kingdom raises further issues (see Warren in Rotherham and Lambert (eds.) (2011)) where conservation managers are trying to decide whether a species should be native to England, Wales, Scotland or some lesser region. In the face of climate change and the inevitable fluxing of species distributions, this is a nonsense and misunderstanding of the serious matters at stake. It is also totally missing the point about the palimpsest nature of historic landscapes and the value of cultural and historical aspects of the environment. Is it relevant that a plant found in Carlisle was not *'native'* in Gretna or beyond, and should it be eradicated if it spreads north? This is a formalising of the old idea of Beech being only native to southern England and so treated as an alien in the northern regions. It has now been found in the early pollen records for North Yorkshire, and a further point is that, in the centuries since the closing of the English Channel, surely Beech would have made its way northwards anyway. In that case, it would now be native in the north as well. There is certainly a case for celebrating and conserving where possible local and regional distinctiveness and character, but regional ecological xenophobia is a dangerous route down which to travel.

Another major problem in dealing with the apparently simple matters of alien and exotic invaders is in the difficult relationships between conservation and 1) the cultivation of exotic trees for forestry and for amenity; and 2) with farming, horticulture and gardening. In all situations, there is blending of nature and culture that makes many assertions of native or exotic status fraught with problems. Both 1) and 2) are major contributors to the undoubted problems caused by alien invasions. Nevertheless, this does not mean that all the impacts are negative, or even that the bad effects are significant or important in all cases and in all situations.

A lesson of the British experience is also that perceptions of what is a problem, what is alien or native, and even who is responsible for any management or control, varies dramatically over decades and even over centuries. Furthermore, issues of exotic and invasive cannot be separated from the wider fluxes of society, economy and environment; so where and when we consider a particular species has a huge effect on our perceptions of it as a positive or negative influence on ecology, economy and society. It can be argued that, as Western imperialism spread globally during the 1800s and into the 1900s, many of these attitudes and a lot of 'native' plants and animals from 'home' were exported. The twin desires to 'improve' and to 'adorn' created many of the invasion and extinction problems witnessed today.

Chapter 12

References

Barker, G. (ed.) (2000) *Ecological Recombination in Urban Areas: Implications for Nature Conservation*. English Nature: Peterborough.

Davis, M.A., K. Thompson and J.P. Grime (2001) 'Charles S. Elton and the dissociation of invasion ecology from the rest of ecology'. *Diversity and Distribution* 7: 97–102.

Rotherham, I.D. (2005) 'Alien Plants and the Human Touch'. *Journal of Practical Ecology and Conservation Special Series*, No. 4: 63–76.

Rotherham, I.D. (2009) 'The Importance of Cultural Severance in Landscape Ecology Research', in A. Dupont and H. Jacobs (eds) *Landscape Ecology Research Trends*. Nova Science Publishers: Hauppauge, NY.

Rotherham, I.D. (2013) 'Searching for Shadows and Ghosts', in I.D. Rotherham, C. Handley, M. Agnoletti and T. Samoljik (eds) *Trees Beyond the Wood – an Exploration of Concepts of Woods, Forests and Trees*. Wildtrack Publishing: Sheffield. pp. 1–16.

Rotherham, I.D. and R.A. Lambert (eds) (2011) *Invasive and Introduced Plants and Animals: Human Perceptions, Attitudes and Approaches to Management*. EARTHSCAN: London.

Vera, F. (2000) *Grazing Ecology and Forest History*. CABI: Wallingford.

13.

CLIMATE CHANGE AND ECOLOGY

Introduction

There is a huge literature regarding issues of climate, climate change and their impacts on people and nature – past, present and future. There is little point in attempting to summarise this wealth of sources in an account such as this, and mostly they are easily available and fully reviewed elsewhere. Climate and weather are influenced by globally experienced phenomena such as solar activity; by 'greenhouse' gases in the atmosphere, which hold in heat otherwise radiated back into space; by the major heat transfer systems of the oceans and atmosphere such as the jet streams, the Gulf Stream and El Niño; and by the path of the planet around the sun. The surface covering of the earth in terms of, say, white snow-sheets or green forests also affects absorption or reflection of heat. The intention here is to summarise some key points to set the context, and to ask pertinent questions in relation to conservation and ecology.

Britain's climate and weather

'Climate' can be taken to be the overall status of weather phenomena at a particular time and 'weather' as the manifestation of climate at specific points; both vary through time and each has extremes, which are more or less frequent. In Britain, our overall climate and short-term weather events are hugely influenced by the oceanic current of the Atlantic called the North Atlantic Drift, or Gulf Stream. This massive heat transfer system carries warm waters and air in a north-easterly direction from the tropics to north-western Europe, and especially Britain. The main consequence of this heat engine is that in Britain we have generally mild, damp winters, and moderately warm, wet summers. We are warmer and wetter than would otherwise be the case. In the absence of the Gulf Stream, our winters would be more like those of Moscow, for example. The influence of the Gulf Stream on native wildlife species was demonstrated very elegantly by long-term observations of Bluebell flowering times in woodlands, by the late Professor Arthur Willis. He showed that, as the current moved slightly north or south of its general trajectory (it wobbles), the date of Bluebell flowering was earlier or later as a consequence.

Perhaps the most surprising thing about climate changing is that humans seem perpetually surprised and taken aback by the fluctuations. Somehow, we expect and anticipate stability when the reality is very different. Indeed, evidence from geology, from palaeo-ecology and palaeo-botany, from ice-cores and from written records, all indicate dramatic fluctuations through history and pre-history. The geology that underlies Britain's landscapes tells stories of radically changing climates and dramatic extinctions and migrations of plants and animals in response.

The lesson is harsh: that climate, and hence weather, changes hugely over time and species come and go in response. The clearest episodes of global climate change are probably the five full 'Ice Ages' which the planet has experienced, the earliest around two billion years ago. Technically, we are still in an ice age, the Pliocene-Quaternary glaciation, which started about 2.58 million years ago during the late Pliocene. At that time, the spread of ice sheets in the Northern Hemisphere began and, since then, the planet has undergone cycles of 'glaciation' with ice sheets advancing and retreating on 40,000-year and 100,000-year time scales. These expansions of ice are called glacial periods, glacials or glacial advances, and the warmer times are interglacial periods, interglacials or glacial retreats. Presently we are in an interglacial and the last proper 'glacial period' ended about 10,000 years ago. Today, all that remains of the continental ice sheets are the Greenland and Antarctic ice sheets and smaller glaciers such as on Baffin Island. The fluctuations are each made up of a long, cold, 'glacial' period and a shorter warm 'interglacial'. The latter may be anything from around 10,000 years long to maybe 50,000 years, and the cold, ice-bound glacials are longer (Macdougall, 2004).

The ebb and flow of warm and cold is catastrophic to many species; some adapt to milder weather or move to warmer climes and others, unable to adapt, perish. Similarly, species of cold areas suffer as the weather warms and mammals like the Woolly Rhinoceros and the Woolly Mammoth perished after the last ice age as Europe warmed. More recently, whilst many climatologists do not like the name, medieval Europe experienced what is called the 'Little Ice Age'. This was a period or more-or-less intense cold with maybe three particularly intensive freezes and warmer times in between. People across Europe starved, became smaller in stature and abandoned peripheral areas. Bad storms washed away extensive coastal zones and flooding was widespread. Plants and animals responded and moved back and forth as the weather zones fluxed.

Climate Change and Ecology

The Little Ice Age

This period of cooling occurred after the Medieval Warm Period or the Medieval Climate Optimum. Whilst it was not really an ice age in the purest sense, in 1939, it was described as such by François E. Matthes and the name stuck. The extent of the period affected is also debated but it is generally regarded as having run from the sixteenth to the nineteenth centuries, though sometimes from around 1350 AD to about 1850 AD. There is variation between evidence from climatologists and historians working on local records with differences according to local conditions. A cold period was defined by NASA as having run from 1550 AD to 1850 AD, with three especially cold times. The intense cold was about 1650, about 1770 and lastly in 1850. Slight warming followed each intense cold period. The Third Assessment Report of the Intergovernmental Panel on Climate Change felt that

Buddleia.

Photograph: Ian D. Rotherham.

this event was essentially independent, regional, climate change, as opposed to globally synchronous increased glaciation, i.e. global climate change. The causes of this cooling of the Northern Hemisphere may have been increased volcanic activity, cyclical lows in solar radiation, changed oceanic circulation, simply fluxing of global climate or even decreases in the human population.

Some researchers have proposed that human influences on climate began earlier than is normally supposed and that major population declines in Eurasia and the Americas reduced this impact, leading to a cooling trend. William Ruddiman suggested that decreased human populations in Europe, East Asia, and the Middle East, following the impacts of the Black Death, led to decreased agriculture and the spread of forest cover. This, he argues, generated uptake of atmospheric carbon dioxide and that might have triggered the Little Ice Age cooling. Similarly, population reduction in Central and North America after European colonisation in the early sixteenth century may have had a similar effect. People had cleared large areas of forest for agriculture to support growing populations, but European contact triggered destructive epidemics of diseases like smallpox and associated population collapse.

Plants and animals again followed climatic trends and moved north or south and upslope or downslope as the weather changed. Birds such as the north sub-species of Carrion Crow, the Hooded Crow, moved southwards and, since the warmer times of the twentieth century, have been progressively retreating northwards. Historic records, written accounts and evidence from palaeo-ecological studies (animal remains) and palaeo-botanical research (pollen profiles) provide insights into the fluxes of species as climate has varied over centuries and millennia. There are numerous accounts providing overviews of these phenomena which, over the decades, have become incredibly fine-grained in their application. Sir Harry Godwin's 1984 book on the history of Britain's vegetation provides a thorough and accessible account. In terms of the fauna of Britain, there is abundant evidence, from the invertebrate remains in peat bogs to the animal and bird bones found in ancient sediments. Changes in faunas demonstrated by studies of these phenomena reflect climatic changes, habitat losses and human influences. The occurrence of wetland birds such as Spoonbills, Egrets, Cranes and even Dalmation Pelicans in the English Fenlands, for example, probably reflects a vastly greater habitat extent and a warmer climate. The northern form of Carrion Crow, the Hooded Crow, is still retreating northwards as Britain's weather has warmed and is now restricted to parts of north Ireland, Scotland and the Isles. Smaller birds such as Dartford

Warbler and Marsh Warbler, for example, also respond to weather patterns as they move north with warmer weather and suffer during extreme cold winters. Common species such as Blackcap and Chiffchaff have altered their behaviour in recent decades to become regular over-wintering birds where they were once mostly summer migrant visitors. The situation for birdlife is summarised by excellent volumes such as Yalden and Albarella (2009) and Harrison (1988) and clearly, for birds, mobility is the key to recolonising a region when conditions become suitable.

For mammals, the situation is more complicated, since mobility with the ability to recolonise Britain was restricted by sea level rises, which cut off Britain from Europe. Yalden (1999) describes the dramatic fluxing of mammal populations in Britain, with the post-glacial colonisation by mammals around 15,000 years ago. The fauna included Reindeer, Wild Horses, Woolly Mammoths, Moose, Wolves, Brown Bears, Lynxes and Wolverines. These species subsequently became extinct, to be replaced by others moving in from the south.

Nightjar.

Photograph: Paul Hobson.

Chapter 13

Climate change today and future biodiversity

That climate is changing cannot be questioned, but there is a big issue about why, where and by how much. Important too, is the need for awareness that climates have always changed and that stability, whilst convenient to human populations in particular, cannot be assumed to be the norm. People appear desperately naïve in their expectations of environmental stability when we live in a changing world and our actions seem hell-bent on changing it more and faster, and on diminishing the ability of the natural world to mollify or mitigate such changes. Put in simple terms, whatever the causes of climate change today, human actions certainly exacerbate the processes and decrease planetary balancing systems. Furthermore, through the impacts of cultural severance and of massive ecosystem disruption and fragmentation, we reduce or even destroy the abilities of species to move in the landscape and to adapt to climatic flux. Worse still, through environmental change and globalisation we move species around the planet, resulting in the homogenisation of ecology and 'Disneyfication' of landscapes. Trapped by habitat loss and isolation, by competition with new invaders and by changing environmental baselines such as climate, many species are nose-diving to extinction and many more are likely to follow.

Conclusions

Climate, experienced as weather, has huge influences and impacts on fauna and flora. These trends and changes have occurred throughout history and they will continue to do so. However, human impact has not only exacerbated climate change trends, but has compromised the ability of nature to respond in a homeostatic way. Thus, species are less able to respond to the challenges of accelerating climatic shifts and ecosystems are themselves limited in terms of their mitigation and balancing of climatic changes.

References

Godwin, Sir H. (1984) *History of the British Flora: A Factual Basis for Phytogeography.* 2nd edition. Cambridge University Press: Cambridge.

Harrison, C. (1988) *The History of the Birds of Britain.* Collins: London.

Ladurie, E. Le R. (1971) *Times of Feast, Times of Famine: a History of Climate Since the Year 1000.* Trans. Barbara Bray. Garden City, NY: Doubleday.

Lamb, H.H. (1972) 'The Cold Little Ice Age Climate of about 1550 to 1800', in *Climate: Present, Past and Future.* Methuen: London.

Macdougall, D. (2004) *Frozen Earth: The Once and Future Story of Ice Ages.* University of California Press: Berkeley.

Rotherham, I.D. (2008) 'Landscape, Water and History'. *Practical Ecology and Conservation* 7: 138–152.

Rotherham, I.D. (2008) 'Floods and Water: A Landscape-scale Response'. *Practical Ecology and Conservation* 7: 128–137.

Rotherham, I.D. (2009) 'The Importance of Cultural Severance in Landscape Ecology Research', in A. Dupont and H. Jacobs (eds) *Landscape Ecology Research Trends.* Nova Science Publishers: Hauppauge, NY.

Yalden, D.W. (2002) *The History of British Mammals.* T. & A.D. Poyser Ltd: London

Yalden, D.W. and U. Albarella (2009) *The History of British Birds.* Oxford University Press: Oxford.

14.

REBUILDING THE JIGSAW – RESTORATION ECOLOGY

Introduction

One response to the environmental impacts of agriculture, forestry, industry and urbanisation is to attempt to reconstruct environments, habitats and functioning ecosystems where opportunities arise.

British projects include landscape-scale attempts to 'recreate' extensive conservation areas, like the Cambridgeshire fenland, with Britain's largest-ever, lottery-funded conservation project. Such efforts are because people recognise landscape-scale requirements for plants and animals to respond to climate change, obligations to offset carbon emissions and the need to mitigate and moderate flood risk. These major restoration projects are also intended to help economic development, especially in post-industrial and depressed rural areas. Such restoration projects go far beyond 1970s and 1980s reclamation efforts in Britain and aim to regenerate sustainable landscapes. The intention is to embed these landscapes in the regional environmental matrix and to reinvigorate the regional economy and communities.

In some cases, this task involves improvements in management to established nature reserves and in others it may be ambitious projects to restore, reclaim or reconstruct habitats in lands despoiled by industry, such as former mining sites and quarries. Examples are found across the country in former mining and quarrying sites. Occasionally, agricultural or forestry land also comes out of production for various reasons and, again, there are projects to recreate functioning ecosystems. With knowledge and expertise gained over the last fifty years or so, it is now possible to create exciting and often species-rich habitats and communities on these sites. In some cases, there has been considerable success in attracting back rare species of birds or mammals from the brink of local, regional or even national extinction.

Current projects to recreate wetlands in England's former fenlands include major new southern sites around Wicken Fen – the Great Fen Project – and in the north across the Humberhead Levels, Wheldrake Ings, Potteric Carr and Old Moor. Taken together, these amount to some tens of square kilometres and birds such as the Crane, the Bittern and many others

Chapter 14

Grey Heron.
Author's collection.

are already responding. However, if we consider that the drainage since the 1600s was of the order of maybe 6,000 to 8,000 square kilometres of wetland, then the scale of the task of restoration becomes clear. Furthermore, with human-induced changes across the wider landscape too, the impacts of agricultural 'improvement' and intensification have been enormous. The scale of the challenge in order to make a real impact thus remains frighteningly large and the effective economics of the new landscapes and their maintenance are questions yet to be resolved.

Since many restoration projects are undertaken with little knowledge of local cultural history, there are often serious flaws in the approaches. The driving forces that shaped and manipulated these ecosystems for centuries or millennia are mostly overlooked and this omission undermines ecological, social and economic sustainability.

Cultural landscapes, conservation and restoration

As noted earlier, the traditional and 'cultural' uses of natural resources and their consequent impacts on landscapes and their ecology are generally overlooked. Even major landscape-scale effects, like the formation of England's Norfolk Broads by medieval peat cutting to supply fuel to Norwich and other areas, went unrecognised until recently (Rotherham et al., 1997, 2013). Such landscapes and associated ecologies are often mistakenly considered 'natural' (Lambert et al., 1961). Other examples include ancient woodlands, among Britain's most highly valued conservation sites. Yet former management as coppice for fuelwood and charcoal is often unnoticed and historic drivers of change that determine the contemporary ecology frequently ignored. These drivers are dynamic forces of politics, economics and society at local and, frequently, subsistence levels. This lack of historical context is troubling because medieval woods, heaths, commons and bogs across western and Mediterranean Europe supplied most people with fuel, building materials and food for many centuries. Local landscapes provided community needs in traditional agrarian, early industrial and subsistence societies. Most people depended on limited land resources, often held in common, for arable pasture, fuel and building materials. Understanding the implications of historic land use and its impacts, both drastic and subtle, on soils, water and vegetation is important in informing future management. Many sites now managed for conservation are unrelated to former cultural uses. Others are intensified or abandoned; in all situations the original ecology, altered, slips away or is destroyed outright. In the 1940s, James Wentworth-Day, described how the National Trust might try to manage the Wicken Fen Nature Reserve to safeguard the rare and declining fauna and flora, but opined that this was doomed to failure since the fenman had been taken out of the fen. Wentworth-Day could see how the site and its habitats would inexorably change in the absence of use by local people. (See Rotherham, 2013 for more detailed explanation).

Restoration, re-creation, or reclamation

In this chapter, I examine recent projects and their shortcomings and suggest how they could be more successful. Specifically, I highlight a need to link culture and ecology, history and economy, in bold landscapes, larger and more dynamic than (with a few exceptions) anything previously attempted in British or European conservation. Projects must be economically robust and sustainable. Furthermore, in order to deliver the desired outputs of biodiversity effectively, these created systems need at least to mimic the original landscape conditions. Most projects do not do this.

Furthermore, it is important to consider whether a project really aims to restore (which is very difficult and, with cultural severance, may be impossible) or whether this is a case of creation of something new. This may seem like splitting hairs, but in terms of the outcomes and benchmarks for major projects, it is important. The idea of restoration or even recreation implies we can turn back the clock to a former condition. With environmental flux, including global climate change, with habitat fragmentation and other human impacts and with the consequences of human cultural severance, this is simply not possible. Micro-scale disturbance and the removal of biomass, and hence nutrients, are essential to many specialist plants and animals but absent in most of these created systems. As nutrients and biomass accumulate, competitors that are more aggressive squeeze the stress tolerators out, and this is the nature of ecological successional processes. There are things we can do to intervene in project landscape design and though ongoing management in order to tip the balance towards the stress tolerators. However, in terms of site management, and for big projects especially, the intervention must be economically driven if it is to be long-term sustainable and anything more than locally cosmetic.

This situation presents great challenges for 'restoration' but it should not deter ambitious habitat creation projects. However, it does imply that some of the desired outcomes may not be achievable. The sites and created ecosystems may be exciting, biodiverse and ecologically rich, but we should not kid ourselves that they will necessarily replace the losses of relict areas destroyed or abandoned to successional change. Additionally, it is a huge task to remediate the sheer scale of loss (see Rotherham, 2013 for example) that has occurred through the environmental destruction of the nineteenth and twentieth centuries.

Overcoming cultural severance through traditional management practices

In 2006, I wrote about four case studies with specific sites and groups of sites, all in northern-central England (Rotherham, 2006). These included dry heathland and ancient woodland (Wharncliffe Heath and Wood), riverine meadow landscape (Woodhouse Washlands), acidic grassland and relict woodland (Westwood) and ancient coppice woods (Ecclesall Woods, Gleadless Valley Woods, and Owler Carr Wood). These studies generated broad

Harvest Mouse.

Photograph: Peter Wolstenholme.

Chapter 14

conclusions and common threads, the areas reflecting inextricable links between landscape history, site utilisation and subsequent abandonment. Recognition by conservationists was followed by a desire to restore or recreate in part the former ecological character as perceived by the stakeholders. However, this raised key issues about economic history and the relationships between environmental resources and local people. It posed questions about how people value and use sites both now and formerly. These landscapes were once exploited but conserved because they were essential to sustainable local living. Today, they are valued for leisure, recreation and conservation, but not

Wood Anemone – an excellent indicator of an old woodland.

Photograph: Ian D. Rotherham.

Rebuilding the Jigsaw – Restoration Ecology

necessarily managed; and, if they are, it is in radically different ways from in the past. The individual projects helped demonstrate huge potential for landscape recovery, but also identified concerns and tensions.

Cultural severance has major impacts on large-scale restoration projects. For maximum success in sustainable outcomes, and to embed projects in regional cultural history, knowledge of former landscapes and their history should inform site restoration. Techniques considered in long-term studies include site restoration and recovery through reinstatement of sympathetic and traditional management at such sites as Woodhouse Washlands and Wharncliffe Heath. Additionally, new sites can be developed within landscape creation schemes, wherever possible using seed and materials from regional donor sites. Case study examples include an opencast coal-mining site at Tankersley and a wetland nature reserve at Blackburn Meadows.

The case studies demonstrated across a number of habitat types the potential for recovery but also the problems of severance from local, subsistence and traditional utilisation. Across wetlands, woodlands and heaths, even in the most unpromising of circumstances, there was remarkable potential for species recovery. Clearly, this improvement was possible even in relatively small sites, but larger areas were better buffered against adverse influences.

Wood Sorrel – an indicator of ancient woods and relicts and often in upland areas.

Photograph: Ian D. Rotherham.

The potential of post-industrial recovery

An irony of the late twentieth-century label of 'brownfield' applied to most post-industrial derelict sites is that many are rich in native, threatened wildlife species which are the stress tolerant plants and animals driven out of the wider landscape. In some cases, this ecology was taken into industrial complexes in the land grabs of the 1700s and 1800s and simply never used. Then, separated from the landscape beyond, these areas avoided the 'improvement' and fertiliser pollution of twentieth-century farming. The evolution of post-industrial sites may therefore give them unique context and value. This is not always the case and they are not always either of interest or sustainable. It is therefore important to be able to discriminate based on good information.

The occurrence of water and waterlogged areas may give considerably enhanced value to a site. However, for areas such as post-coaling landscapes the occurrence of extensive areas of open, bare ground may be a unique feature. Associated with extreme conditions (drought, seasonal waterlogging, contamination, extreme pH etc), such wildlife habitat can be hugely important. Depending on aspect, bare ground can foster microhabitat that is essential for unusual and rare species, particularly invertebrates. Many of these cannot survive outside such areas and these conditions become ever rarer in our increasingly eutrophic environment.

In many cases, such as abandoned limestone quarries rich in orchids, successional processes do occur and biodiversity declines rapidly as biomass increases and nutrients support the competitors. However, in sites with extreme soil conditions and low nutrient levels, the pace of succession may be slowed and the rare species have chance to survive. The coincidence of relict habitats and post-industrial opportunities presents the best chance for successful conservation of these rare and declining species in many parts of Britain. Sadly, viewed as hostile and derelict areas, these sites are frequently targeted for 'reclamation and remediation'.

Holding back the waters

In the 1980s, I approached the Peak District National Park Authority with a request to initiate a programme of drain blocking on a site called Leash Fen. Here, a major raised mire was desiccating due to massive drains cut into it during the middle and late twentieth century. It is now in public ownership and scheduled as a Site of Special Scientific Interest; my concern was to restore the water levels and to allow the site to recover. The reaction from the Peak Park's ecologists was swift and negative, as they suggested that attempts to re-wet the publicly owned site would somehow cause water to back 'upwards' and flood the farmland uphill of the bog. Their experts were also convinced that the suggestion that this was indeed derelict raised mire was wrong and misinformed. Within a year, the main authority from the then Nature Conservancy Council confirmed my assertion that the site was both a raised mire, and effectively on its knees due to ongoing drainage. A programme of modest ditch blocking and re-wetting was then set in motion.

By the new millennium, the idea of grip blocking of cut-over and drained bogs was gaining acceptability and today thousands of upland drains have been closed across the Peak District and the Pennine hills. By the time of the 2007 floods across England, the realisation of the impacts of upland drainage on lowland flooding had dawned. The 'Moors for the Future Project' is one such example of a multi-million pound initiative to re-wet a desiccated landscape. In the lowlands, similar initiatives are occurring around Wicken Fen and The Great Fen Project in Cambridgeshire and across large areas of the Humberhead Levels in Yorkshire and Lincolnshire. The problem in the lowlands is that individual landowners, through their blocking votes in the Internal Drainage Boards, can still prevent landscape-scale re-wetting.

Summary

Creation and 'restoration' projects offer significant opportunities for remediating long-term damage to ecosystems and loss of species. However, there remain major challenges in terms of long-term finance of initiatives and in that recovery will not necessary help the stress tolerant species that have declined or been lost. Post-industrial sites present major potential for effective conservation but opportunities are frequently missed because the sites are seen as of little inherent worth and are targeted for landscape 'improvement' (generally soil bunding and expensive tree planting projects).

Some wetland 'restoration' and creation projects are amongst the biggest environmental recovery schemes ever attempted in Britain. There remain question marks over implementation and long-term finance.

Chapter 14

References

Lambert, J.M., J.N. Jennings, C.T. Smith, C. Green and J.N. Hutchinson (1961) *The Making of the Broads. A Reconsideration of their Origin in the Light of New Evidence.* John Murray Ltd.: London.

Rotherham, I.D. (2006) 'Historic Landscape Restoration: Case Studies of Site Recovery in Post-industrial South Yorkshire, England', in M. Agnoletti (ed.) *The Conservation of Cultural Landscapes.* CABI: Wallingford. pp. 211–224.

Rotherham, I.D. (2011) 'The Implications of Landscape History and Cultural Severance in Environmental Restoration in England', in D. Egan, E. Hjerpe and J. Abrams (eds) *Integrating Nature and Culture: The Human Dimensions of Ecological Restoration.* Island Press: Washington, DC. pp. 277–287.

Rotherham, I.D. (2013) *The Lost Fens: England's Greatest Ecological Disaster.* The History Press: Stroud.

Rotherham, I.D. and J. Bradley (eds) (2011) *Lowland Heaths: Ecology, History, Restoration and Management.* Wildtrack Publishing: Sheffield.

Rotherham, I.D. and J. Lunn (2012) 'Positive Restoration in a "Green Belt" opencast coaling site: the conservation and community benefits of a sympathetic scheme in Barnsley, South Yorkshire', in I.D. Rotherham and C. Handley (eds) *Between a Rock and A Hard Place.* Landscape Archaeology and Ecology Special Series. Papers from the Landscape Conservation Forum, (2). Wildtrack Publishing: Sheffield. pp. 69–80.

Rotherham, I.D., J. Lunn and F. Spode (2012) 'Wildlife and Coal – the nature conservation value of post-mining sites in South Yorkshire', in I.D. Rotherham and C. Handley (eds) *Dynamic Landscape Restoration.* Landscape Archaeology and Ecology Special Series. Papers from the Landscape Conservation Forum, (1). Wildtrack Publishing: Sheffield. pp. 30–64.

Rotherham, I.D., J.C. Rose and C. Percy (2012) 'The dynamic influence of history and ecology on the restoration of a major urban heathland at Wharncliffe, South Yorkshire', in I.D. Rotherham and C. Handley (eds) *Wild by Design and Ploughing on Regardless.* Landscape Archaeology and Ecology Special Series. Papers from the Landscape Conservation Forum, (3). Wildtrack Publishing: Sheffield. pp. 22–36.

Rotherham, I.D., F. Spode and D. Fraser (2003) 'Post–coalmining landscapes: an under-appreciated resource for wildlife, people and heritage', in H.M. Moore, H.R. Fox and S. Elliot (eds) *Land Reclamation: Extending the Boundaries.* A.A. Balkema Publishers: Lisse. pp. 93–99.

Wentworth-Day, J. (1954) *History of the Fens.* George Harrap & Co. Ltd.: London.

PART 4.

FUTURE, PAST AND CONCLUSIONS

15.

WILDING, CULTURAL SEVERANCE AND THE END OF TRADITION

The world is too much with us; late and soon,
Getting and spending, we lay waste our powers;
Little we see in Nature that is ours;
We have given our hearts away, a sordid boon!
This Sea that bares her bosom to the moon;
The winds that will be howling at all hours,
And are up-gathered now like sleeping flowers,
For this, for everything, we are out of tune;

William Wordsworth, 'The World is Too Much with Us'.

Corncrake.

Author's collection.

Chapter 15

Introduction

Along with the major impacts and changes already described, a fundamental shift in the way that the landscape is managed is occurring all over the world. The timeline for Britain demonstrates elements of this, but the real implications and both the scale and the fundamental nature of the consequent challenges are hardly recognised by most nature conservationists. For countless centuries, the interactions between people and the land in traditional and generally subsistence economies were deeply embedded at the most local levels. Resources had to be managed carefully and sustainably, and when this failed people and communities, even whole societies, died. Nevertheless, it was this most intimate of relationships between people and nature that, over vast periods, generated the complex and often biodiverse ecologies of the world. From the late medieval period onwards in Western Europe, and at other times elsewhere, there has been a shift from traditions to agri-industrial farming, urbanised dwelling and industry and agri-forestry. This process has been gathering momentum almost exponentially over the last few centuries.

Konik pony grazing a wetland nature reserve.
Photograph: Ian D. Rotherham.

Wilding, Cultural Severance and the End of Tradition

Now in the early twenty-first century the impacts and sheer scale of these changes are becoming apparent with what may be called '*cultural severance*' – the end of tradition and of customary practice. Large swathes of landscapes are simply being abandoned to become 'wild'. Yet this process of abandonment is often greeted by nature conservationists as 're-wilding' and so inherently good. This is not the case. There is a place for newly wild areas and reconstructed landscapes 're-natured' in the twenty-first century, but abandonment and neglect of tradition is not 're-wilding'. Heaths, commons and grasslands that somehow escaped the ravages of enclosure, intensification and urbanisation are now simply abandoned and their ecologies progress along entirely predictable ecological successions. Some of these 'series' of the ecological process have considerable nature conservation interest but this is entirely transient and in no way replaces that lost from the traditionally managed landscapes. The implications of this widespread abandonment have not yet been recognised by conservation bodies and, along with the spread of exotic species, the globalisation and 'Disneyfication' of ecologies and the drivers of climate and other environmental change, pose serious problems for those seeking sustainability.

Overgrown common heath SSSI.

Photograph: Ian D. Rotherham.

Chapter 15

Re-wilding and re-naturing

Ideas of so-called re-wilding have proved attractive and have undoubtedly caught the imaginations of both public and of practitioners (e.g. Buissink, 2007; Fraser, 2009). However, whilst 'wilding' and wilder landscapes offer great potential and exciting possibilities, the suggestion that we are re-wilding is a myth. Essentially, the problem lies with the prefix 're-' because this implies taking the environment back to a prior state, which, put simply, is impossible. Because of the environmental impacts of humanity in the pre-petrochemical age, the landscapes, their habitats and the ecologies they contain are not natural but eco-cultural. Thus, simply removing people from the landscape will not restore it to a prior condition, but will just release a predictable series of ecological successions. The outcomes of the changes can be forecast with considerable reliability by reference to the work of Philip Grime and colleagues or, for example, to Ellenberg's indicators (Hill et al., 1999).

There is a further, serious flaw in the reasoning that simply letting go of the landscape today will allow nature to recover to become some Uto-

Overgrown heath.

Photograph: Ian D. Rotherham.

pian, ecologically rich and diverse world. With human impact on ecology, following petro-chemically driven revolutions in agriculture and in industry, the landscapes and remaining habitats are fragmented, impoverished and grossly contaminated by, for example, nitrogen and other nutrients. Ending site management and conservation as some now advocate, will lead to rapid and irreversible successional changes in ecology. This has already been witnessed in response to cultural severance, a problem now sweeping across the globe, and will be further exacerbated by a release of landscapes from use or management. The impacts, which rapidly manifest themselves, are increasing biomass, decreasing biodiversity and, in vulnerable environments, hugely damaging wildfires.

However, the concept of 're-wilding' or 're-naturing' that has emerged recently does raise the possibility of 'wilding' rural landscapes in various ways and forms. This should be a vision which, whilst informed by a knowledge and understanding of the past, is looking forwards to new, emerging landscapes and ecologies. In Europe, the approach was begun in response

Overgrown wet commonland SSSI.

Photograph: Ian D. Rotherham.

to Frans Vera's ideas about the origins and nature of European landscapes (Vera, 2000). Yet most of the concepts, visions and projects presently being implemented, overlook the cultural links between Vera's landscape and the early modern period. This is a fundamental error and means that those leading the projects do not realise the significance of the cultural ecology that is descended from Vera's primeval landscape (Rotherham, 2012, 2013). Additionally, a more recent sub-group in the wilding debate appears to veer towards abandonment to supposedly 'feral' ecologies. Vera's ideas, fermented in the environment of the Dutch polders, were essentially to do with the possible roles and impacts of large grazing herbivores in European ecology. The new 'feral' vision rejects intervention with herbivores and advocates letting nature takes its course, to find its own way.

Furthermore, there is a danger that projects for re-wilding and re-introduction of large grazing herbivores fail to understand the ecosystem carrying capacity, landscape cultural history or likely economic impacts of so-called 'ecotourism' (Rotherham, 2008). Locked into a now widespread myth that release from farming leads to landscape 're-wilding' or 're-naturing' and is inherently good for wildlife, it is suggested that once farmed areas

Peat wastage dust storm over the Isle of Ely, 1949.

From Asbury 1958.

can be abandoned and their economies will be powered by ecotourism. It is true that some species benefit from abandonment and ebb and flow with successional change. However, in many cases, abandonment of cultural or working landscapes is dereliction, as seen across the Mediterranean where rural areas depopulate, with resulting social and environmental problems (Agnoletti, 2006). Favourably located landscapes may acquire veneers of tourism affluence or commuter-belt sophistication, but most go into steep decline. With derelict landscapes, no working rural community, degraded ecology and abandoned cultural heritage, these regions discourage tourism or leisure visitors (Doncaster et al., 2006, Rotherham 2008).

Summary

Wilder landscapes offer huge benefits to wildlife and to people if they can be made to work. However, the myth of a return to some magical 'golden age' of ecology needs to be challenged if we are not to make an already catastrophic loss of habitats even worse. Visions for future landscapes need to be progressive and forward-thinking, based on good science and a thorough understanding of history, its lessons and its drivers.

Abandonment of landscapes weakens local tourism economies based on traditional landscapes and communities, without replacing them. Tourists do not pay to see dereliction. Furthermore, released from the constraints of management, be it conservation or local utilisation, the ecologies will spin off along predictable eutrophic trajectories. On grasslands, heaths and commons, the successions will be to rank grass and tall herbs, then species-poor scrub and secondary woodland. On moors, drier bogs and heaths, the shift will be to birch scrub and woodland, and often towards dense, mono-specific bracken beds. The latter are frequently a successional endpoint, which may persist for many centuries. In fire-sensitive areas, wildfires become common and hugely destructive.

On the other hand, there are many abandoned urban sites, which are too manicured for ecology to survive and that would benefit enormously by a degree of wildlife. This was advocated by writers such as Oliver Gilbert (1989, 1992) and George Barker (2000), in the 1980s and 1990s, but is largely now forgotten.

References

Agnoletti, M. (ed.) (2006) *The Conservation of Cultural Landscapes*. CABI: Wallingford.

Barker, G. (ed.) (2000) *Ecological Recombination in Urban Areas: Implications for Nature Conservation*. English Nature: Peterborough.

Buissink, F. (2007) *Wilderness in Europe: What Really Goes on between the Beasts and the Trees*. Staatsbosbeheer: Dreibergen, The Netherlands.

Doncaster, S., D. Egan, I.D. Rotherham and K. Harrison. (2006) 'The tourism economic argument for wetlands: a case study approach'. Proceedings of the IALE Conference, *Water and the Landscape: The Landscape Ecology of Freshwater Ecosystems*. pp. 296–300.

Fraser, C. (2010) *Rewilding the World: Dispatches from the Conservation Revolution*. Metropolitan Press: New York.

Gilbert, O.L. (1989) *The Ecology of Urban Habitats*. Chapman and Hall: London.

Gilbert, O.L. (1992) *The Flowering of the Cities ... The Natural Flora of 'Urban Commons'*. English Nature: Peterborough.

Grime, J.P. (2003) 'Plants hold the key. Ecosystems in a changing world'. *Biologist* **50** (2): 87–91.

Grime, J.P., J.G. Hodgson and R. Hunt (2007) *Comparative Plant Ecology. A Functional Approach to Common British Species*. Second Edition. Castlepoint Press: Dalbeattie.

Hill, M.O., J.O. Mountford, D.B. Roy and R.G.H. Bunce (1999) *Ellenberg's Indicator Values for British Plants*. ECOFACT 2a Technical Annex. Centre for Ecology and Hydrology: Wallingford.

Rotherham, I.D. (2008) 'Tourism and recreation as economic drivers in future uplands'. *Aspects of Applied Biology* **85**, *Shaping a vision for the uplands*: 93–98.

Rotherham, I.D. (2009) 'The Importance of Cultural Severance in Landscape Ecology Research', in A. Dupont and H. Jacobs (eds) *Landscape Ecology Research Trends*. Nova Science Publishers: Hauppauge, NY.

Rotherham, I.D. (2012) 'Traditional Woodland Management: the Implications of Cultural Severance and Knowledge Loss', in I.D. Rotherham, M. Jones and C. Handley (eds) *Working and Walking in the Footsteps of Ghosts. Volume 1: the Wooded Landscape*. Wildtrack Publishing: Sheffield. pp. 223–264.

Rotherham, I.D. (ed.) (2013) *Trees, Forested Landscapes and Grazing Animals: A European Perspective on Woodlands and Grazed Treescapes*. EARTHSCAN: London.

Rotherham, I.D. (2013) *Ancient Woodland: History, Industry and Crafts*. Shire Publications: Oxford.

Rotherham, I.D. (2013) 'Searching for Shadows and Ghosts', in I.D. Rotherham, C. Handley, M. Agnoletti and T. Samoljik (eds) *Trees Beyond the Wood – an Exploration of Concepts of Woods, Forests and Trees*. Wildtrack Publishing: Sheffield. pp. 1–16.

Vera, F. (2000) *Grazing Ecology and Forest History*. CABI: Wallingford.

16.

DEMOCRACY, ACCOUNTABILITY AND ENVIRONMENTALISM

Introduction

In order to address the issues of the decline of environmental quality and the accelerating losses of biodiversity it is important to take coherent and effective actions. However, the evidence presented in the time-line, and the context explained above, suggest that a response on the scale required will be at the least very challenging. In the first place the understanding of the issues by key decision-makers can be questioned and the single-theme or single-issue agencies and NGOs often do not address the broader issues of ecology etched deeply into socio-economic and political processes. In recent years, there has even been an increasing split between traditional nature conservationists and the modern environmental movement. So-called 'green energy' developments can cause damage to ecosystems and biodiversity on a par with older industrial processes. Many policies pay lip service to conservation but do little to address the fundamental causes of declines through the ways that human society interacts with ecosystems. Perhaps the most frightening aspect of this is the way in which, in little over a hundred years, people and nature have been separated. This does not mean that people no longer appreciate or enjoy nature; indeed in many ways more people take part in wildlife watching and nature leisure activities than ever before. However, this is a nature separate from us, a nature to be watched and to be conserved where possible, but somehow different and distant from day-to-day survival. People and natural resources such as farmland, forest and common have been de-coupled and production and consumption are separated. Viewers 'consume' wildlife and nature on television, but these do not underpin daily existence. Landscapes of leisure and recreation have replaced those of production and subsistence, with production concentrated into agri-industrial and agri-forest zones.

A separation from nature

This separation has meant a lessened awareness of the fundamental links and interdependences between people and nature, which must be at the heart of any concept of sustainability. The divide also affects the way in which people engage with nature and biodiversity and the way in which the land is managed. Put simply, most people today do not have a clue about land management, farming, forestry or conservation management, and so effective democratic processes relating to managing the land and delivering future biodiversity are almost impossible.

Bittern.

Author's collection.

There are major successes in nature conservation and, taking the British example, the memberships of conservation bodies and the scale of restoration projects are unprecedented. However, these still fail to address the problems of an inherently flawed system. There are spectacular successes, such as the reintroduction of the Red Kite and the re-creation of relatively large lowland fens in South Yorkshire and Cambridgeshire. Some of the new wetland sites will be several squares miles of water and fen, a seemingly massive achievement for conservation. Yet, if we consider that the losses since 1700 amount to over 6,000 square miles of fenland then the scale and reality of the challenge becomes more apparent. Furthermore, these 6,000 square miles were largely managed in a sustainable way for hundreds of years by local people. Highly valued for their economic returns, they were protected *'politically'* and socially.

The new landscapes are smaller and more fragmented, and isolated in effect from both local people and the local economy. These are created areas for conservation and related leisure, not cultural landscapes essential for survival. The successes in nature conservation are to be applauded and the impacts on biodiversity and nature conservation must be welcomed. Nevertheless, the fundamental problems remain, even down to the processes of decision-making and democracy, which determine future landscapes and their biodiversity. For democracy to work, it is essential that people are informed and understand the issues, that they are engaged in the processes and thus become empowered to take responsibility. Inspection of the British conservation time-line shows the opposite occurring. Local ownership of the landscape diminishes to be replaced by largely absentee property owners who are mostly government agencies, NGOs or corporate industrial agricultural enterprises. Links to local culture and tradition may be celebrated and demonstrated to leisure visitors but they are no longer etched into the local landscape or reflected in the local ecology. Local distinctiveness and character decline and the processes of simplification and 'Disneyfication' continue. In this context, it is hardly surprising that exotic species thrive and invade, powered by ecological disruption and gross eutrophication.

Looking for solutions

In order to find long-term solutions where ecology and landscape once again reflect local traditions and communities it is important first to recognise the nature and scale of the problems. Very often, and Britain is an excellent case of this, the special and national sites and species are protected but the local and commonplace are neglected and abandoned. The first step is to stop further declines and the second is to establish new systems to take the resource forwards sustainably. Understanding the links between culture and tradition, history and ecology is central to this. The British government had *Biodiversity Action Plans* and *Target Species*, with a commitment to end the decline of biodiversity by the year 2010. It is now admitted that there was never any chance of it achieving this and the recent austerity measures and cuts have confirmed that situation even more starkly.

It seems the challenge is to effectively re-couple the landscape and ecology with long-term economic and political processes. This needs to be at every level but especially that of local and once commonplace sites. Instead of starting at the top and ignoring the lower tiers of the environmental resource there needs to be genuine recognition and commitment to protect, to reinstate and to manage effectively key landscape elements at the everyday level. There has been much talk of protecting and enhancing at the local level, but in reality this amounts to 'eco-babble' of little substance.

Kaye Meadow campaigners trying to safeguard a wildflower grassland in Sheffield.

Photograph: Ian D. Rotherham.

Democracy, Accountability and Environmentalism

In making a commitment, the challenge to politicians and decision-makers is to embed such recovery effectively in long-term economic and social processes. There are opportunities to do this through catchment-wide water management guided by the EU Water Framework Directive. Such an approach can link to needs to alleviate both flood and drought and the delivery of so-called ecosystem services. The economic incentives of carbon-traded credits and carbon-sequestration can also be major economic drivers in the landscape-scale responses that are needed, but these must bring with them effective engagement of local people in delivering sustainable landscapes for the future. In today's harsh and wildlife unfriendly political environment, it seems we remain a long way from any satisfactory or genuinely sustainable solution. When environmentalists are regarded 'as a sort of Taliban' (according to George Osborne) and conservation laws and planning guidance 'as environmental red tape', then we have reason to fear the worst.

The Peak District National Park, Britain's first and still an evocative landscape.

Photograph: Ian D. Rotherham.

Chapter 16

Reaping the benefits

There are huge opportunities through the delivery of health benefits via contact with nature and high-quality environments, and in growing economic benefits of nature-based and heritage leisure and tourism. However to deliver the biodiversity and landscape quality that is required, leisure and tourism must cease to be parasitic on the resources and instead seek to support the delivery of necessary management to sustain them. The model

The robin – a powerful and engaging image for many ordinary people.

Photograph: Ian D. Rotherham.

is there in the past landscapes and traditions, which created the biodiversity we wish to sustain, but the challenge is to generate new economically sustainable systems to deliver this into the future.

Summary

The evidence of cultural severance and of observations in traditionally managed landscapes is that communities, given authority, empowerment, responsibility and knowledge, can be vital components of sustainable ecosystems. Once local ownership and usage are threatened and diminished by external forces such as capital economics, centralised ownership and absentee decision–makers, then ecology is under threat. Indeed, once the local community has no vested interest in maintaining the ecosystem and its resources, then these are either abandoned or destroyed by intensified exploitation.

Despite considerable evidence about ecosystem services and other benefits such as tourism economics, health and wellbeing, there is little sign of any deep-rooted and meaningful long-term change in our exploitative approach to nature. Furthermore, with political changes consequent on the global economic downturn, a more positive attitude to nature seems ever more out of reach. Globally we are now in the 'Anthropocene Era', a time when nature is forged by humanity. Perhaps a tiny footnote will be that from the 1960s to the early 2000s, Britain experienced the 'Age of Environmentalism and Nature Conservation', a time when people and politicians began to care about the wider world and nature and really do something about it. This did not last long before the movement's opponents, developers and politicians, ensured that swingeing cuts to local government and public services ended it. The rest, as they say, is history.

References

Cutter, S.L. and W.H. Renwick. (1999) *Exploitation, Conservation, Preservation – A Geographic Perspective on Natural Resource Use.* Third edition. John Wiley & Sons Ltd.: New York.

Evans, D. (1997) *A History of Nature Conservation in Britain.* Second edition. Routledge: London.

Chapter 16

Freedman, B. (1995) *Environmental Ecology – The Effects of Pollution, Disturbance and Other Stresses.* Second Edition. Academic Press: San Diego.

Goldsmith, E. and R. Allen (with Help from M. Allaby, J. Davoll and S. Lawrence) (1972) *A Blueprint for Survival. Ecologist* **2**(1). Also published by Penguin Books Ltd.: Harmondsworth.

Meadows, D.H., D.L. Meadows, J. Randers and W.W. Behrens (1972) *The Limits to Growth.* Pan Books: London.

Mellanby, K. (1967) *Pesticides and Pollution.* Collins New Naturalist: London.

Pepper, D. (1996) *Modern Environmentalism.* Routledge: London.

Ponting, C. (1991) *A Green History of the World.* Sinclair-Stevenson Ltd.: London.

17.

CONCLUSIONS AND FINAL THOUGHTS

And I have felt,
A presence that disturbs me with the joy,
Of elevated thoughts; a sense sublime,
Of something far more deeply interfused,
Whose dwelling is the light of setting suns,
And the round ocean and the living air,
And the blue sky, and in the mind of man

William Wordsworth

Bracken infestation.

Photograph: Ian D. Rotherham.

Box 17.1. Ecosystem Services

Undeveloped Land and Ecosystem Function Value

In recent years, there has been a growing awareness of the huge services provided by ecosystems such as wetlands. With an increasing research literature on issues of land values and semi-natural ecosystems, guidance from the former Office of the Deputy Prime Minister (ODPM) proved useful in linking such assessments to real economic process and the competing demands of development. With derelict land such as at RSPB Dearne Valley in South Yorkshire, or perhaps agricultural land considered surplus to food production, as in the Southern Fens, the Treasury Green Book gives detailed and helpful guidance. In an attempt to give economic and functional values to undeveloped land, either as open countryside unaffected by industry or as land from reclamation projects, monetary figures allow comparisons and evaluations. The values differ with the habitat-type considered. The logic is as follows:

Changes in the provision of environmental goods and services may arise in a number of contexts resulting from a 3R intervention (Regeneration, Renewal and Regional Development). Projects that remediate contaminated land need to consider the environmental benefits (amenity, ecological etc.) that might arise from soft end-use restoration (e.g. parkland) and that could be lost with a hard end-use option (such as commercial development). Similarly, such issues are relevant in considering, for example, the impact of liveability and quality of environments and the role these factors play in encouraging or discouraging private investment.

A recent review of the literature on the value of Greenfield land suggests a range of present values (£/ha) for different types of undeveloped land:

Urban core public space (city park) £10.8 million
Urban fringe (greenbelt) £0.2 million
Urban fringe (forested land) £0.5 million
Rural (forested land, amenity) £1.3 million
Agricultural land (extensive) £0.6m
Agricultural land (intensive) £0.02m
Natural and semi-natural land (wetlands) £1.3m

Source: ODPM (2002). Valuing the External Benefits of Undeveloped Land – A Review of the Literature.

Using this approach we can place a value on the habitat creation at Old Moor (75 ha x £1.3m = £97.5m) and ultimately for RSPB Dearne Valley (200 ha x £1.3 m = £260 m). HLF support to RSPB and partners for this project has therefore generated an ecological service value of around £98 million. This will ultimately rise to around £350 million.

A further economic value can be placed on the absorption of carbon dioxide by wet grassland and wetland environments created and conserved. This occurs from the moment the first wetland is created and organic matter begins to accumulate. This helps meet the UK Government and regional Greenhouse Gas targets. The water management and flood alleviation benefits are also obvious and then there are fantastic landscapes and wonderful wildlife that are priceless. Conservationists have probably been guilty of assuming that being able to place a monetary value on nature means money will be forthcoming. However, this is not real cash but recognition of worth. Nevertheless, failure to invest in and to conserve sites does mean real costs through, for example, flood damage or other consequences of lost ecosystem services. ❧

Introduction

The diversity of natural life, known most widely as 'biodiversity', reflects underlying ecology and ecological processes. For a particular region, in this case the example of the British Isles, the diversity in total reflects a matrix of geographical spaces or habitats with parochial sets of environmental conditions in varying stages and states of flux and stability. The overall 'biodiversity' reflects the summation of these myriad sites, some species-rich, some species-poor and together amounting to our national ecology. However, this resource is fixed in neither time nor space, but shifts, drifts and fluxes with human influences and natural changes in forces such as climate. Over longer timescales evolutionary processes help generate new species and further the extinction of those that exist today. In even longer periods, geological shifts force massive movements of continents around the planet with major extinctions and times of rapid evolution. These latter trends are beyond the scope of this short book, but should be held by the reader in the back of the mind, as a context for the 'bigger picture'.

Over countless centuries, humans have interacted with nature in ways that modify and sometimes destroy environmental resources. However, much human management has led to recognisable 'cultural landscapes', which merge natural and anthropogenic, and many of these have typically been managed according to customary or traditional ways. The result in the pre-petrochemical age was traditional landscapes often with species-rich habitats maintained by long-established techniques varying little in method or timing from year to year, from decade to decade. These traditional,

Chapter 17

'unimproved' landscapes have for centuries held a biodiversity, and ecology, descended from analogous 'habitats' in the ancient, primeval, 'natural' landscape of Europe. The complex interrelationships and ecologies of these habitats and their ecosystems result from this interaction and the longevity of the nature–human interaction.

Since people became more settled in the landscape and their numbers grew, they needed to manage, maintain and, in essence, to conserve, their resources. Indeed, in a subsistence economy, failure to do this was catastrophic. 'Conservation' as we know it emerged in Britain during the early mediaeval period, linked to sustainable allocation of resources for exploitation in the landscape through 'commons' and other designations; and to the leisure and pleasure of landowners and the monarch through great hunting parks, forests and chases. As human populations grew prior to the impact of Black Death in the fourteenth century and later, the need for careful resource control and management became more pressing.

Over the subsequent centuries, landscapes and their ecologies were affected by exploitation and persecution through both hunting and control (of for example, predators) and by landscape transformations associated

Floods at Bentley Doncaster 1932.

Author's collection.

with land-use. These processes varied with human population pressures, social and political changes and the availability of technologies and finance to bring about 'land improvements'. Watershed events included the advent of the parliamentary enclosures in the eighteenth and nineteenth censures, revolutions in agriculture and industry, rapid urbanisation and pollution in the nineteenth and twentieth centuries. The development of coal-based energy and then petrochemical industries and energy sources revolutionised the technologies and processes of transformation, which then occurred in a rapidly accelerating manner. Landscapes and ecology, reflected in measures of biodiversity, were shattered, fragmented, eradicated and replaced.

Those areas remaining were subject to the processes of cultural severance and gross pollution from water and air. The results have been accelerating successional changes in the sites that remain intact and rapid declines in conservation target species. The actual losses of plants, animals and ecosystems are almost beyond comprehension. During the nineteenth and twentieth centuries, industrial and urban pollution and environmental degradation took increasing tolls on the natural world. Then, especially from the 1950s onwards, technologically driven, industrial agriculture and forestry added to the despoliation of landscapes and ecologies. Globalisation followed imperialism in adding invasive, alien and exotic plants, animals and diseases to a recombinant ecological stew.

However, during the early part of the twentieth century a burgeoning environmental and nature conservation movement was a reaction to the now very apparent decline in nature and in environmental quality. The need to plan for nature and people in a crowded, island community such as Britain was growing more obvious and receiving serious attention. Over the latter part of the century, laws were passed and enacted to address matters of pollution, conservation, protection for landscapes, planning controls and strategies and access to the countryside. By the beginning of the twenty-first century, even ideas of positive relationships between health and good environmental quality and recreation or leisure activities in natural areas or interacting with nature were accepted by decision-makers. Even just seeing a pleasant 'natural' landscape makes people feel happier and be healthier. Many of these ideas, which for many people would just be common sense, were now supported by robust scientific evidence. Furthermore, in a country ever more prone to droughts and floods and other environmental problems, landscapes were suddenly perceived as valuable in delivering so-called 'ecosystem services'. Good, functioning ecosystems help to climate-proof and to flood-proof the country and this is worth a fortune in savings on damage and on radiation of damage. Such landscapes also deliver health and other social benefits for communities that again save the government and the taxpayer many millions of pounds in expenditure on health care and other social services. Even the educational benefits of a rich natural environment are worth millions of pounds a year.

In parallel to these trends, wildlife and nature have moved upwards in the public profile to become some of the most popular subjects on television or radio and membership of conservation organisations has rocketed. Conservation organisations like the RSPB, the Wildlife Trusts and the National Trust each have around a million or more members, well in excess of any political party in Britain. The leisure, recreational and tourism activities of these members and others has now grown to the point where it has become a significant contribution to many local and regional economies. In some cases, such as the Lower Dearne Valley in Barnsley, entire regeneration projects have had new green environments and nature reserves at their core. In this example, the RSPB Nature Reserve now generates a tourism economy of around 100,000 visitors per year.

Then, perhaps as a reaction to the colossal environmental damage by farming, agriculture, urbanisation, transport and pollution which was obvious to everyone by the 1980s, laws were tightened and some bold visions emerged on how to redress the balance. With towns and cities increasingly threatened by floodwaters, and continuing declines in biodiversity, there was finally recognition by politicians and decision-makers that these were big issues and required bold responses. Some examples of major land restoration and habitat creation projects include the Great Fen Project and Wicken Fen in Cambridgeshire, the Humberhead Levels, Potteric Carr, and nearby the Old Moor Nature Reserve and the Green Heart Project in the Lower Dearne Valley, all in South Yorkshire. In the uplands, there are major initiatives such as the Moors for the Future Project, to halt the declines in peat bogs and in some cases restore active peat growth. Community Forests and organisations such as the Woodland Trust have championed the cause of woods and especially ancient woods and the Ancient Tree Forum has campaigned to both find and safeguard older trees.

Reintroduction programmes for birds such as Red Kites have proved hugely successful and other species like Common Buzzard, Raven and Peregrine Falcon have recovered through protection and control of persecution and the removal of pollution. In wetland areas Marsh Harriers, Bitterns, and even Cranes are now re-establishing. In south Cornwall, the Cornish Chough has returned in numbers.

Conclusions and Final Thoughts

Gannets Restaurant at RSPB Dearne Valley Nature Reserve.

Photograph: Ian D. Rotherham.

Chapter 17

Box 17.2. The Great Fen Project and the Drainage of Whittlesey Mere

A consequence of the processes and histories described in this book is that we need to develop large-scale, landscape level restoration and remediation. A major driver of this response is the loss of massive eco-system services provided by landscape, which we have long taken for granted. However, today with climate changing, sea levels rising, storm events becoming more severe and lowlands increasingly threatened by inundation, ecosystem services have become big news.

The Great Fen Project is one such response. This is a landscape-scale restoration project located in the western area of the Southern Fens between Peterborough and Huntingdon. It is the latest of a series of dramatic changes that have affected the area and follows a history of large-scale drainage – of perhaps 4,000 square kilometres of wetland. This ground-breaking project aims restore 3,000 hectares of farmland to become new wetland and other habitats in order to protect the im-portant National Nature Reserves of Woodwalton Fen and Holme Fen. It is a partnership between the Environment Agency, Huntingdonshire District Council, the Middle Level Commissioners, Natural England and the Wildlife Trust.

As noted, the term 'ecosystem services' describes the various benefits that semi-natural and even artificial ecosystems provide for society. The term is relevant to the Fens since the landscape provides many wider socio-economic and environmental benefits. These include flood storage to protect local farmland and property. The Great Fen Project is located on the site of the once great Whittlesey Mere, southern En-gland's largest natural lake. It seems appropriate that extensive open water will once again dominate parts of this big sky landscape. Not far away, guided by the National Trust, Wicken Fen is also at the heart of another landscape-scale habitat creation initiative. ☙

Across the country, Badger conservation groups and the Badger Trust have successfully promoted Badger protection and conservation. People have been educated and laws have been changed to support badg-ers and to prevent persecution or other damage. Populations have recov-ered and people across the country now feel privileged to glimpse a Badger crossing the road or even in their garden. Bats too have their champions and regional groups campaign for their welfare and help the application of strict planning controls and protection legislation. Other groups of ani-mals to benefit from strict legal protection include birds subject to special protection, but also Water Voles and Great Crested Newts, Adders and Slow Worms. Indeed, with the increasing profiles and popularity of wildlife species, with big projects and active campaign groups and with legislative protection, with might think that all is now well in terms of biodiversity and its conservation. However, this is not necessarily so.

Despite widespread support for conservation and even awareness now of the economic benefits, which come with nature and ecology, after the first decade of a new millennium, nature is probably as much under threat in Britain as it has ever been. With a period of banking-induced financial collapse and austerity, funding to many projects has been cut and provision of things like local authority country parks and countryside services has been axed. Government agencies responsible for environmental protection and conservation have had their budgets brutally chopped; many of the more experienced, and knowledgeable officers have gone. These changes have occurred against a backdrop of a government, which considers nature protection legislation to be 'environmental red tape', and environmentalists to be a 'sort of Taliban'. Planning controls are being 'loosened' and the planning system is directed to be more-or-less 'pro-development'. To cap this all off, the government, despite all the senior scientific advice to the contrary, has now given permission to proceed with the legitimate shooting or gassing of Badgers under license. In just a few years, environmentalism and nature conservation have been driven backwards into a corporate and political Dark Ages.

Urban sprawl still threatens many areas of countryside and many landscapes are suffering the long-term impacts of cultural severance and abandonment or of intensified farming and forestry. Biofuel extraction is wrecking many ancient woodland sites and upland pastures and heaths are targeted for wind-farms. The proposed high-speed rail system HS2 threatens to rip through the heartland of the English countryside including many ancient woodlands and other supposedly protected areas. Even in many conservation sites, because of low funding availability and a lack of personnel with a clear grasp of conservation management issues, priorities are often to manage and improve access rather than to conserve wildlife and nature.

Ironically, given the high profile of wildlife on television and in other media, we now have a society that is largely ecologically illiterate and few people can name more than a handful of species of wild flowers or of animals. The OPAL project based at Imperial College has highlighted this issue and has made some efforts to address it, but those will be massively counteracted by cuts to local government countryside staff whose jobs were doing exactly this sort of community engagement work. Schools and parents paranoid about health and safety issues associated with outdoor activities, and children focused on computers and afraid of dirt, combine with a generation of teachers themselves severed from nature to give little room for optimism. Organisations like the RSPB and the Wildlife Trusts are doing great things, but we need more.

The 'Case Study of the Breeding Birds of Yorkshire' appended to this chapter provides an example of the trends in a particular taxonomic group across a specific region, the county of Yorkshire in northern England. This illustrates the changes that have occurred in recent history, their causes and the challenges that remain. Much of this brief account encapsulates the main themes and thrusts of the book across a much wider landscape canvas.

Summary

Some broad conclusions from the Yorkshire case study

Today, there are more species of bird breeding in Yorkshire than for a century. Targeted intervention and creation of a network of large nature reserves has helped the recovery and recolonisation of many species, back from the edge of regional extinction. However, their decline has been a classic case of cultural severance and the many nature reserves required now to support them are both isolated and expensive to manage.

Furthermore, in spite of notable conservation successes, declining populations of once commonplace bird species continue to be typical of our wider countryside. Farming conservation payments have often had little effect on the wider declines and so significant challenges remain. To overcome these challenges there is a need for a greater awareness of the fundamental causes and drivers of the shifts in baseline ecology. There need to be bold visions to address the changes and to do this from the local level to a much wider landscape scale. In order to achieve the scale of remediation necessary to ensure that these systems are long-term sustainable, the wider public need to be informed, engaged, empowered and enthused about the issues and the solutions. Moreover, the solutions need to be economically viable and self-sufficient.

Birds of prey, along with mammals like Badger, Polecat, and Pine Marten, have suffered from high levels of persecution leading to extinction across much of the county. These impacts were compounded by pollution from pesticides such as DDT and by massive loss of habitats. Mostly, the persecution

Conclusions and Final Thoughts

has now been much reduced and these species either have recovered or are in the process of so doing. However, the glaring example of the removal of Hen Harrier as an upland breeding bird remains as evidence of widespread, illegal persecution by some sectors of the game shooting industry.

The wider situation

Across the whole of the British Isles, we can see the major trends of change in ecology and biodiversity and, more recently, in the conservation response. Human impacts historically probably led to diversification of landscapes and, when influenced by locally controlled, largely subsistence communities, the survival of species from the primeval European savannah. These plants and animals persisted and even thrived in the eco-cultural analogues of their original habitats before major human influences. With micro-disturbances and regular, predictable interventions of human management,

Tewksbury Abbey viewed from the south-west with the River Swilgate in flood.

Author's collection.

Chapter 17

Box 17.3. The Future – An Example from Suffolk

In May 2007, Common Cranes were found breeding in the East Anglian Fens. This was for the first time in four hundred years. These huge birds were nesting at the RSPB's Lakenheath Fen Nature Reserve in Suffolk, an arable field used to grow carrots until the Society bought it only eleven years earlier. Thus began its transformation into a square mile of marsh and fen. The RSPB staff found the Cranes' nest by chance whilst undertaking a routine site survey; the eggs were about to hatch. The nesting pair of Cranes seemed to attract other Cranes to visit the area.

Lakenheath Fen and plans for the future

There is more habitat creation on the way, with the RSPB planning to create almost twenty square miles (5,000 hectares) of new wetlands in the East Anglian Fens over the next twenty years. They are a part of the Wet Fens Partnership that is promoting wetland creation and, with a newly-opened £700,000 visitor centre at Lakenheath Fen, the Society hopes this will be a 'Gateway to the Fens' and will bring wildlife viewing opportunities for tens of thousands of people. The target is visitor numbers increasing from 15,000 to 60,000 per year.

The main aim of Lakenheath Fen was to form a landscape-scale wetland suitable for breeding Bitterns, and the Cranes are a fortunate accident. Between 1996 and 2002, the RSPB converted over 200 hectares (500 acres) of arable land into reed-beds and damp meadows by carrying out extensive excavations and by planting a third of a million reeds.

Other wildlife at Lakenheath Fen

As well as Common Cranes, Lakenheath Fen has around six pairs of breeding Marsh Harriers and the area has long been the stronghold of the brightly coloured Golden Oriole. The re-created Fen has over a hundred species of aquatic plants, whose seeds had lain dormant in the cultivated soils.

Watching the Cranes at Lakenheath

The RSPB manage visitor access to the reserve to minimise disturbance to the rare birds especially the Cranes. Visitors have the opportunity to watch for them at a designated viewing point, with staff and volunteers on hand to provide information.

The East Anglian Fens

This wetland habitat formerly covered about 1,300 square miles approximately between Peterborough, Lincoln, Cambridge, and King's

Conclusions and Final Thoughts

Lynn. In the seventeenth century, the huge expanses of wetland were drained almost entirely and, by about 1600, this, along with hunting, led to the disappearance of breeding Cranes from England.

The RSPB now manages wet grazing marshes at the Ouse and Nene Washes in Cambridgeshire. They are creating new freshwater wetlands at Lakenheath Fen in Suffolk, at the Hanson-RSPB wetland project at Needingworth in Cambridgeshire and adjacent to the Wash at Freiston Shore and Frampton Marsh, both in Lincolnshire.

This is the scale of habitat remediation required across Britain. These fenland projects are the first tentative steps – not the end of the journey. Importantly, projects such as these must contribute both ecosystem services and real cash contributions to farming and tourism economies. ♒

in the pre-industrial, pre-petro-chemically subsidised economies there was limited scope for massive landscape change and levels of available nutrients were generally restricted. This lack of macronutrients like nitrogen meant that eutrophication and consequent ecological, successional shifts towards catholic, competitive species was already very limited.

By the later medieval and early industrial periods, this scenario changed with the development of political, economic and technological systems able to transform permanently entire ecosystems. Social drivers also changed to reflect these opportunities and the commons were taken from their commoners. Persecution of predators would always have been an issue in a settled, pastoral landscape, but with enclosure and the development of sporting games interests, predator control became a fine art. Across the bulk of the country, large predators, both birds and mammals, were eradicated. The final nail in the coffin of these species came with twentieth-century pollution, particularly from persistent pesticides. With the ability to pump water with engines powered by steam, then electricity, wetlands could be tamed and drained. With the advent of track, diesel vehicles and deep ploughs, rough grounds of heaths, commons and moors might be transformed into productive farmland or forestry plantation.

Urban sprawl and associated impacts spread throughout the land, particularly in southeast England and around the major industrial centres of the Midlands and the north. These expansions rapidly consumed the natural and eco-cultural landscapes and had impacts on the lands around, where farming or woodland management was no longer viable – another example of cultural severance. A zone around the expanding town or city becomes untenable and then abandoned. This leaves it vulnerable to the next wave of development as the city sweeps out across the countryside. Roads, motorways and railways increasingly fragment and dissect the lands that remain to leave the relict sites fragmented, isolated and impoverished.

The overall trends are most apparent in the southern lowlands and least so in the great upland zones of the north and the west. These changes in terms of basic ecology have been assessed by Grime and colleagues (e.g. Hodgson, 1986) and the general trends of declining stress tolerant species and stress tolerant ruderals and increasing competitors are exactly what might be predicted. The differences between the northern and western upland zones and the southern and southeastern lowland zones are also suggested by Grime's work. The changes and the declining biodiversity occur in the uplands too, but are simply slower and less obvious than in the lowlands.

The declines of habitats and species are well known for the nine-teenth and twentieth centuries and the reader is directed to the standard texts. However, in the last few decades there has been a partial halt to many declines and recovery to a degree of some species. Indeed, for birds such as Red Kite, Common Buzzard and Peregrine Falcon, the recovery has been spectacular. At many wetland nature reserves the public can view excit-ing wildlife spectaculars and the breeding of unusual and once nationally extinct birds. This is a remarkable testimony to the work of conservation bodies creating the conditions and the species themselves bouncing back to recovery. However, the highly visible, headline species sometimes disguise the longer-term backdrop of an inexorable decline of the specialist birds, mammals and plants, often Grime's stress tolerators and stress tolerant rud-erals. With cultural severance, the insidious influence of eutrophication, the continuing fragmentation of landscapes and habitats and the abandonment of traditional, economically viable management, ecology still changes and the associated biodiversity continues to decline.

Whilst some strikingly successful projects have come about, the idea of embedding these at a grassroots level across a wider landscape has been dealt a significant blow by cuts to local authority and government agency support for countryside services and for environmental planning. In the age of the so-called 'Big Society', we now have a very small vision. In place of environmental protection and legislation, Britain has descended into a new environmental Dark Age in which conservation laws are red tape and cam-paigners are sidelined. There is even a new environmental language of a sort of 'double-speak' in which things are 'green' and 'environmentally-friendly' even when they destroy wildlife and nature. The HS2 rail system is described as 'green' transport and essential to regional economies. That it drives a wedge through ancient woodlands and other wildlife habitats, and that its real economic impacts are questionable, is neglected. Furthermore, and perhaps most significant, is there has been zero opportunity for meaningful public debate and that local environmental democracy has been steam-rollered. Promises and policies to conserve and to protect wildlife are being ignored or overturned at every level from national to local on the grounds of economic necessity or that the developments are 'environmentally-friendly', 'green' projects. Ancient woodlands, for twenty years or so having had a reasonable degree of protection, are once more under threat as planning regulations are relaxed. Highly paid consultant ecologists queue up to facilitate and enable these most questionable developments to take place and give assurances about ecological mitigation and compensation.

Even worse is the case of many conservation schemes funded by the public purse through Environmental Stewardship grants. In the past, EU-funded Countryside Stewardship was used to bring about some dramatic recoveries of sites and species. However, in the last decade, with a haemorrhaging of skilled and experienced staff from local authorities and governmental environment agencies, those administering projects and grants often have little or no experience of field ecology or of site management. The results have been disastrous, with in many cases public funds for conservation leading directly to major site damage and the decline or even local extinction of the species for which a site was designated. The loss of key officers often means that the damage is simply not seen or recognised. Indeed, in the check lists of site reporting these projects are often given a clean bill of health and are described, outrageously, as in good or favourable condition. All the while, the decline continues.

The case study of the British Isles is informative in terms of the trends and the issues. A key point to emerge is that the drivers of change are long-term trends often linked to social, economic and political forces and influences. Many conservation initiatives of the last forty years were believed to be permanent changes for the good but, viewed today, from the perspective of the environmental historian they turned out to be paper tigers. For conservationists there is a lesson to be learned here. Mostly, following campaigns, people expect the policies and agreements or strategies to stand for all time. They do not. Indeed, policies and commitments at local and national levels last only as long as their champions do. Not even overturned, many nature conservation commitments are now just being ignored or overlooked. This is what an understanding of cultural severance might predict, since the key is informed local ownership and empowerment with regard to countryside and the environment. With local people less informed, less empowered and less engaged on local environmental issues, the future looks bleak.

Surprisingly, for ecology and biodiversity conservation in the British Isles, this is a very negative outlook. Written even just ten years ago, the prediction would have been far more positive. However, the changes in the global economy and in national politics have caused seismic changes in the nature conservation movement and neither the media nor the main actors in the environment have noticed these. The changes provide a real insight into the short-term impacts of the conservation movement of the late twentieth century and the fundamental drivers of politics and economics in cultural severance. This is turn raises huge issues of the long-term nature and the necessity of 'sustainability' and of realistic attempts to climate-proof the landscape and all that depends on it – including humanity.

References

Chislett, R. (1952) *Yorkshire Birds*. A. Brown and Sons, London.

Clarkson, K. (2013) 'The Changing Face of Breeding Birds in Yorkshire – a Brief Review 2012', in M. Atherden, C. Handley and I. Rotherham (eds) *Back From The Edge – The Fall and Rise of Yorkshire's Wildlife*. PLACE: York. pp. 29–36.

Gibbons, D.W, J.B. Reid and R.A. Chapman (1993) *The New Atlas of Breeding Birds in Britain and Ireland: 1988–1991*. T. & A.D. Poyser: London

Grime, J.P. (2003) 'Plants hold the key. Ecosystems in a changing world'. *Biologist* 50(2): 87–91.

Grime, J.P., J.G. Hodgson and R. Hunt (2007) *Comparative Plant Ecology. A Functional Approach to Common British Species*. Second Edition. Castlepoint Press: Dalbeattie.

Hodgson, J.G. (1986) 'Commonness and Rarity in Plants with Special Reference to the Sheffield Flora'. *Biological Conservation* 36(3): 199–252.

Holloway, S. (1996) *The Historical Atlas of Breeding Birds in Britain and Ireland: 1875–1900*. T. & A.D. Poyser: London.

Mather, J.R. (1986) *The Birds of Yorkshire*. Croom Helm: London.

Nelson, T.H. (1907) *The Birds of Yorkshire*. A. Brown and Sons: London.

Rotherham, I.D. (2010) *Yorkshire's Forgotten Fenland*. Wharncliffe Books: Barnsley.

Sharrock, J.T.R. (1976) *The Atlas of Breeding Birds in Britain and Ireland*. T. & A.D. Poyser: London.

Thomas, C.C. (2012) *Yorkshire Bird Report 2010*. Yorkshire Naturalists' Union: York.

A CASE STUDY OF THE BREEDING BIRDS OF YORKSHIRE

Changes in the diversity of breeding birds

In the early twentieth century, there were 123 species of birds recorded as breeding in Yorkshire (Nelson 1907). During the nineteenth century, Bittern, Great Bustard, Red Kite, Avocet, Stone Curlew, Ruff, Black-tailed Godwit, Wryneck and Chough had been lost as breeding birds. By the 1950s, the number of species had increased to 134 species (Chislett, 1952). However, Woodlark, Red-backed Shrike and Raven had been lost. By the 1980s, there were 138 breeding species (Mather, 1986). Clarkson (2013) discusses these issues in detail.

Recent additions during the latter half of the twentieth century include Common Crane, Wigeon, Goosander, Goshawk, Common Gull, Fieldfare, Siskin and Collared Dove. Spotted Crake and Corncrake were additional losses from this period. Since the 1980s, the total number of species known to breed or to have attempted to breed has increased to around 160 species. Egyptian Goose, Mandarin Duck, Little Egret, Red Kite, Spotted Crake, Corncrake, Common Crane, Avocet, Mediterranean Gull, Ring-necked Parakeet, Cetti's Warbler, Savi's Warbler, Marsh Warbler, Golden Oriole, Raven and Common Rosefinch are amongst the new arrivals or recolonisers. At the same time, Hen Harrier, Nightingale and Black Redstart have been lost or at least not been recorded (Thomas, 2012).

According to Clarkson (2013), the factors causing these changes in Yorkshire bird populations are complex but include wetland loss, agricultural intensification, afforestation, human persecution and natural fluctuations of species breeding at the edges of their geographic range; this latter factor is clearly exacerbated by climatic fluxes. Up to and through the mid-twentieth century, massive losses of heaths and commons in lowland areas, and the abandonment or conversion of coppice woodlands, took a major toll on breeding birds.

There are winners and losers. Recent trends, for, for example, 2011 show that of 49 monitored species, Rook shows the greatest decline and Oystercatcher the greatest increase. Moorhen, Woodpigeon, Coal Tit, Long-tailed Tit, Blackbird and Reed Bunting have all shown greater increases than in other English regions. Yorkshire is the British region for which Skylark

Ian D. Rotherham

has not declined. Great Spotted Woodpecker and Common Whitethroat increased less, but Grey Heron, Kestrel, Magpie, Rook and Pied Wagtail all declined more, than in other regions.

Factors behind the changes in Yorkshire's breeding birds

Climate Change

Across Europe, many species associated with warmer climates demonstrate positive trends especially when compared with those found in cooler areas. Obviously, for those also associated with particular habitats which have declined or been abandoned, the trends are not positive. By 2009, Little Egret bred in Yorkshire for the first time since the medieval period. In 2008, a male Dartford Warbler held territory on a Peak District moorland fringe. Hobby, Woodlark and Cetti's Warbler have maintained their northwards expansion. Stonechat and Pied Flycatcher are typically species that display dramatic expansions and contractions in their ranges, from their predominantly western habitats. The former has shown spectacular increases in its Yorkshire breeding range in recent decades.

Changing patterns of agricultural and intensification

Post-war agricultural intensification, specifically land improvement and then the use of herbicides and pesticides, has caused major declines in many formerly common species. Altered seasonality of crops, and particularly the move to autumn sown cereals with resulting loss of winter stubbles, combined with loss or neglect of hedgerows has been especially damaging. In particular, the loss of mixed farming systems, with hay meadows, permanent pasture and arable in close proximity has reduced landscape heterogeneity. This has further exacerbated declines of farmland birds and, in upland areas, loss of hay meadows and of small arable fields and general programmes of land drainage have all contributed to falling numbers and diversity.

The farmland bird indicator has steadily declined with Grey Partridge, Skylark, Yellowhammer, Corn Bunting and Yellow Wagtail all much reduced and Starling and Rook both particularly badly affected. Eight farmland bird species have increased, with Goldfinch, Wood Pigeon, Stock Dove and Jackdaw having the greatest rises.

In the upland areas, particularly the moorland fringe, losses in excess of 75 to 80 per cent of hay meadows have resulted in the virtual extinction of Twite from most of its former range. Indeed, the English breeding population has been reduced to a mere 100 pairs. Seventy of these pairs breed in the Halifax area of Yorkshire, supported by artificial feeding schemes. In the wider landscape, publicly funded agri-environment schemes have largely failed to deliver recoveries of specialist breeding birds of farmland.

Wetland habitat loss, creation and management

Yorkshire wetlands and their breeding birds demonstrate a story of long-term decline, with catastrophic losses during the nineteenth and twentieth centuries and a degree of partial recovery in recent decades.

In the last 400 years, the lowland landscape of much of Yorkshire has changed beyond recognition. In 1626, Vermuyden and his Dutch adventurers began the serious drainage of the 70,000 acre fenlands of Hatfield Chase, whilst 4,000 acres of Potteric Carr fell to Smeaton and his engineers in 1764. Elsewhere farmers drained the Vales of Pickering, York and Mowbray, the Hull Valley and Holderness and the wider Humberhead Levels (Rotherham, 2010). The draining of Yorkshire's great fenlands led to the loss of breeding Bittern, Marsh Harrier, Crane, Ruff, Black-tailed Godwit and Bearded Tit. In upland moors, bogs and pastures, systematic cutting of moorland drainage grips across blanket peat and other 'improvements' triggered major declines in the number of breeding Teal, Snipe, Redshank, Dunlin and Black-headed Gull.

However, during the latter part of the twentieth and the early twenty-first centuries, Yorkshire has witnessed a remarkably successful conservation recovery story. A network of wetland nature reserves has been established across the county. These sites include Blacktoft Sands on the Humber, Fairburn Ings and St Aidan's in the Aire Valley, Old Moor, Edderthorpe, Adwick and Houghton Washlands in the Dearne Valley, the Lower Derwent Valley and Wheldrake Ings, Thorne and Hatfield Moors (Humberhead Levels) National Nature Reserves, Potteric Carr, North Cave Wetlands, Woodhouse Washlands and Rother Valley Country Park on the River Rother, a group of created wetlands around the Ure and Swale, plus numerous smaller sites and reservoirs.

The results of this ambitious approach to restoration and re-creation has been the recovery and return of breeding Bitterns, with at least five pairs in 2012; Marsh Harrier numbers increased to at least 33 pairs in 2011; Spotted Crake had six territorial males in 2011; there were around 50 pairs of Avocets in 2011; and two pairs of Common Crane in 2012. There was a pair of Mediterranean Gulls in 2011, two pairs of Cetti's Warbler in 2012 and three reeling Savi's Warblers in 2011. Yorkshire also holds Britain's the second highest population of Black-necked Grebes.

Changing woods: Abandonment of traditional woodland management

Nearly one third of woodland bird species have declined since the 1950s. In particular, Garden Warbler, Willow Tit, Wood Warbler, Common Redstart and both Pied and Spotted Flycatchers have suffered falling populations and reduced ranges. Much of the decline occurred since the 1970s, despite extensive creation of deciduous plantations. It is believed that two factors may be at play here, and the most significant is the reduced heterogeneity in woodland structure and loss of understory habitat. The major issue is the lack of woodland management, with effects probably compounded by deer browsing which has increased dramatically in recent decades. Deer impacts include lowered invertebrate availability and fewer potential nest sites. However, other birds, like Lesser Spotted Woodpecker and Hawfinch, have also fallen in numbers and this is not linked to deer numbers but perhaps to competition from birds that have increased. Great Spotted Woodpecker, Nuthatch, Chiffchaff, Robin, Blue Tit, Great Tit and Blackbird have all increased. Other mammals, particularly the exotic Grey Squirrel, may be responsible for increased predation together with competition for food and nest-sites.

Extensive twentieth-century planting of commercial forestry across large parts of Yorkshire has also had significant impacts and, for birds, not all are bad. With introduced larch, pines, spruces and firs, there have been spectacular expansions by Siskins and Crossbills. In some areas, the creation of open clear-fell areas in mature plantations provides temporary sites for Nightjars.

Introduced and exotic birds

A number of the additions to Yorkshire's avifauna are non-natives, introduced at some point by humans, either deliberately or as escapees. Little Owl and Common Pheasant are examples of long-established introductions. Other long established species include Canada Goose, Greylag Goose and Ruddy Duck, which established in the 1970s. Mandarin Duck, Ring-necked Parakeet, feral Barnacle Goose and Egyptian Goose are arrivals that are more recent.

TIMELINE

GLOSSARY

BIBLIOGRAPHIES

INDEX

TIMELINE.
SELECTED KEY STAGES IN THE HISTORY OF NATURE CONSERVATION IN BRITAIN

Date	Event	Impacts	Comments
		Domesday, feudalism and hunting parks	
1,000 AD	A time of limited legal controls over land use and exploitation. Some legal controls on hunting mammals especially deer.	Enclosure of land as deer parks, and for smaller game in warrens. Since the demise of the Romano-British systems around 500 AD, little major land reclamation except by monastic houses.	The landscape was dominated by extensive tracts of wood pasture, forest, heath, bog, fen and marsh. Areas around settlements would be enclosed and farmed as arable and as common pasture or meadow on a communal system. The landscape was inherently 'fluid' with different land uses and associated vegetation grading one into the next and fluctuating through time. The natural wealth and what we now term 'biodiversity' was rich, diverse and extensive.
1066	Duke William ('The Bastard') of Normandy conquered England and became King William I.	Perhaps the most famous moment in English history was also a turning point in the history of biodiversity and in the 'conservation' or 'preservation' of selected species, namely 'game' and especially deer.	Many areas that became 'forests' were woodland, heath and furze 'waste' with sparsely scattered farms and homesteads.
1079	The 'New Forest' was one of a number of Royal Forests created by William I as Royal hunting preserves.	Forest laws were set up to protect 'beasts of the chase' and their habitat, with punishments for transgression ranging from death to fines.	Indigenous peasants were prohibited from enclosing their land but by common right were allowed to graze certain domestic animals throughout Forest.

1086	The *Domesday Book* was produced and provides a unique look at the English landscape which the Normans wrested from the Saxons after 1066. This detailed audit provided a rational basis for the future control and planned exploitation of the natural resources of the land. The survey suggests that only 15 per cent of England was wooded in the way that the surveyors would have recognised and defined woodland.	The survey generally describes a landscape that was managed in places quite intensively in the Iron Age period and more so by the Romano-British, but with some release from use during the Anglo-Saxon and Viking times.	By the late Saxon period the landscape was populated by numerous small villages each with common arable fields, shared pasture and meadow along riversides and open unenclosed heaths, moors, bogs, fens and wooded landscapes. Some woods were managed as coppice but most as wood pasture with pollarding and grazing. There were large deer parks enclosed by the late Saxon period, but these were still rare.
1217	The *Charter of the Forest* is a little-known charter sealed in England by King Henry III. *Carta de Foresta* was part of the great constitutional reforms imposed by his barons upon King John.	It was issued in 1217 as a supplement to *Magna Carta*, which King John wished to repudiate and annul with Papal authority as a 'shameful and demeaning agreement, forced upon the king by violence and fear', and revised in 1225.	In comparison with *Magna Carta*, it provided some real rights, privileges and protections for the common people against abuses of encroaching aristocracy.

The 'Magna Carta' of the landscape

1235 AD	*Statute of Merton* issued by King Henry III amended and enforced by Edward I.	Set down the rights of the Lord of the Manor to enclose lands and to legally define wastes, commons, woods and pastures. This recognised and defined open lands and enclosures.	At this time the enclosure of 'coppice woods' and of other productive areas in the landscape is formalised. The once 'fluid' dynamics of discrete habitat areas and landscapes became fixed within the feudal manorial system.

Timeline

1273	A royal decree was passed to prohibit the burning of 'sea coal' (mineral coal) because of its noxious fumes, especially when burn on an open hearth and without a chimney. The effects were unpleasant and potentially deadly. This is believed to be the first anti-pollution legislation in the world.	This action was necessary because of the tendency to burn mineral coal in urban areas. Generally most people relied on turf fuel or wood, and the great houses on charcoal.	Burning of coal was practiced since Roman times but only locally. It would not be until the 1700s and 1800s that it would become widespread with a catastrophic impact on landscapes, on biodiversity and ultimately even on climate.

The Medieval landscape

1400s	The last Wolf in England was reputedly killed in the fourteenth century at Humphrey Head in Cumbria.	Later records persist, often without firm evidence.	The loss of wolves removed a key top carnivore from England's ecosystems.
1100–1500 AD	Legal controls over exploitation of wildlife which provided food and/or sport – notably deer, fish and wildfowl.	Some attempts to drain and reclaim lands but with limited success.	The warm weather which dominated the region during the earlier part of this period deteriorated rapidly towards the late 1400s to become the 'Little Ice Age', with drastically reduced temperatures lasting for several centuries. This had major impacts on biodiversity, with northern species extending southwards and southern species becoming extinct. It also affected human land use and impacts as people retreated from more extreme environments.

1400s –1500s	Piecemeal enclosure of open land was occurring either by unscrupulous landlords taking in areas of common land or by individual peasant or yeoman farmers gradually assarting areas for cultivation.	Local enforcement may have taken some lands back, but much must have gradually been absorbed into individual farmed properties. Royal Forests were strictly protected and those caught making incursions into the unenclosed forest were prosecuted in Forest Courts.	
1483	First English Act passed which addressed the growing of timber trees. This legislation was to ensure that, after felling for timber or cutting for coppice, woods were to be enclosed to ensure regeneration.	The enclosed lands were later to be opened up when the young trees had outgrown danger from cattle grazing and browsing and the act was described as providing for 'rolling powers' of enclosure. New woodland areas were enclosed as mature woods were thrown open.	The process of forestry management for timber was beginning and would continue for centuries.
1600 –1700	**The beginnings of the 'age of improvement'**		
1600– 1700	The beginnings of 'improvement'. The beginnings of globalisation developed as European seafarers travelled the world, taking animals and plants with them and bringing back scores of others for gardens and for naturalisation.	Driven by population pressure, by extreme weather and constant threats of starvation, there was a need for more effective farming systems. With support sometimes from the Crown and at other times from major landowners, there began attempts to drain and to improve of reclaim lands. Capital was needed for investment and this was often raised by 'Gentlemen Adventurers' in return for lands and profits.	Gradually at first, and often suffering major reversals, the inexorable squeeze was beginning on wildlife habitats and also on the commons of the poorer people. From the earlier 'enclosures' following the Statute of Merton, the landscape and wildlife habitats were increasingly fixed in the landscape. As land reclamation and improvement took place, habitats became more fragmented and there was less potential for species to move to adjacent areas.

Timeline

1611	There was the first recorded felling of timber for the Royal Navy in the New Forest.	Also times and fashions were changing and after James I in the New Forest for example, there was no record of any sovereign hunting deer.	With shortage of domestic fuel and of wood for charcoal to smelt iron, competition with the Navy for timber became an acute pressure.
1600s -1800s	Parliamentary Acts of Enclosure to provide a legal basis for the taking of common and heath, waste, wood, bog or fen for private cultivation. This was the beginning of the major phase of agricultural 'improvement'.		
1602	Under this new system of Parliamentary Acts the First Enclosure Act was passed for Radpole near Weymouth in Dorset. This enabled the landlord to enclose his or her land, sometimes with the support of land-owning peasants but often against the wishes of smaller owners and tenants. The landless poor had no say in this process, even though it was the common resource upon which they depended.	From 1700–1760 AD, a further 208 Acts were passed, with 2,000 by the year 1800. By 1860, the process was largely complete and the enclosure of nearly half of England and large parts of lowland Scotland had been achieved. Enclosure by Parliamentary Act was a major factor which led to the development of professional surveying. In some more enlightened situations, 'poor lands' were set aside for the maintenance of the village paupers and the poorer peasants. These provided necessary fuel and often grazing for animals.	The process took the wider landscape from being a resource on which the poorer people could subsist, to being the exclusive domain of the wealthy and powerful. This would be reflected in future battles between poachers and gamekeepers, and, in biodiversity terms, the import and importation of exotic game birds such as pheasants and the ruthless eradication of native predators.
1600s	With Wolves still present, except in England, the government of King James I set down guidelines for Wolf extermination and how much reward should be paid as a bounty for each one killed.	This plan was never implemented but it led to actions under Oliver Cromwell to exterminate perhaps hundreds if not thousands of Wolves in Ireland.	As in England before, this removed an important top carnivore from the food-chain and is in part responsible for over-population by wild deer today.

1668	Parliament passed 'An Act for the Increase and Preservation of Timber within the Forest of Dean', under which 11,000 acres of 'wasteland' were to be enclosed and converted to timber-growing woodland.	Lack of both wood for fuel and timber for construction was becoming very acute.	The centuries which followed would witness increasingly sophisticated and extensive forestry for timber.
1698	'An Act for the Increase and Preservation of Timber in New Forest': this 1698 Act of William III allowed enclosure of a further 6,000 acres for growing naval timber.	Rolling powers meant this could increase, to the detriment of Commoners' grazing rights.	The pressures on open and common land tightened.
1700–1800	**Enclosures, improvement and industrialisation: urbanisation, industry, farming and forestry**		
1700–1800	The age of the enclosures, with land improvement, industry, science and enlightenment.	The processes of landscape change begun in the 1500s and 1600s took full shape. With new technologies, and the appliance of coal-generated energy via steam power, and the powerful political and economic drivers of Parliamentary enclosures, the environment was transformed.	Communities began the ever increasing drift to the new towns and cities that emerged on the back of industry. These urban settlements continued to drive the agricultural revolution to supply the increasing populations with food and other resources. Huge swathes of wildlife habitat are lost and the first major impacts of environmental pollution are beginning to be felt.
	The technology of hunting was changing and the availability of guns had major implications for game species and others such as waterfowl.	Hunting and improvements began to take a major toll on wildlife species.	

Timeline

	Globalisation was gaining speed.	Travel and the collection and introduction to Britain of exotic plants and animals escalated.	
1743	The claimed killing of the last Wolf (*Canis lupus*) in mainland Britain, in Scotland. Wolves were certainly exterminated from Britain after centuries of persecution and survived latest in the Scottish Highlands.	The legend is that the last individual was killed there in 1743, by a man called MacQueen.	As in England and Wales before, the impact of the loss of a key top carnivore would be significant. Now, in the twenty-first century, there are moves to reintroduce top carnivores to Britain.
1776	Not native south of the Scottish border for many centuries, Scots Pine (*Pinus sylvestris*) was introduced to the New Forest, for example at Ocknell and Bolderwood and elsewhere.	In many former hunting forests, the production of timber for the navy was now more important than the ancient hunting rights.	Productive forests for timber would change to become largely dominated by exotic conifers.
1764	This was another important year for the introduction of exotic and invasive species to Britain, with the importation from Gibraltar of the now infamous *Rhododendron ponticum*.		
1786	The last Wolf in Ireland was killed in County Carlow after a farmer lost a number of sheep to a lone Wolf on Mount Leinster.		

Ian D. Rotherham

The beginnings of modern natural history			
1788–9	*The Natural History of Selbourne* written by Gilbert White was published in this year. The book was to become one of the most reprinted and widely read books in the English language and contains many original observations of wildlife and natural history.	White's work was based on meticulous observation and recording of natural history in his clerical parish of Selborne in Hampshire. He corresponded with many of the most eminent and educated natural scientists of his generation and the book was based around letters and mock letters to these individuals.	The emergence of scientific natural history and of original observation. Gilbert White's *Natural History of Selbourne* began a popular interest in wildlife that parallels the academic developments of Charles Darwin and his contemporaries.
1700s	Landscapes of leisure and pleasure.	Landscaped parks and gardens were set out across the country as adornments for great and more modest houses and halls.	The seeds were set for a great escape of new and exotic plants and animals into the wider countryside.
1700s	Commercial high forestry began in earnest.	Large areas of land set aside for new plantations to provide for the production of timber and of game. Now excluded from what was the common land, peasants became poachers and were often ruthlessly and violently suppressed.	Native landscapes were replaced by alien plantations and many exotic plants began the process of naturalisation. Gamekeepers were employed to rigorously exterminate all predatory birds and mammals. In the lowlands the Common Partridge and the Ring-necked Pheasant became the keystone species in the landscape; in the uplands it was the Red Grouse.
1800–1900	Urbanisation, improvement, industry, pollution and natural history collecting		
1800–1900	Urbanisation, improvement, industry, pollution and natural history collecting.	The massive improvement and expansion of agricultural land continued but with ever-increasing intensity. By the mid 1800s, Whittlesey Mere, the biggest of the fenland lakes and the largest natural lake in southern England was drained and turned to arable land.	The consequences of habitat loss, of increasingly sophisticated hunting, and also of collection by and for gentleman naturalists led to catastrophic collapses of many species and regional and national extinctions.

Timeline

1813	Charles Waterton of Wakefield returned from his travels in South America and began to turn his Yorkshire estate into a sanctuary for all wild birds.		This was possibly the world's first wildlife conservation reserve.
1826	Access to countryside for recreational purposes was now becoming a political issue. The Manchester Preservation of Ancient Footpaths Society was formed with the aim of opening up lost and closed footpaths.	The demand for access to open space and hence to the experience of contact with nature was to be a major driver for change throughout the next two hundred years.	
1828	The conflicts between landowners and dispossessed commoners began to go underground and hand-in-hand with game preservation came poaching. Parliament passed the Night Poaching Act in 1828. This legislation was sub-titled: An Act for the more effectual Prevention of Persons going armed by Night for the Destruction of Game.	This Act included the stipulation that: 'Persons taking or destroying game by Night to be committed, for the 1st Offence, for 3 Months, and kept to hard labour, and to find Sureties; 2d Offence, 6 months, and kept to hard labour, and to find sureties; 3d Offence, to be liable to transportation'.	In Britain, as in many other countries, it is not easy to separate nature conservation from game preservation and from competition for vital resources. Commoners and paupers, displaced from their rights of usage, drifted to towns, became paid farm labourers, or went to the poor house.
1831-32	With the spread of huge conurbations but poor sanitation, and also the dramatic increases in world travel and trade, came the fear of disease and plagues. The histories of pollution and of conservation are often closely entwined – as are health, disease and pollution.	The 1830s saw the first outbreak of cholera in England with around 50,000 deaths attributed to the disease. There were public riots about the causes of and responses to the disease and medical opinion was split, with most feeling that the disease was spread by 'miasmas' which emanated from damp and dank areas such as bogs and swamps.	Developments in engineering and technology began to enable effective drainage of foul waters and also of natural water-bodies. Water pollution was to become an increasingly acute problem for over 150 years.

1831-34	On the Duchess of Sutherland's Highland estate in Scotland, the loss of wildlife to gamekeepers was colossal.	During this period 224 Eagles, 1,155 Hawks and Kites, 900 Ravens, 200 Foxes, and 900 Wild Cats, Polecats and Pine Martens were slaughtered on this one estate alone.	Control of predators and 'pests' would drive many species to extinction.
1842	Canadian Pondweed (*Elodea Canadensis*) was introduced into Great Britain and reputedly made its escape to the wild after being poured down the sink of a Cambridge Don's rooms and so via the drains into the River Cam. The rest, as they say, is history.	Exotic species both plants and animals would spread throughout Britain's waterways and wetlands over the next 150 years.	
1843	Formerly present across many areas of the lowlands, the last certain account of the Wild Cat (*Felis sylvestris*) in England was in this year.		

Timeline

1850–1900	The beginnings of nature conservation. With the increasing awareness of human impact on the environment and the growing abhorrence of urban degradation there were the first stirrings of organised conservation.	The Commons and Open Spaces Preservation Society was formed to resist further enclosures and the group take direct action to halt the process. The embryonic National Trust was founded in the late 1800s. The Royal Society for the Protection of Birds emerged from the Fur and Feather Group formed in Manchester in 1889 to protest against the massive use of exotic feathers, particularly in the hat trade. In 1891 it merged with other groups to become the Society for the Protection of Birds. By 1900 it had 25,000 members, a paid secretary and, in 1904, a royal charter.	The major phase of the enclosures of common land ended, in part through community action and demonstration in opposition to enclosures of what are now recreational commons around the expanding metropolis of London. Another major reason for the slowing of enclosure was simply that most of the sites had now gone. The first bird protection legislation of modern times was passed in order to safeguard seabirds from persecution by recreational sportsmen. Hundreds of nesting seabirds being shot on the cliffs at Flamborough and Bempton in Yorkshire sparked public concerns.
1858	The British Ornithologists' Union was established by a small body of 'gentlemen attached to the study of Ornithology'.	This gentleman's pursuit would be taken up by large numbers of amateur naturalists.	Popular ornithological writer Charles Dixon would soon be advocating using opera glasses to observe the birds rather than shooting them in order to obtain a skin to support a recorded sighting.

Ian D. Rotherham

1859	This was a defining year in both the scientific study of natural history and also in the level of public perception and awareness, with the publication of Charles Darwin's *The Origin of Species*.		
1865	The Commons, Open Spaces and Footpath Preservation Society formed, (now the Open Spaces Society).	In the early years this society rescued vital commons like Hampstead Heath, Wimbledon Common and Epping Forest from enclosure and the threat of building.	Often said to be the world's first environmental group and a pioneer of direct action in the cause of conservation.
1866	The Metropolitan Commons Act was passed.	In some cases after the Metropolitan Commons Act of 1866 was passed, the Lord of the Manor, on behalf of all the freeholders, disputed the right of the Metropolitan Board of Works to take land without compensation to the owners.	Many of the commons were Lammas Lands. The freeholders, of which there were a large number, had the use of the land from the 6 April until 12 August and the copyhold tenants of the manor had the right of grazing during the remainder of the year.
1868	The Association for the Protection of Sea-Birds (APSB) was formed by Rev. Henry Frederick Barnes the vicar of Bridlington between 1849 and 1874.	During the 1860s, the Victorian obsession with egg collecting and shooting wild animals, especially birds, had reached a peak. The slaughter of sea birds for 'sport' was widespread and a notable site for this was the belt of high cliffs at Bempton and Flamborough on the Yorkshire coast just north of Bridlington. The mass destruction by sea-borne parties from Bridlington was graphically described by Charles Waterton in his *Essays on Natural History* (1838).	It was estimated that in the 18 miles of coast between Bridlington and Scarborough between the months of April and August some 120,000 birds were taken annually, of which about 108,000 were shot. Day-trippers, many from the Sheffield region, were particularly active in this way. There was also commercial exploitation of birds and their feathers for the millinery trade. John Cordeaux's interest was perhaps sparked by his own visits to Flamborough. After one of these in April 1865 he noted that a party of five had shot 600 Guillemots and Razorbills in one day. In October 1867, one man boasted to him that he had killed 4,000 gulls that season.

Timeline

1869	The Sea Birds Preservation Act was passed.	In June 1869, this Act reached the Statute Book and provided protection for 35 species by introducing a closed season running annually from 1 April to 1 August. The first successful prosecution under the Act took place in Bridlington on 10 July 1869. A Mr Tasker of Sheffield had deliberately shot 28 birds and was fined a total of £3 19s.	
1870	The Red Kite became extinct as a breeding bird in England.		130 years later the Red Kite would return.
1872	The Wild Birds Preservation Act was passed.	This extended protection to a much wider list of bird species. This began a sequence of increasingly comprehensive Acts to protect birds from illegal hunting, bird egg collecting and other persecution. Certain pest species were exempted and game was covered by separate legislation.	
1874	The Little Owl (*Athene noctua*) was one of many species released into the wild in Britain by the Acclimatisation Societies.	Around forty Little Owls were collected from France and released in Kent between 1874 and 1880.	They are still sometimes known as 'Frenchies' or 'Frenchmen'.
1876	The Wild Fowl Preservation Act was passed.		
1876	The Commons Act was passed.	This was an Act for facilitating the regulation and improvement of Commons, and for amending the Acts relating to the Inclosure of Commons and was passed on 11 August 1876.	

1876	The freedom to roam movement began with the formation of the Hayfield and Kinder Scout Ancient Footpaths Association.		
1880	The first Bird Protection Act, giving comprehensive protection to particular wild birds with some exemptions and exclusions.		
1884	The Access to Mountains and Moorlands (Scotland) Bill was presented to Parliament but failed. Lawyer James Bryce, an Aberdeenshire MP introduced his first abortive Bill in 1884.	Over his 27 years at Westminster there were a twelve such attempts, of which eight were from Bryce. All were withdrawn through lack of support, largely due to Parliament being dominated by landowning interests.	An Access to Mountains Act did eventually reach the statute books in 1939. It originated from a Private Member's Bill and was repealed ten years later.
1885	The Plumage League was formed.	This led to the Society for the Protection of Birds in 1891.	
1891	The Society for the Protection of Birds was formally established; founded by women in Didsbury, Manchester, who sought to influence and persuade their own well-to-do peers that the fashionable trade in bird feathers for the adornment of hats should be stopped.	This fashion was causing the slaughter of many birds including Egrets and Grebes. Queen Victoria helped the cause by endorsing an agreement stopping the military wearing Egret plumes, though the wearing of genuine 'bear-skin' hats continues with the Guards Regiments to this day.	
1891	British Pteridological Society was formed to promote the study of ferns. During the Victorian period the so-called 'Fern Craze' of collecting wild ferns for gardens and for inside displays in specially constructed glass cabinets decimated many species.		

Timeline

1893	Giant Hogweed (*Heracleum mantegazzianum*) was introduced to British gardens from the Caucasus.	This was one of a number of spectacular plants promoted by the 'Wild Garden movement' and encouraged by the writings of leading Victorian garden writer and designer William Robinson.	The Wild Garden Movement actively promoted the naturalisation of spectacular exotic plants 'to good effect' in wild gardens and landscapes. The Acclimatisation Societies devoted themselves to the introduction and naturalisation of exotic birds and mammals.
1895	Emerging from the work of the Commons Preservation Society, The National Trust was formed as the The National Trust for Places of Historic Interest and Natural Beauty.		
1898	The Coal Smoke Abatement Society was formed (now National Society for Clean Air) to combat the now dreadful levels of coal-generated pollution in and around urban areas.	The impacts of coal-generated air pollution were catastrophic for a number of taxonomic groups but most famously for the lichens. These were simply obliterated from huge areas of the landscape.	Previously unknown and pollution-tolerant lichen species emerged from the pall of smoke to dominate the drastically impoverished lichen communities.
1899	The National Trust acquired Wicken Fen as a Nature Reserve.	This is often claimed to be the first nature reserve in Britain, though it was around sixty years after Charles Waterton's efforts.	
	Many authors, such as W.H. Hudson and Richard Jefferies, and artists, such as John Gould and Thomas Bewick, captured the public imagination and helped grow a huge interest in natural history.	This was mirrored by a burgeoning of amateur natural history and also rambling groups and societies. These cut across class barriers, with both the educated middle classes and the workers taking part.	Collecting for natural history purposes became a craze and many species, across a whole range of taxa, were driven to extinction.

Ian D. Rotherham

1900–1920	Urban sprawl, agri-industrial farming and forestry: great estates and game management and the beginnings or organised nature conservation		
1900	The Red Kite became extinct in Scotland.		
1900–1920	The emergence of modern agriculture and urban infrastructures with roads and rail.	Massive loss of habitats and degradation due to uncontrolled pollution of land, water and air.	
1903	The Society for the Preservation of the Wild Fauna of the Empire was formed.		It is now called the Flora and Fauna Preservation Society.
1904	The Society for the Protection of Birds became the Royal Society for the Protection of Birds.		
1904	Arthur Tansley, a distinguished plant ecologist who was later knighted, founded the British Vegetation Committee in 1904 to map Britain's vegetation.	This led to the formation of the British Ecological Society in 1913.	
1905	British Empire Naturalists' Association set up and later became the British Naturalists' Association.		
1906	First described in the 1770s, the Mazarine Blue Butterfly (*Polyommatus semiargus*) became extinct at some point between 1906 and 1920, though the exact date of its final demise is unknown.	Despite being widespread and fairly common on the continent, this butterfly is extinct in Britain. Its habitat was open damp, flowery grassland and, though widespread in southern England, it was always scarce.	The last known breeding colony was in 1904. It is likely that enclosures, land improvement for agriculture and associated drainage were the main culprits, with collection by entomologists no doubt speeding its final demise.

Timeline

1907	The National Trust reconstituted as a statutory body by an Act of Parliament.	Through a Private Bill approved by Parliament the Trust had the power to declare property inalienable.	
1912	The Society for the Promotion of Nature Reserves (SPNR) was established.	Founded by wealthy banker the Hon. Charles Rothschild and his acquaintances, the intention was to identify key areas worthy of protection, organise their acquisition and subsequent transfer to the National Trust.	
1915	White-tailed Eagle bred in Great Britain for the last time until they were reintroduced to Scotland in the 1980s.		
1916	The SPNR received its Royal charter from King George V.	The Society also published the first list of important wildlife sites.	
1919	The Forestry Commission set up. During the First World War over 4,000,000 acres of woodland were felled.	The Commission was set up to make good the losses. The Forestry Commission was responsible to the Ministry of Agriculture.	
1919	The SPNR acquires Woodwalton Fen: their first reserve but established by Rothschild in 1910.		
1920– 1940	**Land-use planning, the break up of the great estate, and the end of tradition**		
1920– 1940	A time of change	Some of the great hunting estates were still fashionable and remained so until the outbreak of the Second World War. Predatory birds and mammals were still rigorously controlled on hunting estates, and land was managed to favour game species.	In the uplands, for example, huge areas of land were actively drained to reduce wet peat bogs and encourage a monoculture of heather (*Calluna vulgaris*).

Ian D. Rotherham

	With popular literature on natural history and collecting, hobbies such as the collection of bird's eggs were legal and popular.	Trapping wild birds and either eating or keeping them in cages was widespread.	
	The abandonment of the rural estates.	For reasons of both fashion and finance many great and lesser rural houses and halls and their landed estates were sold. Buildings were often demolished and gardens became derelict.	This triggered a great escape of exotic plants and occasionally of animals too. Species brought into Britain and introduced to managed landscapes were now free to escape and naturalise into the wild. Many did just this, although the ecological impacts were generally not recognised for another fifty years or more.
	Concerns about the scale of habitat loss and wildlife extinction were growing. But there were as yet no effective organisations to take this forward and also no science to support an underpin actions.	The Society for the Promotion of Nature Reserves was formed. Awareness of the scale of loss was often voiced by those in the hunting and shooting lobby who witnessed first-hand the loss of habitats and the rapid declines in, for example, wading birds and wildfowl.	There was some acquisition of small areas of land for conservation by both naturalists and wildfowlers; all with the intention of preservation.
	With the establishment of the Forestry Commission in 1919, to re-establish woodlands and forests depleted by the war efforts, there began a process of drastic land acquisition, drainage and planting of exotic trees.	Traditional coppice woods were being abandoned and converted in plantation woods of often-exotic conifers.	As a part of this process, the traditional crafts and skills associated with the old woods were rapidly lost, thus ending in a few decades traditions going back to before Domesday.
1925	The Law of Property Act was passed.	This gave the public right of access for 'air and exercise' to all commons in urban areas in England and Wales.	

1926	The first County Naturalists' Trust was formed in what is probably England's premier wildlife county, Norfolk.		
1926	The Council for the Preservation of Rural England (CPRE) was formed. The word 'Preservation' was later changed to 'Protection'.	This was a powerful and influential lobby for mechanisms such as Green Belts.	
1927	One of the most spectacular fenland butterflies, the Large Copper (*Lycaena dispar*), was driven to extinction by mass drainage of the Cambridgeshire Fens.	There was an attempted reintroduction to the Fens from Holland in 1927.	This was the culmination of 300 years of drainage.
1929	The Royal Society for the Protection of Birds (RSPB) acquired its first nature reserve at Dungeness in Kent.		
1930	The Ramblers' Federation formed.		
1932	There were the first organised Mass Trespasses at Kinder Scout in the Peak District.	Six arrests made as several thousand people all trespassed together.	This transformed public opinion over access issues.
1932	Town and Country Planning Act. This is the first time that the term 'country' is used in a British planning context.	The legislation covered both urban and rural areas.	

Ian D. Rotherham

1935	A key development at this time was the idea of access to the countryside and the popular demand for the 'Right to Roam' resulting in the formation of the Ramblers' Movement.	Much of this grew from the emergence of religious non-conformism and self-education in the over-crowded urban industrial cities especially in northern England.	The Ramblers' Association was formed to promote the interests of walkers and others demanding access to the countryside and along established footpaths.
1935	The Marsh Frog (*Rana ridibunda*) was introduced to Britain from Europe to become well established in parts of Kent and Sussex.		
1936	First National Forest Park as a Forestry Commission designation was established in Argyllshire.	Other Forest Parks followed in the Forest of Dean in 1939 and in Snowdonia in 1940.	
1938	Green Belt Act (London and Home Counties).	After years of research and policy formulation the first Green Belts were designated as a means to hold back urban sprawl.	
1938	The Little Ringed Plover (*Charadrius dubius*) was first recorded as breeding in Britain in south and east England especially around gravel pits.	By the 1980s it was relatively common in coal mining areas on abandoned coal spoil heaps, waste slag heaps and on opencast coal mining sites.	
1939	The Access to the Mountains Act was finally passed largely due to the activities of the Mass Trespass in 1932.	It was introduced by a Labour MP for Shipley in Yorkshire, but was repealed and replaced by the 1949 National Parks and Access to the Countryside Act.	

Timeline

	Agricultural depression gave something of a reprieve for wildlife habitats under the squeeze of long-term 'improvement'.	This was to provide only temporary respite.	
	In the fens such as at Wicken Fen in Cambridgeshire, there was the first organised and detailed ecological evaluation and monitoring.	This led to the first realisation that acquisition of sites by itself was not enough. Without management the interest of a site such as a fen would be lost anyway.	Specialist plants and animals begin to disappear from the fragmented habitats which still remain.
	Popular natural history and bird watching are emerging and are encouraged by the motorcar.		
	Derived from the self-education and outdoors movements of late Victorian England there is a demand for access to the countryside led by northern ramblers' groups.	The ordinary people begin the long process of reclaiming the commons, but for recreational use and not for subsistence.	Serious problems for biodiversity which relate to the abandonment of traditional site management, but these would not be generally recognised for nearly half a century.
1940–1960	**The war years and beyond: self-sufficiency in an island under siege – technology, petrochemicals, fertilisers and pesticides**		
1940–1960	The war years and beyond.	An immediate impact of the outbreak of war was the need to feed an island community under siege. Often using imported technology from the USA, large areas of previously uncultivated land are drained and ploughed. Animal power for farming was replaced by machinery and oil-power and petrol-power, together with tractors and tracked vehicles, facilitated massive landscape transformation.	After around 500 years of gradual drainage and 'improvement' almost the entirety of the East Anglian Fens, around 4,000 square miles, now totally destroyed. Other areas across the country have followed a similar pattern with a similar fate. Many species of plants and animals are lost.

1940	Snowdonia National Forest Park set up.	
	Plans were already being formulated during the war years to establish National Parks, Nature Reserves and other protected areas.	This was in part to safeguard nature, but also for the recreational benefits of the emerging middle class urban populations.
1941	A major conference was held on Nature Preservation in the Post-War Reconstruction.	There were representatives from over thirty organisations attending and the conference endorsed the need to include Nature Reserves in any post-war national planning scheme.
1942	The Scott Report on land utilisation in rural areas was produced.	Section 178 outlined the need for National Parks and other open spaces, the preservation of the coast and registration of common lands.
1942	The Field Studies Council was set up to promote natural history fieldwork and environmental education.	
1943	The Ministry of Town and Country Planning was set up.	This provided the first co-ordinated approach to land-use planning.
1945	The Norfolk Naturalists'Trust acquired its first nature reserve.	The landmark event was the first for a County Naturalists'Trust.
1945	The Dower Report was produced and under the direction of John Dower.	It produced a list of suggested National Parks and other 'amenity areas'.

Timeline

1946	The Wildfowl Trust formed was formed by war hero and former wildfowler, Peter, later Sir Peter, Scott, British conservationist and artist.	Along with true 'wildfowl' (geese, ducks, and swans), the refuge maintains breeding colonies of four of the world's six known flamingo species and has a special pavilion for exotic ducks and various small birds. The refuge's collection has around 3,000 birds covering about 200 species.	The Trust introduced North American Ruddy Duck (*Oxyura jamaicensis*) to the England. Now widely naturalised, it is accused of threatening the European native White-headed Duck (*Oxyura leucocephala*). There is now a very controversial and hugely expensive programme to eradicate the Ruddy Duck from Britain.
1946	The second County Naturalists' Trust formed in Yorkshire called *Yorkshire Naturalists' Trust*.		
1947	The Town and Country Planning Act was passed and became the principle Act establishing the post-war planning system across Britain.	There were to be development plans prepared by all statutory planning authorities to cover a twenty-year period.	This included the potential to designate Green Belts around major conurbations.
1947	A report of the Wildlife Special Committee stated that there was 'no comprehensive wildlife protection bill for Great Britain as a whole'.	This was a review from a committee initiated by the Government.	
1947	The Hobhouse Report presented findings of a committee formed in 1945 to consider the implications of the Dower Report and to decide which National Parks were to be chosen and promoted to Parliament for approval.	They also decided that not all the areas suggested were to become National Parks and receive special protection. Some would have a lesser status as 'conservation areas'; later designated as Areas of Outstanding Beauty (AONB).	
1948	Lincolnshire Naturalists' Trust founded.		

1949	The National Parks and Access to the Countryside Act was passed by the British Parliament. This was one of the major landmark legislative achievements for British nature conservation.	It led to the setting up of the National Parks Commission (later to become the Nature Conservancy Council). This introduced National Nature Reserves (NNRs) and Sites of Special Scientific Interest (SSSIs), important for their flora and fauna, geology or landform.	This also gave powers to local authorities to create Local Nature Reserves (LNRs), and made provision to establish the mechanism for the production of formal access agreements for recreational use of land.
1951– 1954	This period saw a programme of establishment of major British National Parks.	The first British National Park established in 1951 was the Peak District, followed by the Lake District National Park in the same year, and then Snowdonia.	
1951	In Scotland the first National Nature Reserve in Britain was designated at Beinn Eighe.	This features wonderful mountain scenery and ancient pinewood fragments overlooking Loch Maree.	The reserve is home to typical Highland wildlife, including Red Deer, Golden Eagle and the elusive Pine Marten.
1951	Forestry Act whereby the felling of trees was prohibited unless a licence obtained.	The Act exempted fruit trees and trees under a certain diameter.	
1952	First Local Nature Reserve in England established at Gibraltar Point in Lincolnshire.	The site became a National Nature Reserve in 1984 and is now managed by the County Wildlife Trust.	
1952	The year saw the probable extinction date of the indigenous genotype of the Swallowtail Butterfly (*Papilio machaon*).	This was a consequence of massive habitat destruction, culminating in wartime drainage of the fens in the 1940s.	There have since been attempts to reintroduce it to the Norfolk Broads and to the Fens, but these have met with mixed success.
1954	The Protection of Birds Act was passed and became a landmark piece of conservation legislation.		

Timeline

1956	The first Area of Outstanding Natural Beauty was designated: the Gower in Wales.		
1956	The Clean Air Act was passed by Parliament and established a programme of designated 'clean air zones' or 'smokeless zones' in major cities.	This for the first time in two centuries began to reverse the impacts of air pollution on sensitive species such as lichens.	Many of the more pollution sensitive lichens began a slow recovery and recolonisation into formerly polluted areas.
1957	The first English AONB was designated in the Quantock Hills, Somerset.		
1957	BBC Natural History Unit was formed and from its Bristol base was to be hugely influential in raising awareness and concern for nature over the next fifty years.		
1957	EEC founded (European Economic Community) with six European countries signing the Treaty of Rome.	The consequences were in part to drive intensive farming to become agri-industrial in scale and very damaging to the environment.	Ultimately though, the Union was to foster and promote environmental protection legislation.
1957	The first pair of Collared Doves (*Streptopelia decaocto*) nested in Scotland.	This was part of a long-standing colonisation across Western Europe from the east.	
1958	By now there were seven County Naturalists' Trusts in existence.	This number was to grow to 47 by the end of the century.	

216

Ian D. Rotherham

	The post-war years continued the siege mentality and the drive for self-sufficiency with oil-fuelled agricultural 'improvement' and intensification, the emergence of agri-industrial farming and its equivalent in forestry.		
1960-1980	**Intensification and mechanisation of agriculture and forestry and the emergence of environmentalism**		
1960	There were now 84 National Nature Reserves (NNRs) covering a total of 56,250 ha of land in Britain.		By 2004, there were 215 NNRs in England, covering 879 square kilometres
1962	By September 1,726 SSSIs had been identified.		
1962	Rachel Carson's book *Silent Spring* was published and documented the dangers of pesticides and herbicides. She showed the long-lasting presence of toxic chemicals in water and on land; the presence of DDT even in mothers' milk; and the threat to wildlife such as birds and mammals, especially songbirds.	The agricultural chemical industry called the book 'sinister' and 'hysterical' but the public's concern was captured and the book was a major trigger for the emerging environmental movement worldwide. President John F. Kennedy read *Silent Spring* and initiated a presidential advisory committee; and the US senate opened an investigation of pesticides. Carson died in 1964.	By the early twenty-first century, American agri-industrial writers are once again rubbishing *Silent Spring* and re-advocating the benefits of DDT.
1963	The first 'Countryside in 1970' conference was held.		

Timeline

1965	By this time every county in Great Britain was covered by a County Naturalist's or Conservation Trust.	These organisations would have acquired over 200 nature reserves by the end of the century.	
1965	The Commons Registration Act was passed and so local authorities were bound to compile registers of all common land.	This registration was to be completed by 1970 but disputes continued way beyond that date.	The Commons Registration Act was intended to be the first legislative stage in a process to clarify and strengthen the law and permanently protect Common Land.
1965	The second 'Countryside in 1970s' conference was held.		
1965	The Science and Technology Act passed.	The Nature Conservancy was absorbed into the Natural Environment Research Council (NERC) to cover research into the natural environment. The Nature Conservancy Council (NCC) took on the nature conservation role and the overseeing of related statutory functions.	
1966	The Tees Valley and Cleveland Water Bill passes crucial report stage in the House of Commons, leading to the building of Cow Green Reservoir.	This was a landmark failure by the embryonic conservation movement to halt a very damaging development to an area of unique conservation and scientific value.	Future protests would learn from the mistakes and assumptions made here.
1967	The Torrey Canyon oil tanker ran aground and caused a huge contamination event	The major oil tanker disaster struck deep into public consciousness as the scale of the tragedy, combined with the new media of mass communications via television, brought the Torrey Canyon shipwreck and its oil spill into everybody's living room.	People were appalled as 40,000 tons of crude oil gave rise to an oil slick that covered an area of around 100 miles square. Contaminated seabirds were hauled out of the sea and collected along coastal beaches.

1968	The Countryside Act was passed by Parliament. This set up the Countryside Commission (CoCo) to replace the National Parks Commission (NPC) and to take up the challenge of a much wider remit of public engagement with the countryside. This Act imposed on every minister, government department and public body a duty to have regard for the desirability of conserving the natural beauty and amenity of the countryside. In many ways this was one of the defining Acts of nature conservation in Britain in the latter twentieth century.	This resulted in a major increase in government involvement in landscape conservation and outdoor recreation outside the National Parks. Local authorities were given powers to establish *Country Parks*, picnic sites, and plans for camping and caravans to stop overnight. The intention was to take the pressure off agricultural land, nature reserves and National Parks.	More positive powers were given both to the Forestry Commission and to statutory water undertakings to widen their interest by providing for outdoor recreation on their property. It set up the mechanism for formal Management Agreements to help achieve conservation and recreational objectives. For the first time cyclists were allowed to use 'Bridleways' along with horse riders. The Countryside Commission concentrated on informal recreation in the countryside and the Sports Council was given responsibility for physical recreation and sport in both urban and rural contexts.
1968	The Town and Country Planning Act passed.	This legislation updated the 1947 Act and set down the requirement for the provision of Structure Plans and Local Plans.	
1968	The Nature Conservancy Council (NCC) attempted to re-introduce the Large Copper Butterfly to Woodwalton Fen Nature Reserve in Huntingdonshire.		
1969	The Silsoe Conference brought together for the first time the agricultural and nature conservation interests to debate environmental issues.		

Timeline

1969	The Farming and Wildlife Advisory Group was formed (FWAG).	It has now grown to be nation-wide networks of FWAGs with professional paid officers providing advice on conservation issues to farmers and landowners.	
1969	The first Country Park, The Queen Elizabeth Country Park in Hampshire, was opened and in the same year Elvaston Castle in Derbyshire was also designated.	This began a major trend in the pattern of both conservation and countryside visiting.	
1969	Transported across the Atlantic, Friends of the Earth (UK) was established in London.		
1970	The Conservation Corps became the British Trust for Conservation Volunteers (BTCV).		
1970	Third and final 'Countryside in the 1970s' conference.		
1970	The Great Bustard Trust was founded to promote the re-introduction of this magnificent bird to Britain.	The Bustard became extinct in the 1800s as a consequence of enclosures, of hunting with guns and finally through the efforts of bird collectors.	
1970	The Department of the Environment (DoE) was set up within the Government and replaced the functions of a number of earlier ministries.	The 'environment' was previously the responsibility of several disparate areas of authority. For the first time this governmental structure sought to bring all these interests together.	By 1985, there were 75 executive and advisory bodies including the Nature Conservancy Council and the Countryside Commission.

1971	Responding to massive public concerns the Prevention of Oil Pollution Act was passed.		
1971	The Otter Trust was formed.		
1971	Parliament passes the Wild Creatures and Forest Laws Act.	This was a move towards effective protection for wildlife species.	
1971	The Sandford Committee undertakes review of the functions and management of National Parks.	This ultimately provides policy guidance for the Parks for the next twenty years.	
1972	The Woodland Trust was established to promote the awareness and conservation of woodlands and became a major owner of sites and a big membership organisation.	By the end of the century it owned over 1,000 woodland sites.	
1972	The Nature Conservancy became the Nature Conservancy Council under the Nature Conservancy Council Act. The NCC was now an 'independent council' but received funding through the Department of the Environment.	The NCC was established with three main functions: 1. To advise Government Ministers on nature conservation policy and to provide advice and information generally on nature conservation; 2. To establish and manage National Nature Reserves; 3. To encourage scientific research into nature conservation.	
1972	Driven along by Rotherham MP Peter Hardy, the Badgers Act for the first time gave some legal protection to Badgers.		

Timeline

1973	Britain finally entered the European Economic Community (EEC).	For wildlife this would be the catalyst for a twenty-year period of grant-aided agricultural intensification and massive habitat destruction.	
1973	The Ecology Party was formed.		
1973	There were now forty County Naturalists' and Conservation Trusts established.		
1975	The Conservation of Wild Plants and Wild Creatures Act.	This provided a degree of limited legal protection for a wide range of wildlife species and not just the vertebrates that covered by previous wildlife laws.	
1975	White-tailed Eagles were re-introduced in Britain with birds from Scandinavia released onto the Isle of Rhum in Scotland.		
1975	The Ministry of Agriculture, Fisheries and Food (MAFF) began a Badger gassing programme in order to attempt the reduction of Bovine TB infection in cattle.	This has remained a hugely controversial, ineffective and expensive campaign to this day.	
1976	The Endangered Species Act was passed.		
1976	The Dangerous Wild Animals Act was passed and dealt with the regulation of large exotic carnivores as 'pets'.	One consequence was that many people simply released their 'pets' into the wild and many are rumoured to still be there as breeding populations.	

Ian D. Rotherham

1976	A Royal Charter was granted by Queen Elizabeth II to the Society for the Promotion of Nature Reserves.	It also changed its name and now became the Royal Society for the Promotion of Nature Conservation.	
1976	The Countryside Review Committee (CRC) published The Countryside: Problems & Policies in England & Welsh Countryside.	This stressed the need for consensus on ideas of conservation in Britain.	
1976	The seminal book in two volumes *A Nature Conservation Review* was published.	This provided the first thorough and authoritative account and evaluation of sites of natural importance for nature conservation in Britain.	
1976	A new system for NNR's and SSSIs was proposed under the NCC's Site Protection Policy, with sites graded according to value.		
1976	Otters were finally given legal protection in England and Wales. Remarkably they were not given legal protection under the 1975 Protection of Wildflowers and Creatures Act. In 1975 the otter was on the verge of extinction in France, Italy and Switzerland and was protected in almost every European country apart from Eire and Britain.	It was odd that the otter was not included in the 1975 Act but the politically powerful 'field sports' lobby threatened to object, seeing this as the beginning of the end for all field sports, including fox hunting.	The hunting, shooting and trapping of otters was permitted in 1975 with nine active otter hunting packs in Great Britain. Therefore the otter was omitted from the 1975 Act. In January 1978 the legislation was enacted and the otter was added to the list of protected animals.
1976	NCC budget for nature conservation was now at £6 million, double the previous figure.	In a surprising statement the NCC said they were to significantly increase funding to voluntary conservation bodies especially the Society for the Promotion of Nature Conservation.	The financial allocation promised to these voluntary bodies was dramatically reduced and in practice the support announced earlier was not delivered.

Timeline

1976–1978	The culling of seals caused a major controversy and was perhaps unique in British nature conservation history.	To halt the 'crisis', the British government called in Norwegian sealers, armed with rifles and hakapiks.	
1978	The Ecological Parks Trust was formed.	Its first major undertaking was to convert a derelict industrial site in inner city London into a wildlife park.	
1979	The Large Blue Butterfly (*Maculinea arion*) was declared extinct in this year and it turned out that the cause was the loss of habitat and also of the traditional management of its favoured grasslands.	Protection of the areas had led to a change in vegetation; an alteration of micro-climatic conditions favouring the 'wrong' species of ant whilst that on which the young butterflies depended was lost.	Unfortunately for the Large Blue Butterfly, the scientists of the time got it wrong. By the 1990s, with careful habitat management, the species made a comeback through a reintroduction programme using the closely-related European variety.
1979	The British Association of Nature Conservationists (BANC) was formed.	This was to develop the philosophy of conservation and to open up debates on issues and politics.	
1979	On 20 June, the newly elected Conservative Government announced the forthcoming introduction of Wildlife and Countryside Bill; to Parliament.		This was a follow-up to the previous government's proposed *Countryside Bill*.
1980-2000	**Emergence of sustainability, of professional nature conservationists, the growth of the urban wildlife movement and of public protest**		
1980	The World Conservation Strategy was launched on 5 March in London and in 32 other countries around the world.	The Strategy was prepared by the IUCN and commissioned by UNEP following extensive consultation with governmental agencies, non-governmental organisations (NGOs), and key individuals.	A popular paperback was produced to explain the Strategy and called *How to Save the World*.

1980	On 25 November the Wildlife and Countryside Bill was introduced to Parliament to replace the Protection of Birds Act 1975 and the Wildlife and Wild Plants Act 1975.		
1980	The NCC budget was now £7.5 million per year or about 14p per person, whereas farm subsidies were around £5 billion per year by 1981.		
1980	There were now 42 County Nature Conservation Trusts including in Avon, the first Urban Wildlife Trust.	The Urban Wildlife Group was formed in Birmingham and began campaigning for wildlife conservation in the West Midlands.	
1980	The World Wildlife Fund launched a £2 million Land Fund in order to support land acquisition for conservation.		
1981	The 1981 Wildlife and Countryside Act was passed by Parliament.	This was the first comprehensive wildlife legislation in Britain.	Importantly the legislation provided for the protection of habitats.
1981	SPNC formally becomes the Royal Society for Nature Conservation (RSNC), the The Wildlife Trusts Partnership, or simply The Wildlife Trusts; a federation of 47 local Wildlife Trusts in the United Kingdom plus the Isle of Man and Alderney.	The partnership's member trusts, between them, look after 2,500 nature reserves covering 800 square kilometres. By 2005 they had a combined membership of 530,000 members.	Wildlife Trusts are local and regional organisations of differing size, history and origins and can vary greatly in their constitution, activities and membership. All wildlife trusts share a common interest in wildlife and biodiversity, rooted in a practical tradition of land management and conservation.

Timeline

1981	The Forestry Act gave Ministers the power to sell publicly-owned forestry land (with the exclusion of the Forest of Dean).	As a consequence, between 1982 and 1986, the Forestry Commission sold off 100,000 acres of public land.	
1982	The Countryside Commission changed status on 1 April, following a third of a century as part of the civil service, to become an independent agency grant aided by DoE.		
1982	England's second largest fenland, the Somerset Levels, is the scene of major confrontation between conservationists and farmers over the designation of much of the area as Sites of Special Scientific Interest.		
1985	The Wildlife and Countryside (Amendment) Act was passed to strengthen further the protection for SSSI by making designation operative on notification by the NCC.	This closed the so-called 3-month loophole.	However, many sites were needlessly destroyed because of this bureaucratic mix-up.
1985	NCC produced 'Nature Conservation in Great Britain'.	This was an important document which set out past failures with present and suggested future policies.	Reading this document brings home how much has changed – and how quickly.
1985	For the first time, the Ministry of Agriculture Fisheries and Food (MAFF) accepts the duty to 'balance' agriculture and conservation interests.	There still followed several years of serious conflicts of interest.	

1985	The 200th NNR was declared this year.		
1985	After ten years of a managed reintroduction and conservation programme, the first young White-tailed Eagles to breed in the wild for 70 years.		
1985	Ecological Parks Trust becomes Trust for Urban Ecology.		
1985	Agriculture Act allows the Ministry of Agriculture to designate Environmentally Sensitive Areas (ESA).	The areas initially chosen in England were Breckland, North Peak, The Pennine Dales, The Shropshire Borders, The Somerset Levels, The Test Valley and West Penwith.	This ultimately paved the way for Environmental Stewardship and Single Farm Payment schemes.
1985	Britain's first Marine Nature Reserve is declared for the seas and seabed around the tiny island of Lundy in the Bristol Channel.	Negotiations continue for MNRs at Skomer, the Menai Strait in Wales and Loch Sween in Scotland.	
1987	The Large Blue Butterfly, which became extinct in Britain in 1978/9, becomes the subject of a special WWF campaign.	A £20,000 appeal raises funds to bring back eggs of this rare butterfly from Sweden.	This was the most closely-related genotype to the original British variety.
1987	New government circular issued by the Department of the Environment: on Nature Conservation (27/87). This replaces Circular 108/77.	These were the effective way in which government policy on the interpretation of legislation was to be put into action by organisations such as Local Authorities and other public bodies. They were later to be known as Planning Policy Guidance.	

Timeline

1987	Mori Poll commissioned by FOE and World Wide Fund for Nature.	81 per cent of the public felt that the Government should give a higher priority to the protection of the environment.	
1988	Seal Tragedy: thousands of Grey Seals died from a rare form of Canine Distemper. Nearly 2,000 dead seals were recovered from British waters alone. Around 17,000 seals died off the coast of Northern Europe. The virus killed 73 per cent of Sweden's Common Seals and 80 per cent of Denmark's seal population.	The 1988 seal plague was the largest recorded case of mass mortality in any marine mammal. Pollution-related stress may have been a factor.	
1988	Shetland suffered Britain's greatest seabird disaster, with hundreds of thousands of birds, mainly young Arctic Terns, Arctic Skuas, Kittiwakes, Puffins, Great Skuas and Red-Throated Divers lost through breeding failures on an unprecedented scale.	The problem seemed to be a mix of weather or climate and over-fishing and pollution affecting the main fish in the food-chain, particularly the once super-abundant Sand Eels.	
1989	The Plantlife charity is launched as an organisation dedicated to saving plants which are vital to our survival and quality of life, and to putting wildflowers back into British countryside.		

1989	The Government proposal to split the Nature Conservancy Council into separate organisations for England, Scotland and Wales was announced.	This joined the Countryside Commission in Scotland and Wales. In Wales the merged organisation will be called the Countryside Council for Wales, and in Scotland it was Scottish Natural Heritage.	A major driver for this was believed to be a punitive response to the supposed interference by NCC in the conservation of extensive Scottish peat bogs. The actions particularly annoyed a senior Scottish Conservative Government minister and he set about 'emasculating' the agency.
1989	The Community Forests scheme was officially launched by the Countryside Commission and the Forestry Commission.	This targeted major, funded new forest planted areas in urban fringe and former industrial zones. It complemented the New National Forest.	
1990	The Red Kite was re-established in England and Scotland after an absence of 100 years.	Eleven young kites from Spain were released in secret locations.	Up to this time the species only clung on in mid Wales.
1990	The Government White Paper *This Common Inheritance* was published.	The document provided a very thorough and informative account of conservation and environmental issues.	
1990	The Somerset Levels became Britain's 236th National Nature Reserve.	Farmers and peat-cutters had previously burnt effigies of the Nature Conservancy Council Officers.	
1990	The Environmental Protection Act was passed.	This Act established three conservation councils and the Joint Nature Conservation Committee to succeed the Nature Conservancy Council; and provide further protection of SSSIs.	
1990	For the first time, people sent to prison for 'badger digging'.		

Timeline

1991	The Nature Conservancy Council became English Nature under the Environment Protection Act.	The NCC was replaced by single-country agencies in England, Scotland and Wales.	
1992	The United Nations Conference on the Environment & Development (UNCED) was held in Rio de Janeiro, twenty years after the Stockholm Conference on the Human Environment.	Representatives from over 185 countries were invited, over 150 attended and 103 heads of state gathered at the final ceremony.	
1992	There was increased protection for SSSIs within the land use planning system. It withdrew permitted development rights for certain temporary uses of land and indicated that the Secretary of State would generally call in and determine planning applications which would significantly affect sites of national and international conservation importance.	It also provided additional advice on the need for Environmental Assessment, and required local planning authorities to consult the conservation agencies about planning applications on land near to and likely to affect a SSSI.	
1992	Thirty-one young Red Kites fledged from nests in England and Scotland.		
1994	The European Union Habitats Directive on the Conservation of Natural Habitats and Wild Flora & Fauna came into force in October this year.		

1995	The name 'The Wildlife Trusts' was chosen as the name by which the partnership of local Trusts was to become known.	Many County Trusts changed their name to include 'Wildlife Trust' and began using the badger logo as part of the UK identity.	
1995	The Carnivore Trust proposed to re-introduce wolves back into the Highlands of Scotland.		
1995	The Countryside Movement was launched and promised £5 million by country sports industries and private individuals to support hunting.		
1996	The Government establishes the concept of Biodiversity Action Plans or BAPS.	This derived from the 1992 Earth Summit and the Convention on Biological Diversity.	
1996	The Osprey (*Pandion haliaetus*) bred in England for the first time since 1843.		
1997	The Department of Environment, Transport and Regions (DETR) was formed with a huge remit covering housing, environmental pollution, rail transport, road transport, local government, planning including green belts, National Parks, AONBs.	It appointed and supervised the work of the Countryside Agency, the Environment Agency, English Nature and many other bodies.	It would last about 5 years.

Timeline

1998	250,000 people marched through central London organised by the Countryside Alliance to protest against the proposed ban on Fox hunting.		
1998	The British Government published Action Plans for the conservation of over 400 priority species.		
1999	The Countryside Agency was established on 1 April 1999. The new agency resulted from a merger of the Rural Development Commission and the Countryside Commission.	This new statutory body was to work to: 1. Conserve and enhance the countryside; 2. Promote social equity and economic opportunity for the people who live there; 3. Help everyone wherever they live to enjoy this national asset.	It lasted about 8 years.
1999	The Woodland Trust acquired its thousandth wood.		
2000	Parliament passed the Countryside and Rights of Way Act 2000 (CRoW Act 2000), which applies to England and Wales and	The Act enabled public access on foot to particular categories of land, refined the law on Public Rights of Way, increased protection for Sites of Special Scientific Interest (SSSIs) and strengthened wildlife enforcement legislation.	This legislation at last began to redress some of the losses in terms of access to land which had ben taken away in earlier centuries. It provides the firm foundation for the principle of the 'right to roam'.
2000	The EU Water Framework Directive was agreed.	This required member governments to improve water management for people and wildlife by 2015.	

| 2000 | Natura 2000 is the European Union-wide network of nature conservation sites to be established under the Council Directive on the conservation of natural habitats and of wild fauna and flora (92/43/EEC) (Habitats Directive). | It includes Special Areas of Conservation (SACs) designated under that Directive and Special Protection Areas (SPAs) under the Council Directive on the conservation of wild birds (79/409/EEC). | This symbolises the conservation of precious natural resources for the year 2000 and into the twenty-first century. |

SUMMARY OF THE SITUATION IN THE YEAR 2000

By 2000 we could see:

The emergence of professional nature conservation

The development of mass appeal and interest in wildlife and conservation

The implementation of exciting and high profile conservation projects

The proliferation of legislation

The proliferation of NGOs and in short-lived government agencies with ever-changing roles and responsibilities

Serious continuing problems of biodiversity loss and environmental quality decline

Wildlife and environmental laws extensive yet not comprehensive and often with limited logic

Enforcement of legislation often difficult

Funding for management of conservation resources and especially for scientific monitoring very limited and generally short-term

Limited understanding of nature conservation and biodiversity in relation to human history, economics and politics

Separation of nature from community and long-term issues of cultural severance and eutrophication

GLOSSARY

Biodiversity

The diversity of living organisms expressed by the number, abundance and composition of genotypes, populations, species, functional types and landscape units; often described in relation to a particular ecosystem, region or landscape.

Climate Change

A term used to imply a significant change from one climatic state to another and which may reflect natural and human-induced influences.

Conservation

The active management of environmental resources to maintain and enhance diversity and identified natural interest such as threatened or rare species.

Cultural ecology

The results of long-term interactions between the environment, history and human tradition often relating to subsistence utilisation of landscapes and their natural resources.

Cultural severance

This refers to the ending of traditional, long-term interactions between people and nature or landscapes often because of the cessation of subsistence or at least local community use of landscape resources.

Ecology

The interactions between living organisms and their physical environment.

Enclosures

When referring to cultivated land this generally means the taking in and enclosure by fences, hedges, walls or ditches of landscape resources previously open and used in common by members of a community. The resulting lands are often then owned and managed by a few privileged individuals.

Environment

The factors which together and in interaction form the surroundings, including physical components such as air, water and land and biological components such as flora, fauna and humans.

Environmental change

Any long-term fluctuations in environmental conditions and their manifestations through landscape and ecology, resulting from natural and human-induced (anthropogenic) influences or combinations of these.

Exotic

Relating to the status of a plant, animal or other living organism deemed as 'not native' to a location at a particular time.

Improvement

A term used to describe human induced changes to agricultural systems which increase production and productivity, normally resulting from innovations in cultivation techniques, transformations of landscapes to facilitate new uses and the imposition of technologies and of modified or new socio-economic structures.

Invasive

A species which is rapidly increasing its biogeographic range, sometimes 'naturally' or associated with human-induced impacts.

Native

Relating to the status of a plant, animal or other living organism deeded as 'naturally' occurring at a given location at a particular time.

Natural

Something generally considered to occur without human influence.

Naturalised

This is applied to a species which, introduced by humans, has increased its biogeographic range to successfully establish in a new area, to the point where it has a self-perpetuating 'wild' population.

Nature and Naturalness

These are expressions of an ecology unfettered by human influence and often placing interactions with people as separate from other components of the ecosystem.

Parliamentary enclosures

Enclosures of agricultural land brought about by individual Acts of Parliament in England between the early 1700s and the late 1800s.

Re-wilding

This term is applied to the concept of allowing a supposed reversion to 'nature' both through deliberate planning and intervention and through abandonment of land management practices.

Semi-natural

A term which recognises the complexity of human–nature interactions in producing landscapes considered of value for nature conservation or for cultural heritage.

Tradition and Traditional use

Long-established uses of natural, wildlife and landscape resources over long periods of time, often distinctive to a region or location and frequently undertaken by a local community and in relation to a subsistence economy.

Wilderness

A concept of landscape and nature with implied freedom from human influence but which in reality is often a matter of the obviousness or easily visible impacts of people.

ANNOTATED BIBLIOGRAPHY

Agnoletti, M. (ed.) (2006) *The Conservation of Cultural Landscapes*. CABI: Wallingford. [This gives a broad overview of cultural landscapes.]

Agnoletti, M., S. Anderson, E. Johann, R. Klein, M. Kulvik, A.V. Kushlin, P. Mayer, C.M. Molina, J. Parrotta, P. Patosaari, I.D. Rotherham and E. Saratsi (2007) Guidelines for the Implementation of Social and Cultural Values in Sustainable Forest Management. A Scientific Contribution to the Implementation of MCPFE – Vienna Resolution 3. IUFRO Occasional Paper No. 19. [This gives a specific regional example of the issues of social and cultural values in relation to sustainable forestry.]

Agnoletti, M., S. Anderson, E. Johann, M. Kulvik, E. Saratsi, A. Kushlin, P. Mayer, C. Montiel, J. Parrotta and I.D. Rotherham (2008) 'The introduction of cultural values in the sustainable management of European forests'. *Global Environment* **2**: 172- 193. [This paper presents examples of the issues of social and cultural values in relation to forest management in Europe.]

Allaby, M. (ed.) (1992) *The Concise Oxford Dictionary of Botany*. Oxford University Press: Oxford. [A useful sourcebook for technical botanical definitions.]

Allen, D.E. (1976) *The Naturalist in Britain – A Social History*. Penguin Books Ltd.: Harmondsworth. [This provides a background to the history of natural history.]

Beard, C. (1997) *Wildlife Conservation and the Roots of Environmentalism. The Facts and Figures*. Privately Published. [This gives an insight into the history of conservation.]

Blackburn, J. (1989) *Charles Waterton – Traveller and Conservationist*. The Bodley Head: London. [The biography of the pioneering nature conservationist who established the world's first nature reserve.]

Bownes, J.S., T.H. Riley, I.D. Rotherham and S.M. Vincent (1991) *Sheffield Nature Conservation Strategy*. Sheffield City Council: Sheffield. [An example of a typical local authority nature conservation strategy.]

Carson, R. (1965) *Silent Spring*. Penguin Books Ltd.: Harmondsworth. [The definitive text on pesticide impacts.]

Çolak, A.H., S. Kirca, I.D. Rotherham and A. Ince (2010) *Restoration and Rehabilitation of Deforested and Degraded Forest Landscapes in Turkey*. Ministry of Environment and Forestry, General Directorate of Afforestation and Erosion Control: Istanbul. [An insight into major restoration issues in Turkey.]

Cutter, S.L. and W.H. Renwick (1999) *Exploitation, Conservation, Preservation – A Geographic Perspective on Natural Resource Use*. Third edition. John Wiley & Sons Ltd.: New York. [A useful overview of conservation issues and challenges.]

Evans, D. (1997) *A History of Nature Conservation in Britain*. Second edition. Routledge: London. [A thorough overview of nature conservation history in Great Britain.]

Fitter, R. and M. Fitter (1978) *The Penguin Dictionary of British Natural History*. Penguin Books Ltd.: London. [A useful sourcebook for British natural history.]

Freedman, B. (1995) *Environmental Ecology – The Effects of Pollution, Disturbance and Other Stresses*. Second Edition. Academic Press: San Diego. [Excellent overview of environmental pollution issues.]

Gaston, K.J. (ed.) (1996) *Biodiversity: A Biology of Numbers and Difference*. Blackwell Science: Oxford. [Significant background text to biodiversity and its assessment.]

Gilbert, O.L. (1989) *The Ecology of Urban Habitats*. Chapman and Hall: London. [Classic introduction to urban ecology.]

Gilbert, O.L. (1992) *The Flowering of the Cities... The Natural Flora of 'Urban Commons'*. English Nature: Peterborough. [Fascinating insight into 'urban commons'.]

Goldsmith, E and R. Allen (with help from M. Allaby, J. Davoll and S. Lawrence, 1972) *A Blueprint for Survival. Ecologist* **2**(1). Also published by Penguin Books Ltd.: Harmondsworth. [Classic environmental text.]

Gutteridge, A.C. (1983) *Cambridge Illustrated Thesaurus of Biology*. Cambridge University Press: Cambridge. [Useful sourcebook.]

Ingrouille, M. (1995) *Historical Ecology of the British Flora*. Chapman & Hall: London. [Good compact account of the history of British flora.]

Jeffries, M.J. (1997) *Biodiversity and Conservation*. Routledge: London. [Accessible introductory volume.]

Lincoln, R.J. and G.A. Boxshall (1987) *The Cambridge Illustrated Dictionary of Natural History*. Cambridge University Press: Cambridge. [Useful sourcebook.]

Meadows, D.H., D.L. Meadows, J. Randers and W.W. Behrens (1972) *The Limits to Growth*. Pan Books: London. [Classic environmental text.]

Mellanby, K. (1967) *Pesticides and Pollution*. Collins New Naturalist: London. [Pioneering introduction to pesticide and pollution impacts.]

Mitchell, A. (1985) *The Complete Guide to Trees of Britain and Northern Europe*. Dragon's World Ltd.: Limpsfield. [Good overview of British trees.]

Myers, N. (Ed.) (1993) *Rainforests*. The Illustrated Library of the Earth, Time-Life Books: Amsterdam. [Useful introductory account.]

Onions, C.T. (1983) *The Shorter Oxford English Dictionary on Historical Principles*. Guild Publishing: London. [Essential background for definitions etc.]

Pepper, D. (1996) *Modern Environmentalism*. Routledge: London. [Good account of the development of environmentalism.]

Perlin, J. (1989) *A Forest Journey*. Harvard University Press: Cambridge, Mass. [Excellent overview of the importance of trees and timber to civilisation.]

Ponting, C. (1991) *A Green History of the World*. Sinclair-Stevenson Ltd.: London. [Useful and accessible introduction to green history.]

Rackham, O. (1986) *The History of the Countryside*. Dent: London. [Classic introduction to the history of the British countryside.]

Richardson (1992) *Pollution Monitoring with Lichens*. Naturalists' Handbooks No. 19, Richmond Publishing Co. Ltd.: Slough. [Wonderful little guide to an important group of taxa used in pollution monitoring.]

Riley, D. and A. Young (1966) *World Vegetation*. Cambridge University Press: Cambridge. [Accessible guide to a complex subject.]

Annotated Bibliography

Rose, F. (1974) 'The epiphytes of oak', in M.G. Morris and F.H. Perring (eds) *The British Oak, its History and Natural History.* Classey: Faringdon. pp. 250–273. [Pioneering study on the ecology of the oak.]

Rose, F. (1976) 'Lichenological indicators of age and environmental continuity in woodlands', in D.H. Brown, D.L. Hawksworth and R.H. Bailey (eds) *Lichenology: Progress and Problems.* Academic Press: London. [Classic study of lichens and air pollution.]

Rose, F. and P.W. James (1974) 'Regional studies on the British lichen flora, 1. The corticolous and lignicolous species of the New Forest, Hampshire'. *Lichenologist* **6**: 1–72. [This gives insight into the impacts of air pollution on lichens and their use and indicators of environmental quality.]

Rotherham, I.D. (1999) 'Peat cutters and their landscapes: fundamental change in a fragile environment'. *Landscape Archaeology and Ecology* **4**: 28–51. [The impacts of peat cutting on landscapes.]

Rotherham, I.D. (1999) 'Urban Environmental History: the importance of relict communities in urban biodiversity conservation'. *Practical Ecology and Conservation* **3** (1): 3–22. [Examples of urban ecology and urban biodiversity.]

Rotherham, I.D. (2005) 'Fuel and Landscape – Exploitation, Environment, Crisis and Continuum'. *Landscape Archaeology and Ecology* **5**: 65–81. [Detailed account of human impact on landscape through exploitation for fuel use.]

Rotherham, I.D. (2005) 'Alien Plants and the Human Touch'. *Journal of Practical Ecology and Conservation Special Series,* No. 4: 63–76. [Essay on people and exotic plants.]

Rotherham, I.D. (2007) 'The implications of perceptions and cultural knowledge loss for the management of wooded landscapes: a UK case-study'. *Forest Ecology and Management* **249**: 100–115. [This paper provides examples of how we are losing cultural knowledge of our landscapes and their past management.]

Rotherham, I.D. (2007) 'The Historical Ecology of Medieval Deer Parks and the Implications for Conservation', in R. Liddiard (ed.) *The Medieval Deer Park: New Perspectives,* Windgather Press: Macclesfield. pp. 79–96. [An account of the historical ecology of medieval parks.]

Rotherham, I.D. (2009) 'The Importance of Cultural Severance in Landscape Ecology Research', in A. Dupont and H. Jacobs (eds) *Landscape Ecology Research Trends.* Nova Science Publishers: Hauppauge, NY. [Introduction to the concept of 'cultural severance'.]

Rotherham, I.D. (2009) *Peat and Peat Cutting.* Shire Publications: Oxford. [A new and unique look at the history of peat and peatlands.]

Rotherham, I.D. (2010) *Yorkshire's Forgotten Fenlands.* Pen & Sword Books Limited: Barnsley. [Account of the destruction of around 3,000 square kilometres of fenland.]

Rotherham, I.D. (2011) 'A Landscape History Approach to the Assessment of Ancient Woodlands', in E.B. Wallace (ed.) *Woodlands: Ecology, Management and Conservation.* Nova Science Publishers: Hauppauge, NY. pp. 161–184. [Describes an emerging new approach to assessing wooded landscapes.]

Rotherham, I.D. (2012) 'History of Conservation and Biodiversity', in M. Agnoletti, E. Johann and S.N. Serneri (eds.) *World Environmental History. Encyclopedia of Life Support Systems (EOLSS),* Developed under the Auspices of the UNESCO, Eolss Publishers: Oxford. [http://www.eolss.net] [Retrieved 17 November 2012] [First published account of the eco-timeline idea]

Ian D. Rotherham

Rotherham, I.D. (2013) *The Lost Fens: England's Greatest Ecological Disaster*. The History Press: Stroud. [Account of the most spectacular ecological destruction ever witnessed in England.]

Rotherham, I.D. and M. Jones (2000) 'The Impact of Economic, Social and Political Factors on the Ecology of Small English Woodlands: a Case Study of the Ancient Woods in South Yorkshire, England', in M. Agnoletti and S. Anderson (eds.) *Forest History: International Studies in Socio-economic and Forest Ecosystem Change*. CABI: Wallingford. pp. 397–410. [Regional example of the evolution of wooded landscapes through time and the influences of social, political and economic factors.]

Rotherham, I.D., D. Egan, and P.A. Ardron. (2004) Fuel economy and the uplands: the effects of peat and turf utilisation on upland landscapes. *Society for Landscape Studies Supplementary Series*, 2, 99–109. [Human impact on upland landscapes through the use of fuel.]

Rotherham, I.D. and D. Egan (2005) 'The Economics of Fuel Wood, Charcoal and Coal: An Interpretation of Coppice Management of British Woodlands', in M. Agnoletti, M. Armiero, S. Barca and G. Corona (eds) *History and Sustainability*. European Society for Environmental History. pp. 100–104. [History of fuel-wood and landscape.]

Rotherham, I.D. and P.A Ardron (2006) 'The Archaeology of Woodland Landscapes: Issues for managers based on the case-study of Sheffield, England and four thousand years of human impact'. *Arboricultural Journal* **29** (4): 229–243. [Human impact in a single, now urban, woodland and extending over around 4,000 years.]

Rotherham, I.D. and D. McCallam (2008) 'Peat Bogs, Marshes and Fen as disputed Landscapes in Late eighteenth-Century France and England', in L. Lyle and D. McCallam (eds.) *Histoires de la Terre: Earth Sciences and French Culture 1740–1940*. Rodopi B.V.: Amsterdam & New York. pp. 75–90. [This gives an insight into cultural and international issues in the approaches to wetlands and peat bogs.]

Rotherham, I.D. and R.A. Lambert (eds) (2011) *Invasive and Introduced Plants and Animals: Human Perceptions, Attitudes and Approaches to Management*. EARTHSCAN: London. [A challenging account of the perceptions, impacts and management of invasive species.]

Rotherham, I.D. and C. Handley (eds) (2011) *Animals, Man and Treescapes*. Wildtrack Publishing: Sheffield. [A collection of chapters on the history and impacts of larger herbivores in wooded landscapes.]

Rotherham, I.D. and J. Bradley (eds) (2011) *Lowland Heaths: Ecology, History, Restoration and Management*. Wildtrack Publishing: Sheffield. [A collection of essays on lowland heaths in England.]

Santos, M.A. (1999) *The Environmental Crisis*. Guides to Historic Events of the Twentieth Century. Greenwood Press: Westport, CT. [Useful overview of the emergence of environmentalism.]

Smout, T.C. (2000) *Nature Contested – Environmental History in Scotland and Northern England Since 1600*. Edinburgh University Press: Edinburgh. [Fascinating introduction to regional and national environmental history.]

Stamp, D. (1969) *Nature Conservation in Britain*. Collins New Naturalist: London. [The original and definitive early introduction to nature conservation in Britain.]

Stokes, J. and D. Rodger (2004) *The Heritage Trees of Britain & Northern Ireland*. Constable: London. [Useful overview.]

Annotated Bibliography

Stott, P. (1981) *Historical Plant Geography. An Introduction.* George Allen & Unwin: London. [Accessible introduction.]

Taylor, G.R. (1972) *The Doomsday Book.* Panther Books Ltd.: London. [Classic environmentalism text.]

Vera, F. (2000) *Grazing Ecology and Forest History.* CABI: Wallingford. [The hugely influential account of the impacts of large grazing herbivores on the landscapes of northern Europe.]

Vincent, P. (1990) *The Biogeography of the British Isles – An Introduction.* Routledge: London. [Good accessible account of British biogeography.]

WCED (1987) *Our Common Future.* The World Commission on Environment and Development. Oxford University Press: Oxford. [Defining statement of intent on a global scale – though almost totally anthropocentric in outlook.]

Wilkinson, G. (1981) *A History of Britain's Trees.* Hutchinson: London. [Accessible account.]

Wilson, E.O. (ed.) (1988) *Biodiversity.* National Academy Press: Washington D.C. [One of the classic ecology texts.]

Wilson, E.O. (ed.) (1992) *The Diversity of Life.* Harvard University Press: Cambridge, Mass. [A follow-on from the above.]

FULL BIBLIOGRAPHY

Agnoletti, M. (ed.) (2006) *The Conservation of Cultural Landscapes*. CABI: Wallingford.

Agnoletti, M., S. Anderson, E. Johann, R. Klein, M. Kulvik, A.V. Kushlin, P. Mayer, C.M. Molina, J. Parrotta, P. Patosaari, I.D. Rotherham and E. Saratsi (2007) Guidelines for the Implementation of Social and Cultural Values in Sustainable Forest Management. A Scientific Contribution to the Implementation of MCPFE – Vienna Resolution 3. IUFRO Occasional Paper No. 19.

Agnoletti, M., S. Anderson, E. Johann, M. Kulvik, E. Saratsi, A. Kushlin, P. Mayer, C. Montiel, J. Parrotta and I.D. Rotherham (2008) 'The introduction of cultural values in the sustainable management of European forests'. *Global Environment* **2**: 172- 193.

Allaby, M. (ed.) (1992) *The Concise Oxford Dictionary of Botany*. Oxford University Press: Oxford.

Allen, D.E. (1976) *The Naturalist in Britain – A Social History*. Penguin Books Ltd.: Harmondsworth, Middlesex.

Ardron, P.A. (1999) 'Peat Cutting in Upland Britain, with Special Reference to the Peak District'. Unpublished Ph.D. Thesis, University of Sheffield, Sheffield.

Ardron, P.A., I.D. Rotherham and O. Gilbert (1999) 'An evaluation of the South Pennines peatlands with reference to the impact of peat cutting'. *Peak District Journal of Natural History and Archaeology* **1**: 67–75.

Barker, G. (ed.) (2000) *Ecological Recombination in Urban Areas: Implications for Nature Conservation*. English Nature: Peterborough.

Beard, C. (1997) *Wildlife Conservation and the Roots of Environmentalism. The Facts and Figures*. Privately Published.

Blackburn, J. (1989) *Charles Waterton – Traveller and Conservationist*. The Bodley Head: London.

Bownes, J.S., T.H. Riley, I.D. Rotherham and S.M. Vincent (1991) *Sheffield Nature Conservation Strategy*. Sheffield City Council: Sheffield.

Buckingham, H., J. Chapman and R. Newman (1999) *Hidden Heaths – A Portrait of Limestone Heaths in the Peak District National Park*. Peak District National Park Authority: Bakewell.

Carson, R. (1965) *Silent Spring*. Penguin Books Ltd.: Harmondsworth.

Çolak, A.H., S. Kirca, I.D. Rotherham and A. Ince (2010) *Restoration and Rehabilitation of Deforested and Degraded Forest Landscapes in Turkey*. Ministry of Environment and Forestry, General Directorate of Afforestation and Erosion Control: Istanbul.

Cutter, S.L. and W.H. Renwick (1999) *Exploitation, Conservation, Preservation – A Geographic Perspective on Natural Resource Use*. Third edition. John Wiley & Sons Ltd.: New York.

Davis, M.A., K. Thompson and J.P. Grime (2001) 'Charles S. Elton and the dissociation of invasion ecology from the rest of ecology'. *Diversity and Distribution* 7: 97–102.

Evans, D. (1997) *A History of Nature Conservation in Britain*. Second edition. Routledge: London.

Fitter, R. and M. Fitter (1978) *The Penguin Dictionary of British Natural History*. Penguin Books Ltd.: London.

Freedman, B. (1995) *Environmental Ecology – The Effects of Pollution, Disturbance and Other Stresses.* Second Edition. Academic Press: San Diego.

Gaston, K.J. (ed.) (1996) *Biodiversity: A Biology of Numbers and Difference.* Blackwell Science: Oxford.

Grime, J.P. (2003) 'Plants hold the key. Ecosystems in a changing world'. *Biologist* **50** (2): 87–91.

Grime, J.P., J.G. Hodgson and R. Hunt (2007) *Comparative Plant Ecology. A Functional Approach to common British Species.* Second Edition. Castlepoint Press: Dalbeattie.

Gilbert, O.L. (1989) *The Ecology of Urban Habitats.* Chapman and Hall: London.

Gilbert, O.L. (1992) *The Flowering of the Cities... The Natural Flora of 'Urban Commons'.* English Nature: Peterborough.

Godwin, Sir H. (1984) *History of the British Flora: A Factual Basis for Phytogeography.* 2nd edition. Cambridge University Press: Cambridge.

Goldsmith, E. and R. Allen (with help from M. Allaby, J. Davoll and S. Lawrence) (1972) *A Blueprint for Survival. Ecologist* **2**(1). Also published by Penguin Books Ltd.: Harmondsworth.

Gutteridge, A.C. (1983) *Cambridge Illustrated Thesaurus of Biology.* Cambridge University Press: Cambridge.

Harrison, C. (1988) *The History of the Birds of Britain.* Collins: London.

Hodgson, J.G. (1986) 'Commonness and Rarity in Plants with Special Reference to the Sheffield Flora'. *Biological Conservation* **36**(3): 199–252.

Ingrouille, M. (1995) *Historical Ecology of the British Flora.* Chapman & Hall: London.

Jeffries, M.J. (1997) *Biodiversity and Conservation.* Routledge: London.

Ladurie, E. Le R. (1971) *Times of Feast, Times of Famine: a History of Climate Since the Year 1000.* Trans. Barbara Bray. Doubleday: Garden City, NY.

Lamb, H.H. (1972) 'The Cold Little Ice Age Climate of about 1550 to 1800', in *Climate: Present, Past and Future.* Methuen: London.

Lambert, J.M., J.N. Jennings, C.T. Smith, C. Green and J.N. Hutchinson (1961) *The Making of the Broads. A Reconsideration of their Origin in the Light of New Evidence.* John Murray Ltd.: London.

Lincoln, R.J. and G.A. Boxshall (1987) *The Cambridge Illustrated Dictionary of Natural History.* Cambridge University Press: Cambridge.

Macdougall, D. (2004) *Frozen Earth: The Once and Future Story of Ice Ages.* University of California Press: Berkeley.

Meadows, D.H., D.L. Meadows, J. Randers and W.W. Behrens (1972) *The Limits to Growth.* Pan Books: London.

Mellanby, K. (1967) *Pesticides and Pollution.* Collins New Naturalist: London.

Mitchell, A. (1985) *The Complete Guide to Trees of Britain and Northern Europe.* Dragon's World Ltd.: Limpsfield.

Myers, N. (ed.) (1993) *Rainforests.* The Illustrated Library of the Earth. Time-Life Books: Amsterdam.

Onions, C.T. (1983) *The Shorter Oxford English Dictionary on Historical Principles.* Guild Publishing: London.

Pepper, D. (1996) *Modern Environmentalism.* Routledge: London.

Perlin, J. (1989) *A Forest Journey.* Harvard University Press: Cambridge, Mass.

Full Bibliography

Peterken, G.F. (1981) *Woodland Conservation and Management.* Chapman and Hall: London.

Peterken, G.F. (1996) *Natural Woodland – Ecology and Conservation in Northern Temperate Regions.* Cambridge University Press: Cambridge.

Ponting, C. (1991) *A Green History of the World.* Sinclair-Stevenson Ltd.: London.

Rackham, O. (1980) *Ancient Woodland: its History, Vegetation and Uses in England.* Edward Arnold: London.

Rackham, O. (1986) *The History of the Countryside.* Dent: London.

Richardson (1992) *Pollution Monitoring with lichens.* Naturalists' Handbooks No. 19. Richmond Publishing Co. Ltd.: Slough.

Riley, D. and A. Young (1966) *World Vegetation.* Cambridge University Press: Cambridge.

Rose, F. (1974) 'The epiphytes of oak', in M.G. Morris and F.H. Perring (eds.) *The British Oak, its History and Natural History.* Classey: Faringdon. pp. 250–273.

Rose, F. (1976) 'Lichenological indicators of age and environmental continuity in woodlands', in D.H. Brown, D.L. Hawksworth and R.H. Bailey (eds.) *Lichenology: Progress and Problems.* Academic Press: London.

Rose, F. and P.W. James (1974) 'Regional studies on the British lichen flora, 1. The corticolous and lignicolous species of the New Forest, Hampshire'. *Lichenologist* **6**: 1–72

Rotherham, I.D. (1999) 'Peat cutters and their landscapes: fundamental change in a fragile environment'. *Landscape Archaeology and Ecology* **4**: 28–51.

Rotherham, I.D. (1999) 'Urban Environmental History: the importance of relict communities in urban biodiversity conservation'. *Practical Ecology and Conservation* **3** (1): 3–22.

Rotherham, I.D. (2005) 'Fuel and Landscape – Exploitation, Environment, Crisis and Continuum'. *Landscape Archaeology and Ecology* **5**: 65–81.

Rotherham, I.D. (ed.) (2005) Crisis and Continuum in the Shaping of Landscapes. *Landscape Archaeology and Ecology* **5**.

Rotherham, I.D. (2005) 'Alien Plants and the Human Touch'. *Journal of Practical Ecology and Conservation Special Series,* No. 4: 63–76.

Rotherham, I.D. (2006) 'Historic Landscape Restoration: Case Studies of Site Recovery in Post-industrial South Yorkshire, England', in M. Agnoletti (ed.) *The Conservation of Cultural Landscapes* CABI: Wallingford. pp. 211–224.

Rotherham, I.D. (2007) 'The implications of perceptions and cultural knowledge loss for the management of wooded landscapes: a UK case-study'. *Forest Ecology and Management* **249**: 100–115.

Rotherham, I.D. (2007) 'The Historical Ecology of Medieval Deer Parks and the Implications for Conservation', in R. Liddiard (ed.) *The Medieval Deer Park: New Perspectives.* Windgather Press: Macclesfield. pp. 79–96.

Rotherham, I.D. (2008) 'Landscape, Water and History'. *Practical Ecology and Conservation* **7**: 138–152.

Rotherham, I.D. (2008) 'Floods and Water: A Landscape-scale Response'. *Practical Ecology and Conservation* **7**: 128–137.

Rotherham, I.D. (2009) 'The Importance of Cultural Severance in Landscape Ecology Research', in A. Dupont and H. Jacobs (eds) *Landscape Ecology Research Trends.* Nova Science Publishers: Hauppauge, NY.

Rotherham, I.D. (2009) *Peat and Peat Cutting*. Shire Publications: Oxford.

Rotherham, I.D. (2010) *Yorkshire's Forgotten Fenlands*. Pen & Sword Books Limited: Barnsley.

Rotherham, I.D. (2011) 'A Landscape History Approach to the Assessment of Ancient Woodlands', in E.B. Wallace (ed.) *Woodlands: Ecology, Management and Conservation*. Nova Science Publishers: Hauppauge, NY. pp. 161–184.

Rotherham, I.D. (2011) 'Hanging by a Thread – a brief overview of the heaths and commons of the north-east midlands of England', in I.D. Rotherham and J. Bradley (eds) (2009) *Lowland Heaths: Ecology, History, Restoration and Management*. Wildtrack Publishing: Sheffield. pp. 30–47.

Rotherham, I.D. (2011) 'The Implications of Landscape History and Cultural Severance in Environmental Restoration in England', in D. Egan, E. Hjerpe and J. Abrams (eds) *Integrating Nature and Culture: The Human Dimensions of Ecological Restoration*. Island Press: Washington DC. pp. 277–287.

Rotherham, I.D. (2011) 'Habitat Fragmentation and Isolation in Relict Urban Heaths – the ecological consequences and future potential', in I.D. Rotherham and J. Bradley (eds) *Lowland Heaths: Ecology, History, Restoration and Management*. Wildtrack Publishing: Sheffield. pp. 106–115.

Rotherham, I.D. (2012) 'Post Coal-mining Landscapes: water, heaths, and commons as a resource for wildlife, people and heritage', in I.D. Rotherham and C. Handley (eds) *Between a Rock and A Hard Place*. Landscape Archaeology and Ecology Special Series. Papers from the Landscape Conservation Forum, (2). Wildtrack Publishing: Sheffield. pp. 49–58.

Rotherham, I.D. (2012) 'Traditional Woodland Management: the Implications of Cultural Severance and Knowledge Loss', in I.D. Rotherham, M. Jones and C. Handley (eds) (2012) *Working & Walking in the Footsteps of Ghosts. Volume 1: the Wooded Landscape*. Wildtrack Publishing: Sheffield. pp. 223–264.

Rotherham, I.D. (ed.) (2013) *Trees, Forested Landscapes and Grazing Animals: A European Perspective on Woodlands and Grazed Treescapes*. EARTHSCAN: London.

Rotherham, I.D. (2013) *Cultural Severance and the Environment. The Ending of Traditional and Customary Practice on Commons and Landscapes Managed in Common*. Springer: Dordrecht.

Rotherham, I.D. (2013) *Ancient Woodland: History, Industry and Crafts*. Shire Publications: Oxford.

Rotherham, I.D. (2013) *The Lost Fens: England's Greatest Ecological Disaster*. The History Press: Stroud.

Rotherham, I.D. (2013) 'Searching for Shadows and Ghosts', in I.D. Rotherham, C. Handley, M. Agnoletti and T. Samoljik (eds) (2013) *Trees Beyond the Wood – an Exploration of Concepts of Woods, Forests and Trees*. Wildtrack Publishing: Sheffield. pp. 1–16.

Rotherham, I.D. and P.A. Ardron (2006) 'The Archaeology of Woodland Landscapes: Issues for Managers based on the Case-study of Sheffield, England and four thousand years of human impact'. *Arboricultural Journal* **29** (4): 229–243.

Rotherham, I.D. and J. Bradley (eds) (2011) *Lowland Heaths: Ecology, History, Restoration and Management*. Wildtrack Publishing: Sheffield.

Rotherham, I.D., D. Egan and P.A. Ardron (2004) 'Fuel economy and the uplands: the effects of peat and turf utilisation on upland landscapes'. *Society for Landscape Studies Supplementary Series*, 2: 99–109.

Full Bibliography

Rotherham, I.D. and D. Egan (2005) 'The Economics of Fuel Wood, Charcoal and Coal: An Interpretation of Coppice Management of British Woodlands', in M. Agnoletti, M. Armiero, S. Barca and G. Corona (eds) *History and Sustainability*. European Society for Environmental History. pp.100–104.

Rotherham, I.D. and C. Handley (eds) (2011) *Animals, Man and Treescapes*. Wildtrack Publishing: Sheffield.

Rotherham, I.D., C. Handley, M. Agnoletti and T. Samoljik (eds) (2013) *Trees Beyond the Wood – an Exploration of Concepts of Woods, Forests and Trees*. Wildtrack Publishing: Sheffield.

Rotherham, I.D. and M. Jones (2000) 'The Impact of Economic, Social and Political Factors on the Ecology of Small English Woodlands: a Case Study of the Ancient Woods in South Yorkshire, England', in M. Agnoletti and S. Anderson (eds.) *Forest History: International Studies in Socio-economic and Forest Ecosystem Change*. CABI: Wallingford. pp. 397–410.

Rotherham, I.D. and R.A. Lambert (eds) (2011) *Invasive and Introduced Plants and Animals: Human Perceptions, Attitudes and Approaches to Management*. EARTHSCAN: London.

Rotherham, I.D. and J. Lunn (2012) 'Positive Restoration in a 'Green Belt' opencast coaling site: the conservation and community benefits of a sympathetic scheme in Barnsley, South Yorkshire', in I.D. Rotherham and C. Handley (eds) *Between a Rock and A Hard Place*. Landscape Archaeology and Ecology Special Series. Papers from the Landscape Conservation Forum, (2). Wildtrack Publishing: Sheffield. pp. 69–80.

Rotherham, I.D., J. Lunn and F. Spode (2012) 'Wildlife and coal – the nature Conservation value of post-mining sites in South Yorkshire', in I.D. Rotherham and C. Handley (eds) *Dynamic Landscape Restoration*. Landscape Archaeology and Ecology Special Series. Papers from the Landscape Conservation Forum, (1). Wildtrack Publishing: Sheffield. pp. 30–64.

Rotherham, I.D. and D. McCallam (2008) 'Peat Bogs, Marshes and Fen as disputed Landscapes in Late eighteenth-Century France and England', in L. Lyle and D. McCallam (eds) *Histoires de la Terre: Earth Sciences and French Culture 1740–1940*. Rodopi B.V.: Amsterdam & New York. pp. 75–90.

Rotherham, I.D., J.C. Rose and C. Percy (2012) 'The dynamic influence of history and ecology on the restoration of a major urban heathland at Wharncliffe, South Yorkshire', in I.D. Rotherham and C. Handley (eds.) (2012) *Wild by Design and Ploughing on Regardless*. Landscape Archaeology and Ecology Special Series. Papers from the Landscape Conservation Forum, (3). Wildtrack Publishing: Sheffield. pp. 22–36.

Rotherham, I.D., F. Spode and D. Fraser (2003) 'Post–coalmining landscapes: an under-appreciated resource for wildlife, people and heritage', in H.M. Moore, H.R. Fox and S. Elliot (eds.) *Land Reclamation: Extending the Boundaries*. A.A. Balkema Publishers: Lisse. pp. 93–99.

Santos, M.A. (1999) *The Environmental Crisis*. Guides to Historic Events of the Twentieth Century. Greenwood Press: Westport, CT.

Sheail, J. (1976) *Nature in Trust. The History of Nature Conservation in Britain*. Blackie: London.

Sheail, J. (1984) 'Wildlife conservation: an historical perspective'. *Geography* **69**: 119–27.

Sheail, J. (1985) *Pesticides and Nature Conservation: the British Perspective, 1950–1975*. Clarendon Press: Oxford.

Sheail, J. (1987) *Seventy-five Years in Ecology: The British Ecological Society*. Blackwell Scientific Publications: Oxford.

Sheail, J. (1993) 'Green history – the evolving agenda'. *Rural History* **4**: 209–23.

Sheail, J. (1998) *Nature Conservation in Britain: the Formative Years.* The Stationery Office: London.

Sheail, J. (2002) *An Environmental History of Twentieth-century Britain.* Palgrave: Basingstoke.

Smout, T.C. (2000) *Nature Contested – Environmental History in Scotland and Northern England Since 1600.* Edinburgh University Press: Edinburgh.

Stamp, D. (1969) *Nature Conservation in Britain.* Collins New Naturalist: London.

Stokes, J. and D. Rodger (2004) *The Heritage Trees of Britain & Northern Ireland.* Constable: London.

Stott, P. (1981) *Historical Plant Geography. An Introduction.* George Allen & Unwin: London.

Taylor, G.R. (1972) *The Doomsday Book.* Panther Books Ltd.: London.

Vera, F. (2000) *Grazing Ecology and Forest History.* CABI: Wallingford.

Vincent, P. (1990) *The Biogeography of the British Isles – An Introduction.* Routledge: London.

WCED (1987) *Our Common Future.* The World Commission on Environment and Development. Oxford University Press: Oxford.

Webb, N.R. (1986) *Heathlands.* Collins: London.

Webb, N.R. (1998) 'The traditional management of European heathlands'. *Journal of Applied Ecology* **35**: 987–990.

Wentworth-Day, J. (1954) *History of the Fens.* George Harrap & Co. Ltd.: London.

Wilkinson, G. (1981) *A History of Britain's Trees.* Hutchinson: London.

Wilson, E.O. (ed.) (1988) *Biodiversity.* National Academy Press: Washington D.C.

Wilson, E.O. (ed.) (1992) *The Diversity of Life.* Harvard University Press: Cambridge, Mass.

Yalden, D.W. (2002) *The History of British Mammals.* T. & A.D. Poyser Ltd: London

Yalden, D.W. and U. Albarella (2009) *The History of British Birds.* Oxford University Press: Oxford.

INDEX

Index

Lightning Source UK Ltd.
Milton Keynes UK
UKOW04f1403041017
310395UK00001B/287/P

9 781874 267812